A Theology of the *Spirit* in Doctrine and Demonstration

Essays in Honor of Wonsuk and Julie Ma

Edited by
Teresa Chai

WIPF & STOCK · Eugene, Oregon

Wipf and Stock Publishers
199 W 8th Ave, Suite 3
Eugene, OR 97401

A Theology of the Spirit in Doctrine and Demonstration
Essays in Honor of Wonsuk and Julie Ma
By Chai, Teresa
Copyright©2014 APTS Press
ISBN 13: 978-1-4982-1764-4
Publication date 2/10/2015
Previously published by APTS Press, 2014

FOREWORD

It is a distinct pleasure and privilege for me to contribute the Foreword of this *Festschrift* in honor of my friends and former colleagues, Drs. Wonsuk and Julie Ma. I am pleased that the APTS Press, a ministry of Asia Pacific Theological Seminary (APTS) in the Philippines, which counts them both as alumni and former faculty, has undertaken to publish it.

I first met the Mas when I came to APTS as Academic Dean in 1991. The Mas had already been at the seminary for a number years, both as students and (Wonsuk) as faculty. They left soon after I arrived to pursue Ph.Ds. at Fuller Seminary under the APTS faculty development program, where Wonsuk studied Old Testament and Julie, Missiology. In 1996, the year I became APTS President, the Mas returned once again to serve at APTS—Wonsuk in the role of Academic Dean and Julie as a member of the faculty.

As any president of an academic institution will attest, the work of the academic dean is critical to the success of the school and his or her effectiveness in that role relieves much pressure from the board and constituency that might otherwise fall on the president. Certainly, Wonsuk fulfilled that expectation. As Academic Dean, he provided outstanding leadership to the growing and diverse APTS faculty, which included both Western and Asian members. He was highly effective in expanding the number of Asian members of the faculty representing a number of nations, and in leading the school through accreditation self-studies and reviews by its three accrediting agencies. His many creative initiatives in looking for ways to expand the programs of the school and in seeking new delivery mechanisms constantly encouraged us toward innovation. At the same time, he was highly valued as a teacher and mentor of students. Julie was also involved in teaching and was especially effective in mentoring students through the writing of master's theses and doctoral dissertations and she was the primary academic supervisor for students doing research in missiology.

During these years, Wonsuk was instrumental in the establishment of two academic journals: the *Asian Journal of Pentecostal Studies* (*AJPS*), published by APTS, and the *Journal of Asian Missions* (*JAM*), published by Asia Graduate School of Theology (AGTS), a consortium of seminaries in the Philippines to which APTS belongs. He co-edited *AJPS* with William Menzies, noted Pentecostal scholar and former APTS President, but it was acknowledged by Menzies that Ma carried the major editorial burden. Wonsuk also served as the first editor of *JAM*, a role that Julie later assumed.

It is rare to find a couple who both have strong academic and practical ministry interests and achievements, but the Mas distinguished themselves in both areas. The location of APTS is in the Cordillera mountain region of Northern Philippines and the influence of the Mas did not end at the gates of the seminary but extended into the far reaches of the mountains where they were involved in planting and nurturing new churches and leading teams of students to contribute to these efforts. Over the years, they were instrumental in establishing more than 150 churches through these endeavors–an accomplishment that many might consider sufficient for a lifetime of ministry. Julie's doctoral research on the history and practice of Pentecostal missions among the Kankana-ey people of Northern Philippines provided a strong missiological basis for this ministry.[1]

In 2006, Wonsuk accepted the invitation to become the Executive Director and Julie a research tutor for the Oxford Centre for Mission Studies (OCMS) in the UK. I felt both a sense of loss as these wonderful friends and colleagues were leaving APTS, but also joy in seeing them expand their influence through contributing to the education of key global Christian leaders through the work of the Centre. Clearly, the years since have witnessed their continuing commitment to scholarship and excellence in theological education, and God has multiplied their effectiveness in significant ways as they teach and mentor students while also maintaining an active program of scholarship and academic writing.

The Mas are people of the Spirit with a strong commitment to the worldwide mission of the church. As such, it is fitting that the articles in this *Festschrift: A Theology of the Spirit in Doctrine and Demonstration* represent the work of scholars from across the globe, including Asia, Africa, Europe and the US. The ministry of the Mas has also had this kind of global reach. In addition, the range of topics included in the volume touch on many of the academic and ministry interests of the Mas, evinced through both their own writings and their continuing involvement in theological education, through which they have guided the development of many emerging theological educators, theologians and missionaries. Significantly, several of the contributors to this volume are former students of the Mas.

No doubt, for anyone involved in theological education, the greatest satisfactions derive from seeing students accomplish

---

[1] Julie C. Ma, *When the Spirit Meets the Spirits: Pentecostal Ministry among the Kankana-ey Tribe in the Philippines.* Frankfurt am Main: Peter Lang, 2000.

significant levels of achievement in their own right. I'm certain that the legacy of Wonsuk and Julie Ma will continue to reverberate around the world as generations of students, who have completed graduate and post-graduate education under their guidance, assume the ministry roles to which God has called them. As such, the lasting impact of the ministry of Wonsuk and Julie Ma has only begun to be realized.

John F. Carter, Ph.D.
President Emeritus, Asia Pacific Theological Seminary

EDITORIAL

by Teresa Chai, PhD

In March 2014, the Asia Pacific Theological Seminary (APTS), Baguio, Philippines celebrated its 50th Anniversary of operations. Two of the key persons in this great institution's journey are Dr. Wonsuk Ma and Dr. Julie Ma. The leadership of the institution believes that one of the 50th Anniversary publications should include this *festschrift* in honor of the Mas' contributions to the missional, academic and ecclesiastical world they have so long been a part of in such an active way. John Carter had kindly agreed to do the *Foreword* to this publication. The *festschrift* is a peculiarly academic genre. It is a celebratory publication in honor of a scholar or scholars. In a *festschrift*, academic peers and former students honor scholars by writing essays on a topic close to their scholarly heart. Thus, this theme reflects for the Mas' what is close to their hearts: *A Theology of the Spirit in Doctrine and Demonstration.*

The ones who are the contributors to this publication are friends of the Mas; they have worked with them, they have been their colleagues and their former students. This is the legacy the Mas leave in the Philippines and the one that Rose Encoy's historical article sketches through interviews and archival research on how the Mas helped plant one hundred mountain churches concurrently with their academic duties at APTS. As she states, "the Mas have an exceptional capacity of valuing both people and ministry and live a balance between academics and spirituality. "

Next is an article by Amos Yong entitled *Incarnation, Pentecost, and Virtual Spiritual Formation: Renewing Theological Education in Global Context*. He challenges theological educators to consider the "digital world" and to build in the aspect of spiritual formation. Still on the topic of spirituality, Robert Menzies, who comes from a missionary point of view, contributes his article *Missional Spirituality: A Pentecostal Contribution to Spiritual Formation*. In his own words, Menzies' dedication of his article is as follows "I feel the following essay on Missional Spirituality is particularly appropriate in this instance, for Dr. Ma was never an ivory tower scholar. Rather, he has always been a missionary at heart, a man driven by the Holy Spirit to take the gospel to those who have not heard."

Veli-Matti Kärkkäinen is from Finland and has served as a missionary in Thailand. His article is entitled *Theological Education in a Pluralistic World: Theological Reflections*. This is his concern, "This brief essay seeks to offer some *theological* (rather than pedagogical) reflections on international theological education with a focus on one particular issue that I find increasingly challenging, namely training ministers in and for a religiously pluralistic world." From Birmingham is Allan Heaton Anderson, who writes an engaging article entitled *Contextualization and Pentecostal-Charismatic Education in a Global Village*. His article captures the essence of the work of the Mas in their missionary ministry and academic contributions.

Another good friend of the Mas' is Harold Hunter. He gives his *Pentecostal Reflections on Apostolicity*. This article is used with permission as it was previously published in JEPTA a journal published in Europe. As Hunter stated "The particular emphasis will be on fidelity to the church of the apostles in terms of teaching and practice while acknowledging that our covenant communities observe sacraments." Next is Kim Kirsteen giving a Pentecostal perspective on *Mission in the Spirit: From Edinburgh* to Canberra and Athens. In honor of the Mas, Kirsteen is writing about ". . . the contribution of Pentecostal-charismatic perspectives to mission spirituality and mission pneumatology through reflection on the mission of the Spirit."

Then from non-Western authors we have three articles. The first is written by J. Kwabena Asamoah-Gyadu about *The Blessing of Abraham: Pentecostalism and Ecumenism in African Perspectives*. Asamoah-Gyadu expresses his appreciation saying, "Wonsuk Ma and his wife Julie are Pentecostals with a wonderful ecumenical spirit and this essay is written to celebrate the fact that their work has impacted Africa too." Next, the article entitled *Pentecostal Feeling in Conversation with William James and Rudolf Otto: A Preliminary Exploration* is written by Ekaputra Tupamahu, a former student of the Mas. Taken from his understanding of Wonsuk Ma, Tupamahu builds upon this premise that what is needed is "a deep conviction that the task of constructing theology has to be undertaken from within a real human context." A former colleague from APTS, R.G. dela Cruz, is a New Testament scholar writing on *Peter, Women and the Spirit in the Bezan Text of Acts*. Dela Cruz is using the "Codex Bezae Cantabrigiensis . . . a major New Testament uncial Greek-Latin bilingual manuscript that has preserved remarkable variant readings in the Acts . . ." to give fresh insights on the topics of Peter, women and the Spirit in the Book of Acts.

Last but not least, Dave Johnson, who was mentored by Julie Ma, gives his contribution of *Baptism in the Holy Spirit vs. Spirit Possession in the Lowland Philippines: Some Considerations for Discipleship*. Johnson, a veteran missionary in Bicol, Philippines, focuses his article on ". . . how Filipinos understand the baptism in the Holy Spirit within their cultural framework." This article serves to give a wonderful bookend and practical application of the theme *A Theology of the Spirit in Doctrine and Demonstration*. May you enjoy reading this festschrift.

Wonsuk and Julie Ma

CONTENTS

iii   Foreword

vii   Editorial

1   A Historical Sketch of Wonsuk and Julie Ma
Rose Engcoy

27   Incarnation, Pentecost, and Virtual Spiritual Formation: Renewing Theological Education in Global Context
Amos Yong

39   Missional Spirituality: A Pentecostal Contribution to Spiritual Formation
Robert P. Menzies

57   Theological Education in a Pluralistic World: *Theological* Reflections
Veli-Matti Kärkkäinen

67   Contextualization and Pentecostal-Charismatic Education in a Global Village
Allan Heaton Anderson

89   Pentecostal Reflections on Apostolicity
Harold D. Hunter

107   Mission in the Spirit: From Edinburgh to Canberra and Athens
Kirsteen Kim

127	The Blessing of Abraham: Pentecostalism and Ecumenism in African Perspectives *J. Kwabena Asamoah-Gyadu*
153	Pentecostal Feeling in Conversation with William James and Rudolf Otto: A Preliminary Exploration *Ekaputra Tupamahu*
177	Peter, Women, and the Holy Spirit in the Bezan Text of Acts *R.G. dela Cruz*
205	Baptism in the Holy Spirit vs. Spirit Possession in the Lowland Philippines: Some Considerations for Discipleship *Dave Johnson*
227	Publications by Wonsuk Ma
231	Publications by Julie Ma
233	Profiles of Contributors

A Historical Sketch of Wonsuk and Julie Ma

by Rose Engcoy

Introduction

How does one discuss in a few pages the legacy of two imminent Asian Pentecostal scholars, educators, missionaries, authors, etc., who have ministered around the globe in a span of more than three decades? The vast ministerial experience and influence of Drs. Wonsuk and Julie Ma make this a most difficult task.

Scope

The Mas are Korean Pentecostal scholars. They are prolific writers with multiplied academic contributions to Asian Pentecostalism. Much has been written by them and about them, however, very little has been written about Wonsuk and Julie as they lived their lives and interacted with people around them during ordinary mundane days. This article aims to fill some of that gap. It will reflect on the impact and influence of the lives of Wonsuk and Julie upon the people they ministered to and ministered with in three specific areas: as administrators at Asia Pacific Theological Seminary (APTS), as missionaries to the mountain tribes of Benguet, and as professors and Executive Director of the Oxford Centre for Mission Studies (OCMS).

Methodology

As stated above, I will focus on how the Mas influenced people whose lives they touched as they went about their daily responsibilities. To do this, I interviewed or emailed questionnaires to colleagues, staff, students, pastors, and church leaders who have worked with this amazing couple. These people's testimonies showed that, indeed, the Mas have an exceptional capacity for valuing both people and ministry and they live with a balance between academics and spirituality.

Background

A short background of the Mas' salvation story and ministry is necessary to appreciate the discussion in this paper.

Wonsuk is a third generation Christian. He was in high school when he received the baptism of the Holy Spirit and while his family attended an Assembly of God (AG) church. During a revival meeting, he dedicated his life to preaching the gospel. To prepare for the ministry, he studied at the Full Gospel Bible College in Seoul.[1] It was there he met his future wife, Julie.[2]

Julie (her Korean name is Jungja Cho[3]) was born to a strongly Buddhist family. When she converted to Christianity, her family persecuted and then disowned her. Thus, she decided to study in a Bible College away from home.[4] There, she met and married Wonsuk, with whom she had two sons, Woolim and Boram.

---

[1] "Profile of a FEAST Instructor," *Pentecostal Evangel,* (23 October 1983): 7.
[2] Wonsuk and Julie C. Ma, "The Making of Korean Pentecostal Missionaries: Our Personal Journey," *Together in One Mission: Pentecostal Cooperation in World Evangelization,* Arto Hamalainen and Grant McClung, eds. (TN: Pathway Press, 2012), 162.
[3] Wonsuk Ma, email message to author, 18 May 2014, Oxford.
[4] Wonsuk and Julie C. Ma, 161-2.

Wonsuk sensed that God wanted him to be trained so he could teach others. This led him to enroll in the Far East Advanced School of Theology (FEAST), the AG Bible College in the Philippines.[5] Julie soon followed and the couple graduated together in 1983. The following school year, Wonsuk joined the FEAST faculty[6] and the Mas became the "very first appointed missionaries of the Korean AG."[7]

When FEAST launched a program for faculty development, Wonsuk, Robert Menzies, and Gary Long joined the program.[8] Wonsuk has the distinction of being the first Asian FEAST faculty member to complete this program.[9] Afterwards, he was granted a sabbatical to pursue higher studies at Fuller Theological Seminary in the United States. In 1992, Wonsuk went back to Fuller, this time with Julie, and they both pursued their PhD degrees. In 1996, Wonsuk and Julie became the first husband and wife to earn their PhDs at Fuller in the same year.[10] Wonsuk earned a PhD in Old Testament while Julie graduated with a PhD in Intercultural Studies.[11] After graduation, both returned to APTS, Wonsuk to serve as Academic Dean (later his title became "Vice President for Academic Affairs"), and Julie as "principal resource person for mission studies."[12] In 2000, the Mas became missionaries of the United States Assemblies of

---

[5]"Profile of a FEAST Instructor," 7.
[6]Dave Johnson, Led By the Spirit: The History of the American Assemblies of God Missionaries in the Philippines (Pasig City, Philippines: ICI Ministries, 2009), 335.
[7]"The Ma Family: Who are They and What Do They Do?" Ma Summer 2000 newsletter.
[8]Ma email.
[9]Johnson, 335.
[10]William W. Menzies and John F. Carter, eds., Zeal with Knowledge (Baguio City, Philippines: APTS Press, 2004), 58.
[11]"Assemblies of God Theological Seminary Doctor of Missiology Program," available at https://www.agts.edu/syllabi/dmiss/2012/mss939(02)stu_wma_fall 2012_dmiss.pdf, accessed May 15, 2014.
[12] Wonsuk and Julie C. Ma, 171.

God's (USAG) Department of Foreign Missions.[13] At the same time, they were also appointed missionaries of the Korean AG.[14]

It was in this new chapter of their lives that the Mas' ministry began to take a sharp upward curve. Their academic perspective played an important role in this growth. They later explained, "As academicians, we paid serious attention to research, conference participation, and publication. They were all 'luxury items' for a developing mission institution. But we reminded ourselves that the Ph.D. degree was only the beginning of a serious academic journey, not the end."[15]

During Wonsuk's tenure as academic dean, APTS' academic program expanded. Two academic journals (the *Asian Journal of Pentecostal Studies* and *Journal of Asian Mission*) began to be published, and the Asian Pentecostal Society was founded. The Mas' published works placed APTS on the academic map. Moreover, they often represented Asian Pentecostal scholars in various academic gatherings. Soon they were sought-after Asian Pentecostal speakers in academic conferences.[16] Furthermore, by the time the Mas left APTS for OCMS, Wonsuk was, and still is, the longest serving faculty of FEAST/APTS (from 1983 to 2006).[17]

In 2006, the Mas moved to OCMS. Wonsuk served as the new OCMS Executive Director, and Julie was a Research Tutor in Missiology.[18] This move enlarged their scope of ministry to global missions.

---

[13] "The Ma Family."
[14] Ma email.
[15] Wonsuk and Julie C. Ma, 171.
[16] Menzies and Carter, 106 ff.; Wonsuk and Julie C. Ma, 172-3.
[17] Johnson, 338.
[18] "Dr Wonsuk Ma," available at http://www.ocms.ac.uk/content/index.php?q=ocms/people/faculty_and_staff/dr_wonsuk_ma, accessed May 15, 2014; "Dr Julie Ma," available at http://www.ocms.ac.uk/content/index.php?q=node/390, accessed May 15, 2014. Note: The OCMS website states that Wonsuk became Executive Director in 2005. The year is actually 2006 as clarified by Wonsuk's email.

Wonsuk's leadership brought in new donors and increased funding for OCMS.[19] His vision "for print media and leading scholarship in theology and mission studies globally," coupled with Regnum Books International, an imprint of OCMS, resulted in the publication of many books and theses—around 20 new titles in a span of twelve months.[20] Moreover, Wonsuk's wide network of friends connected OCMS with various ecumenical and global mission groups and churches.[21] Indeed, as one OCMS staff commented, Wonsuk "has brought OCMS to a wider audience. He has improved the reputation of OCMS."[22] Yet, in Wonsuk's own words, "Our story with OCMS and global mission leadership is still in the making, and we will have to wait to see its full extent."[23]

With this short ministerial background, we begin our reflection on the Mas' impact and influence on other people's lives.

APTS: Administrators

Wonsuk was Registrar when he first joined FEAST (now APTS) faculty. After he earned his PhD, he became APTS Academic Dean, a post he held until he moved on to OCMS. Throughout these years, interaction with the APTS staff was a daily routine. Barbara "Barbs" de la Cruz, Wonsuk's secretary, shares about the Mas' personal traits and how they impacted her life.

---

[19]Carole Glendinning, "Questions re Drs. Wonsuk and Julie Ma," email to author, 29 April 2014, Oxford.
[20]William Prevette, "Questions re Drs. Wonsuk and Julie Ma," email to author, 23 April 2014, Oxford; Judy Berinai, "Questions re Drs. Wonsuk and Julie Ma," email to author, 25 March 2014; "Regnum Books," available at http://www.ocms.ac.uk/regnum/, accessed May 14, 2014.
[21]Berinai.
[22]Glendinning.
[23]Wonsuk and Julie C. Ma, 174-5.

Mild-tempered

Barbs started work in APTS as Wonsuk's secretary in August 1999. She came at a busy time because preparations were being made for accreditation visits by the Association for Theological Education in South East Asia (ATESEA), Asia Pacific Theological Association (APTA), and Asia Theological Association (ATA). Because of the extremely busy schedule, the outgoing secretary was unable to give Barbs sufficient orientation for her new job. Inevitably, she made a lot of mistakes. Despite all her mistakes, Wonsuk never scolded her nor said, "This is wrong." Instead, he would say, "Perhaps, do it this way." He had her redo the task until she understood what he wanted her to do. There were times when she was overwhelmed and frustrated over her many mistakes that she told him, "Sir, I want to quit." Each time, Wonsuk would not answer. Instead, he would give her more work. One time though, when he was irritated with her pessimism, he responded, "Is that the way to improve?" That opened Barbara's eyes. Those were truly learning times for her.[24]

Other APTS staff also declared that in all their years at APTS, they never saw Wonsuk lose his temper.[25] When a staff made a mistake, Wonsuk would talk to the person at fault in an encouraging way. Because of Wonsuk's kindness, the staff sought to give their best. At times when Wonsuk did get upset, he would keep quiet, go out of his office, and walk around the campus with Julie.[26] Even when his face would show his disappointment with a student, he would simply say, "Hey, this is what happened. A student did this." He would explain without using an offending or condemning word. Then he would ask, "What should we do?"

---

[24]Barbara de la Cruz, interview by author, 21 March 2014, APTS, Baguio City, Philippines, transcript in the hand of author, 2.

[25]Jing Aquino, Glo Royeca, Ely Sebiano, and Barbs dela Cruz all attested to this.

[26]Cheryl Joy Aquino, interview by author, 20 March 2014, APTS, Baguio City, Philippines, transcript in the hand of author, 2; Eleanor Sebiano, interview by author, 21 March 2014, APTS, Baguio City, Philippines, transcript in the hand of author, 2.

Under no circumstances would he ever raise his voice.[27] Indeed, Wonsuk has the knack of correcting without making one feel reprimanded.[28]

Visionary

Wonsuk was a visionary and he cast that vision to those around him. His associates enjoyed the personal training and growth from working together with him on the fulfillment of a vision.

As stated above, APTS' academic program expanded under the leadership of Wonsuk. Barbs was there to assist him with all his projects. She not only caught his vision, but she also learned to appreciate her own self more because of the way her "boss" treated her. Wonsuk appreciated her efforts. He respected her and trusted her and she valued that trust as sacred. It helped her grow as a person knowing that somebody was counting on her and appreciated what she was doing. Thus, she was willing to work beyond office hours knowing that her work was a ministry. For Barbs, her six years as Wonsuk's secretary were among the most beneficial years of her life.

Generosity

However, what the staff remembered and treasured most were the Mas' sensitivity to people's needs and their corresponding generous help. Most of the staff interviewed had personal stories of how the Mas extended help to them without being asked. One such staff member was Mercy Panelo.

Mercy was Admission/Immigration Assistant at the Registrar's office in 1998 when she first met the Mas. She often

---

[27]Gloria Royeca, interview by author, 21 March 2014, APTS, Baguio City, Philippines, transcript in the hand of author, 1-2.
[28]Aquino, 1.

saw the couple but had no opportunity for a friendly chat with them.

In January 2001, all three of her kids, aged eight, seven and three, were diagnosed with primary complex. The doctor prescribed one year of medication for all three children. However, Mercy and her husband could not afford the medication. Mercy had no one to turn to but God. She fasted and prayed silently in the office during lunch break. One day, she saw a long white envelope on her desk. Inside was money with a note: "Here's 1,000 pesos to buy medicine for your kids. – Wonsuk."

Mercy was surprised, but grateful! She went to Wonsuk's office to thank him. She asked how he knew she needed money. "I'm starting to discern others," he responded, then laughed. He interviewed Mercy about her situation. He then shared this with the rest of the faculty. As a result, Mercy received a six-month's supply of medicine, food, and vitamins for her kids! How the family praised and thanked God for His faithfulness!

By August, the medicine had run out. After lunch one day, Julie came to Mercy's office and said, "My husband saw you this morning and he asked me to come to see you and ask why you are losing weight." Mercy tried hard to hide her emotions, but Julie immediately hugged her and gave her an envelope with ₱3,000. Moreover, she said, "Please, if this is not enough, don't hesitate to come to us." This generosity of the Mas led to the salvation of Mercy's husband.[29]

Gloria "Glo" Royeca had a similar unforgettable experience as a recipient of the Mas' generosity. The 1990 earthquake that devastated Baguio City forced Glo's family to move down to Pangasinan, but Glo had to remain in Baguio because of her work at APTS. It broke her heart to be separated from her two boys, one four years old and the other three months old. Her baby was still breastfeeding. She planned to go down and visit

---

[29]Mercy Panelo, email to author, 2 May 2014, Baguio City, Philippines.

them every weekend. Julie heard about Glo's predicament and she gave Glo money for her fare. She also gave money for the children's milk. She did this every Friday. Soon Glo became embarrassed to continue to receive the money, but Julie insisted. Sometimes, Julie would have someone hand her the money in an envelope so Glo would not be able to refuse it.

Glo said she would not have been able to visit her family often in those 3 to 4 months if not for the Mas' help. But more than the money, what touched her most was their love and concern for her family.[30]

Working closely with Wonsuk, Barbs had a deeper knowledge of the extent of the Mas' generosity. The Mas' deep love for missions made them sensitive to others' needs. Wonsuk would write solicitation letters seeking sponsors for students, for APTS faculty and for other people, yet he did not write solicitation letters for his family's needs. When students sought his help because they could not pay their bills, he would make a way to help them come up with funds. Often, he gave all he had just to be able to help.[31]

It reached a point when Glo had to have a heart-to-heart talk with Wonsuk about his financial aids. At that time, he was supporting many local pastors who were studying at APTS. Each time they asked for financial aid for tuition, he approved the release of his funds, so much so, that his personal account was already in the red. As the Accounting Supervisor, Glo was concerned that Wonsuk was unaware that he was already in debt to APTS. Wonsuk listened to Glo and thanked her for her concern. He said, "OK, we'll just hold on to these needs first. I have to give you some checks first." In all this generosity, Julie gave Wonsuk her full support. Glo commented that the Mas had

---

[30]Royeca, 2.
[31]dela Cruz, 2.

very big hearts, giving even though they already had none left for themselves.³²

Love for the Staff

For Patricia "Pat" Escuadra, who had few opportunities to interact with the Mas, what struck her most was their humility. Pat joined APTS in 1991. In her work as one of the cleaning ladies, Pat was able to observe the Mas' lifestyle. She saw that the Mas would mingle with the staff, going down to their level. Thus, the staff was not hesitant to talk to them or approach them with questions.³³

Many attest to the Mas' closeness to the staff. When Wonsuk and Julie would return from their mountain ministries with sacks of potatoes, fruits, or vegetables, they would distribute these to the staff or have the kitchen cook the corn or sweet potatoes for the staff's snack at break time.³⁴ The couple would also greet them and ask how they were doing. For Cheryl Joy "Jing" Aquino and her husband Philip, the Mas were like parents who often encouraged them: "Keep up the good work. Just go on. Just trust the Lord." Jing said, "You can just feel God's love through them."³⁵

Thus, among all the numerous missionaries who came and went at APTS during our 11-years' stay in the campus, only the Mas were given a separate *despedida* (going-away party) by the APTS staff: proof of the deep love and gratitude of the staff for them.

---

³²Royeca, 1.
³³Patricia Escuadra, interview by author, 20 March 2014, APTS, Baguio City, Philippines, transcript in the hand of author.
³⁴Royeca, 1.
³⁵Aquino, 1.

Mountain Ministry: Missionaries

One of the things that made the Mas stand out as missionaries at APTS was their involvement in the ministries of local pastors and churches in the Cordilleras. They sponsored kids' schooling and helped waterworks projects up in the mountains.[36] In fact, Walter Caput, South Central Cordillera District Superintendent, deeply appreciates how the Mas worked to empower his people. He said, "I appreciate Brother Ma's spirit in working closely with us and his desire to upgrade ministers and also members."[37]

Training

The Mas helped qualified tribal pastors study at APTS or other Bible schools in the District by finding sponsors for them. Wonsuk and Julie visited and preached at many local churches and encouraged members in their spiritual lives. Wonsuk also helped in training the mountain ministers.[38] His training was done inside and outside the classroom. Tito Inio, one of the Kankana-ey pastors, says Wonsuk trained them to minister by encouraging them to pray for others even if he could do it himself. This way, the local pastors' faith was exercised.[39]

Humility

What the APTS staff saw, the tribal congregations also saw; the Mas were a humble couple.[40] Humility was an adjective commonly used by interviewed staff and pastors to characterize

---

[36]Sebiano, 1.
[37]Walter Caput, interview by author, 3 April 2014, FARM, Roxas City, transcript in the hand of author.
[38]Ibid.
[39]Tito Inio, interview by Eleanor Sebiano, 17 March 2014, Itogon, Benguet, transcript in the hand of author, 1.
[40]Ibid.

the Mas. Some testified: "He was very approachable and always brought Korean Missionaries to visit us . . . He was very much at home and very humble and loving to everyone."[41]

"He is so gentle. The pastors coming to him–they feel comfortable; those from the mountains–he is able to stoop down to their level . . . And the way he would relate with the people. I said, 'Wow, this is Christianity in action. . . . ' He projects himself as, 'I am an ordinary person like you. . . . ' He would come and just be friends."[42]

I wrongly presumed that the Mas were effective in their mountain ministry because they spoke the dialect. But Eleanor "Ely" Sebiano, an APTS staff member who handled the Mas' ministry funds, and a Kankana-ey herself, sees a different reason. Ely explains, "Not necessarily. It's his humble spirit. Even without words, you could feel how they communicate, their body language; even without the language, you could project a welcoming spirit. I don't think it's just the language; it's just the countenance, the welcoming spirit; his speaking the language simply adds up."[43] Ely further states, "And you cannot fake it if you have love for the people. It comes out when you relate…It just comes out naturally. Sister Julie learn[ed] Ilocano and talk[ed] with the women. They [ate] whatever they were served."[44]

Sensitivity to Mountain Culture

Their knowledge of the dialect gave the Mas insights to tribal culture. They were able to integrate missions and theology in the way they handled cultural practices. One tradition in the Cordilleras is the *cañao*. Natives butcher pigs as sacrifices to

---

[41]Teodoro Gaiwen, interview by Imelda P. Sedano, 17 March 2014, La Trinidad, Benguet, transcript in the hand of author, 1
[42]Sebiano, 1, 3.
[43]Ibid., 1.
[44]Ibid., 3.

appease the spirits. So Wonsuk said, "Let's have a *cañao* for thanksgiving instead." He would initiate buying a pig for thanksgiving instead of for fear. Ely explained the impact of this gesture:

> [It] shows generosity in his part, and he teaches the mountain people to be grateful and acknowledge the source of blessing, and that it is OK that we would butcher a pig and direct our thanksgiving to God who has showered us with blessings and not to appease the spirits because of fear of misfortune and sickness. He is also affirming the practices, that it is also good, but directing it to the Creator, and not out fear but out of thanksgiving.[45]

Encouragers

Julie's dissertation, *When the Spirit Meets the Spirits: Pentecostal Ministry Among the Kankana-ey Tribe in the Philippines*, is well-supported by the couple's frequent visits to mountain churches, often during weekends. They helped in evangelistic and church planting ministries of the local pastors. Pastor Inio, at that time a pioneering pastor, was struck by Wonsuk's courage in sharing the gospel and encouraging ordinary church members to do the same.[46]

That was one of the Mas' traits that truly impacted the tribal churches: encouraging others. Wonsuk often encouraged others to serve and to share with others the Word of God.[47] He emphasized that the fruit of the church should be numerical growth. He taught the congregations to love mission work and to desire to be used by God in giving to others.[48] As he taught, so he

---

[45]Ibid.
[46]Inio, 1.
[47]Gaiwen, 2.
[48]Inio, 2.

lived. He was consistent in his words and actions; what he said, he would do.[49] Thus, he was able to draw out the best in a person.[50]

Ely feels very blessed because the Mas trusted and appreciated her. In fact, since she was handling the ministry finances, she had joint checking accounts with them. For her, it was very humbling and she honored that trust. Wonsuk often said, "Ely, it is God's work." She learned faith in God's provision through this couple.[51]

Greatest Contribution to Mountain Ministry

Yet, above all else, for the mountain pastors, the Mas' greatest contribution was the assistance they gave in constructing mountain churches.[52] Wonsuk was not one to simply dole out money. He encouraged partnership. Often he would say, "What can you give? I'll match [it]."[53]

John Vicente, one of the leaders of the tribal pastors, relates how the church building projects started: "One time he came to my place and he said, 'I would like to work with you.' And I answered him, 'Sure, why not?' So every time we have a pioneer work and we bought the lot, I [requested his] assistance for the building. After assessing it, [he would say,] 'OK, you can come and we will buy [the construction materials].'"[54]

There were many building projects. When a pioneer work already had a congregation and a lot had been donated or bought and lumber gathered, that was when the pastors often approached Pastor Vicente and asked him to present the church building project to Wonsuk. Wonsuk often went and did an

---

[49]Sebiano, 3.
[50]Ibid., 4.
[51]Ibid., 3.
[52]John Vicente, interview by author, 3 April 2014, FARM, Roxas City, transcript in the hand of author, 2; Gaiwen, 2; Inio, 2.
[53]Sebiano, 1.
[54]Vicente, 1.

ocular inspection of the site. Pastor Vicente recalls walking with Wonsuk for 24 hours to visit a pioneering work to see if the church and congregation truly existed. Pastor Vicente was surprised that Wonsuk walked faster than he did. Had Wonsuk not walked with him, he would never have walked that far. But Wonsuk's zeal challenged him.

During those visits, they would hold a service. Wonsuk would preach and Pastor Vicente would interpret the message. Later, at the dedication service of the completed church building, Wonsuk would attend the service and preach.

The financial aid that Wonsuk raised to help build churches had a deep impact on the tribal congregations. He was a stranger from far away, not even related to the people, yet because of the Gospel, he gave. This encouraged the members to also give both time and resources toward the completion of their church building.

First-hand Account of a Mountain Trip

The Mas sought to share their vision for the mountain ministry by bringing along students, missionaries, and friends on their mission trips up the mountains. Marlene Yap's account of her experiences in one of those trips gives us a glimpse of the Mas' ministry in the Cordillera Mountains.[55]

It was December 1991. The Mas gave an open invitation to anyone who would join them on a week-long ministry among mountain churches during the Christmas break. Three APTS students, a missionary family, several Malaysian visitors, and an APTS staff member who served as interpreter joined Wonsuk, Julie, and Boram (who was by then a toddler).

---

[55]Unless otherwise stated, all info given in this account is taken from Marlene Yap, interview by author, 4 March 2014, APTS, Baguio City, Philippines, transcript in the hand of author, 1-3.

The group started with a long ride up the mountain. When the vehicle could no longer negotiate the roads, they hiked. Every day they moved from one outreach to another, hiking at least 4 hours by day and having services at night. In one outreach, only the male members of the party went with Wonsuk because they had to go down to the valley and go up another mountain, a good 8-hour hike. No wonder Wonsuk told the group to "travel light."

The group brought sleeping bags, which was good since the mountains got very cold at night. They were housed by Christians. No one took a bath; there were no shower rooms and the water was cold. It also turned out to be good that at night it was very dark, because the toilet was anywhere you could find a spot to relieve yourself. On one particularly long hike, Wonsuk told them to leave their sleeping bags. That night, they were all shivering, yet Wonsuk and Julie did not seem to mind the temperature.

The group ate whatever the natives served them. They usually had rice, noodles, and cabbage—lots of cabbage. There were no canned goods because these were a luxury up in the mountains. The long hikes made them hungry so they usually snacked on boiled cassava. They drank water straight from the faucets since they assumed the mountain water was clean because the natives did not have stomach problems. None from the group suffered from the water, but many did get sick with colds and flu, including Marlene. Still, she said, "It was worth it. I enjoyed it. I'm glad I went."

Everywhere the group went, they held evangelistic meetings at night because people were working during the daytime. There was no sense of scheduled time. People came down the mountain using candles. Then the service started. They preached outdoors, in a small church, or at a basketball court. They preached using candlelight with the people sitting in total darkness. They could not even read the Bible. They had to know the message by heart. Always there was a local pastor coordinating the event.

Marlene appreciated Wonsuk's leadership. He was not bossy, but he told them where they would go and what they would do. Wonsuk had everyone take turns preaching, giving the testimony, etc. Wonsuk made her feel, "OK, I can do this." Afterwards, she felt good that she did do it.

Moreover, observing the Mas, Marlene learned much about relationship with the natives. The people loved the couple. They would gather around the campfire and drink natural boiled coffee. The Mas would converse with the natives, building relationships. "They say the language of the heart speaks louder than the words. So I'm sure the people see their love, because the people enjoyed their company," Marlene concluded.

Pastor Vicente concurs with this observation. He says the Mas were approachable, relating with everybody and spending time with the people. They easily adjusted to the people's culture.[56] Thus, the locals felt that the Mas really liked them.

The Mas' mountain ministry left a lasting legacy. In a 2000 issue, the *Pentecostal Evangel* reported that the Mas have helped establish 70 mountain churches.[57] By the time the Mas left for OCMS in 2006, that number had increased to "somewhere between 140-160."[58] There were so many; the Mas have already lost count.

OCMS: Professors and Executive Director

In OCMS, the Mas flourished all the more in the things they loved to do and the things they were good at. Yet, the same characteristics that endeared them to people in the mountains

---

[56]Vicente, 2.
[57]John W. Kennedy, "Embracing the Challenge," *Pentecostal Evangel*, (June 4, 2000): 12.
[58]Ma email.

remained the same—plus much more. This section will deal with their academic, social, and spiritual impact in OCMS.

Academic

The Mas' academic impact in OCMS is exemplified in the life of one student, Jonathan Libag.[59] Jonathan first met the Mas in June 2001 when he enrolled at APTS to major in missions. Wonsuk was the Academic Dean while Julie was Jonathan's professor in several missions courses. Julie was soft-spoken, so Jonathan always sat in front of the room. He did not want to miss her interesting insights. Julie's book was the textbook in a course in folk religion. When she taught, she used her personal experiences, not just what she read from other textbooks. She always emphasized missiological implications. When you read a book or when you write something, you always think, "What is the practical thing that I can do?" She did not stop at how one views things, but how one can apply what was learned in a very practical way. This greatly influenced Jonathan in his mission ministries outside the Philippines.

In 2008, when Jonathan was in Hawaii, he emailed Christmas greetings to the Mas, telling them he was a staff of Youth with a Mission (YWAM). Wonsuk invited him to come to OCMS to study. Initially, he refused because he still wanted to be in the field. When Wonsuk asked him, "What really makes you do what you do?" he responded, "I want to be like you…I want to experience the world and how God works in my life."

Wonsuk kept encouraging Jonathan to study at OCMS. He said, "We are going to visit Boram in the States. On our way back to London, we'll have 3 hours lay-over in Chicago. I want you to come to Chicago and let us meet. This is your ticket. Come over."

---

[59]Unless otherwise stated, all info given in this section is taken from Jonathan Libag, interview by author, 21 March 2014, APTS, Baguio City, Philippines, transcript in the hand of author.

Jonathan went, although he did not know what Wonsuk saw in him to encourage him to earn his PhD. In Chicago, Wonsuk introduced Jonathan to people from a Catholic Foundation that was willing to support his studies. But Jonathan was noncommittal. His response was, "It's a good idea, but is this what God wants me to do? I really have to pray for this." So, Wonsuk made a proposal. "OK, why not come to Oxford, Jonathan, and see our program, and from there you decide."

It took Jonathan a year to get to OCMS. He loved his YWAM ministry in Hawaii and was not ready to leave it behind. But Wonsuk was very persistent. When Jonathan finally went to Oxford, he found out that OCMS was offering a PhD in Professional Practice. It focuses on the answer to the question, "How will you improve your own practice?"

Wonsuk explained the program. He showed him the numerous theses all on the shelf, commenting that their writers were hoping someday somebody would pick these up and quote one phrase then cite their names. Then he said, "We are looking for somebody who could make a manual, a working manual that people can adopt." The practice-based research was a revolutionary program of OCMS. It was Wonsuk's brain-child.

With many other words, Wonsuk encouraged Jonathan. Finally, Jonathan caught Wonsuk's vision and realized that OCMS was where the Lord wanted him to be at that point in time. He was attracted to the idea, "In your mission now, how will you improve your practice?" This became his research subject. Using his college degree in agriculture, he is currently doing a practice-based research among rural pastors on their socio-economic divisions. Wonsuk serves as one of his mentors. Now Wonsuk pushes him hard in his studies, but each time Jonathan would ask questions, Wonsuk always has clever ways to encourage Jonathan to press on.

Generally, how Wonsuk dealt with Jonathan was also the way he dealt with the rest of the school. His persistence is obviously one major factor for his great accomplishments at OCMS. It brought in more students, more sponsors and more publications. Under his leadership, OCMS grew to 120 PhD research scholars and 12 faculty members.[60] His encouragement made people stay despite the difficulties of academic work. He was likewise great in encouraging others to write, research, and publish.[61] Their increased publications brought OCMS' name to many schools and improved the institution's reputation in academic circles.[62]

David Singh, a Research Tutor, summed up Wonsuk's impact on OCMS in these words:

> OCMS as an institution has acquired a very high level of credibility and reach under Wonsuk's leadership. I am not aware of a single Christian forum of worth across the world which remains untouched by some aspect of it that interfaces with OCMS under his leadership. I think Wonsuk's single most significant contribution has been in solidifying and extending the institutional footprint of OCMS.[63]

Social

The Mas influenced not only the academic life of OCMS, but also the social atmosphere of the institution. Wonsuk's office is one of the first things you see when you open the OCMS door. Often he would invite students to, "Come in, come in."[64] Both Wonsuk and Julie are approachable; they have an "open door policy."[65] They are good listeners and people trust them.[66]

---

[60]Prevette, 1.
[61]Ibid.
[62]Glendinning, 1.
[63]David Singh, "Questions re Drs. Wonsuk and Julie Ma," email to author, 23 April 2014, Oxford.
[64]Libag, 3.
[65]Singh, 1.
[66]Prevette, 1.

Moreover, in Wonsuk's leadership position, his non-judgmental approach is crucial in attaining good working relationships in the school.[67] What amazes people is the fact that both Mas are academically excellent, yet they consider others special. And when they communicate, they express their thoughts in ways that are easy to understand."[68] Although they now occupy the top position in the school, their humility remains. Moreover, OCMS students, staff, and faculty are all recipients of Wonsuk's and Julie's caring and compassionate ways. They readily express sympathy and support during tragedies in their community members' lives.[69] Under Wonsuk's leadership, the culturally diverse OCMS community became more cohesive. Members started caring for each other and depending on one another.[70]

A colleague described them this way: "Wonsuk is intensely person-focused. He has the exceptional ability to affirm others and make others feel they are important and are making significant contributions. Where he thinks there is need for improvement he has his own inimitable way of enabling colleagues to realize their potential."[71]

This colleague goes on to say:

Julie is deeply personable. I have shared many hours of wonderful discussions with her not only one-on-one, but also as part of the more formal weekly lectures and seminars. She has a keen and inquisitive mind, which challenges you to think deeper, but she also has a wonderful emotional side, which allows one to connect with her as a friend.[72]

Another social aspect at OCMS that the Mas influenced was the role of women in the institution. OCMS was male-

---

[67]Glendinning, 1
[68]Singh, 1.
[69]Glendinning, 1
[70]Prevette, 2.
[71]Singh, 1.
[72]Ibid.

dominated; spouses were not allowed to work within the same institution. However, when OCMS offered the top position to Wonsuk, he said, "I will not accept this unless my wife will work with me."[73] Later, people saw that Julie was Wonsuk's greatest confidant.[74]

Julie started as a Research Tutor at OCMS, yet she struggled when they first arrived in the school. It was obviously difficult for some to acknowledge her academic expertise. Yet, slowly attitudes and social dynamics changed. Now, "Julie is the only woman academic in OCMS, but she holds her own not just with her comprehensive knowledge of the Asian and Western contexts but also her rigorous and missionally sound reflections."[75] Moreover, lecturers' wives are now involved in school gatherings. To top it all, more female students are coming to OCMS. Many believe that all these changes are because of Julie's example. It is a tribute to Julie's character that she is now well-loved in the community.[76]

Finally, a significant comment regarding the Mas' social influence was expressed by an OCMS student: "Before he came, OCMS [was] so quiet, so focused on their studies. But now, the dynamics has [have] changed. They are still focused, but now they laugh."[77]

Spiritual

A person's real faith and relationship with God is revealed by sickness and tragedies. One precarious experience proved the Mas to be people of prayer and people of the spirit.[78] When Julie

---

[73] Libag, 3.
[74] Prevette, 1. This was clear even during their APTS days when Wonsuk would be upset and he would release stress by walking around the campus with Julie.
[75] Singh, 1.
[76] Libag, 4.
[77] Ibid., 3.
[78] Prevette, 1.

had a cerebral aneurism in December 2010, the Mas' faith and spiritual strength was a beautiful testimony of the power of prayer and of God's grace and faithfulness.[79] William Prevette, a Research Tutor at OCMS, was an eyewitness to this. He relates the experience in this manner:

> I was by [Wonsuk's] side in December 2010 when Julie was admitted to the JR Hospital in Oxford after suffering a brain aneurism which was life threatening. During that very tense life and death ordeal, I learned that Wonsuk Ma has a very deep and profound relationship with Jesus Christ and that his prayer life is not like most people I know. There were a number of days when the doctors were not sure that Julie would survive and then they were not sure she would ever regain consciousness, let alone walk out of the hospital. Through this time of shadow and darkness, Wonsuk was confident that God was going to restore Julie to full health. I add that he was probably the only one here in Oxford that believed this to the degree he did. Some thought she might live as [an]invalid, others thought she might learn to speak again, few gave her much chance of complete recovery. Three months after her aneurism Julie returned to living at home and today three years later she is back to full health serving as a research tutor at OCMS. This was a 'sign' to those of us at OCMS and around the world that prayed for Julie and Wonsuk that indeed they were under God's sovereign protection and covering.[80]

The Mas' deep spiritual walk has influenced the entire OCMS community. Under Wonsuk's leadership, the whole OCMS community gathers for prayer every Wednesday after

---

[79]"Prayer for Julie Ma," *Prayer Update Epiphany 2011*, available at http://www.ocms.ac.uk/content/sites/default/files/110126%20OCMS%20Prayers.pdf, accessed May 20, 2014.
[80]Prevette, 2.

chapel. They pray for each other's burdens and concerns. This cultivates a sense of togetherness that unites the community.[81]

Judy, a doctoral student mentored by Julie, called Julie her "pillar of strength" while she was writing her thesis for four years. Julie faithfully and earnestly prayed for her and encouraged her until she successfully completed her thesis. Wonsuk, on the other hand, often reminded her, "Our God is rich and money is God's least problem." These words encouraged her and indeed God faithfully provided all her needs. Judy is amazed by the Mas' Christian faith and prayer life. She likens them to "yeast," very humble yet making "a mind-blowing difference" wherever they are. She considers herself truly blessed to have been "discipled" by them during her studies in OCMS.[82]

When Our Strength Becomes Our Weakness

In counseling parlance, one's strength can also be one's weakness. Unfortunately, in some aspects, this was true with the Mas. The Mas' generosity and compassion, especially toward the poor and underprivileged, are well-known. However, their generosity had at times led to unrestrained giving which compromised their personal finances. Furthermore, some of those they helped tended to look to them instead of to the Lord for their provision.

Another strength of the Mas is their focus on Asians, which in OCMS has enlarged into the Global South.[83] Their passion is to give voice to Asian Pentecostals and to develop them theologically and academically. However, at times their emphasis

---

[81]Ibid., 1.
[82]Berinai, 1.
[83]The Global South refers to less developed countries while the Global North or "core" countries are from the developed world, which are the rich countries that control the means of production and a vastly larger percentage of wealth in comparison to the poorest countries. "Intro to the Global North vs. Global South," available at http://shesoverseas.com/2011/07/02/intro-to-the-global-north-vs-global-south/, accessed May 18, 2014.

on Asians has been misconstrued as a bias and as an aversion to westerners.

At present, the Mas are pouring out their lives into OCMS. Hopefully, they have also reserved some time for themselves. We do not want to see the Mas burning their candles from both ends. They still have a lot of visions and projects for the expansion of God's kingdom waiting to be fulfilled.

Wonsuk and Julie are not perfect; no one is aside from God. Yet their lives will ever be a legacy and a great example for others to follow in serving God.

Conclusion

I would like to conclude this article with personal thanks to the whole Ma family from my own family. Lem and I were among those that Wonsuk invited to join APTS's Faculty Development Program. When we moved to APTS, the Mas made our whole family, our son and daughter included, feel part of their family. Throughout our postgraduate academic journey, from our masters programs all the way to our doctorates, the Mas were there, giving encouragement, financial support when needed, and lots and lots of prayers. Even though they were halfway across the globe when I was doing my PhD studies, still their love and concern reached me.

This article is my expression of gratitude to a couple who believed in us and generously invested time and resources into our lives. Wonsuk and Julie have a big part in whatever we have attained in our academic life and in our ministry.

To Wonsuk and Julie, on behalf of all those whose lives you have touched and encouraged, I say with deep gratitude, THANK YOU AND GOD BLESS YOU!

Incarnation, Pentecost, and Virtual Spiritual Formation: Renewing Theological Education in Global Context

by Amos Yong

There has been in the last generation a steady and ongoing "virtualization" and "digitization" of theological education in global context. The groundwork was laid with theological education by extension starting in the 1960s. It was advanced through correspondence processes involving written and audio media, and it has continued to expand more recently with the advent of computer technologies. Developments in this area have been driven by the need to make theological education accessible, not to mention affordable, to larger numbers of people in order to meet the needs of an exploding global Christianity. The major challenges, of course, have related to quality control: how can ministers, missionaries, and church leaders be formed from a distance, or via online venues? Theological accrediting bodies put the question this way: can distance or online educational programs achieve the same outcomes and foster the same competencies as those in traditional, face-to-face classrooms? These matters are not trivial since theological education has always involved a dimension of personal, moral and spiritual formation that involves much more than mere transference of cognitive data.[1]

---

[1] Virginia Samuel Cetuk, *What to Expect in Seminary: Theological Education as Spiritual Formation* (Nashville: Abingdon Press, 1998). I should note that while part of my focus in this paper is on spiritual formation, I do not claim to have mastered the extensive literature on this important topic; for an

At one level, any defense of the digitization of theological education will have to be made operationally via empirical indications that such formation can and does occur in online environments. Yet theologians should neither be impelled only by such pragmatic exigencies nor depend only on such practical warrants for their educational practices. Hence, the emergence of more explicitly Christian theological reflection on virtual education is to be welcomed. Some have made the case scripturally, calling attention to how apostolic epistolary writings are themselves instances of theological education from a distance, and that they involved extensive theoretical and practical considerations about formation of moral and spiritual agents that can guide contemporary thinking about such matters.[2] Others have taken a more substantively theological approach. For instance, some would argue that as a theology of incarnation is irreducible to underwriting the goodness of the material or created order but also involves a pedagogical aspect regarding divine revelation meeting creatures on their contextual terms, so also does online education provide a medium for contextualizing theological education for those who for various reasons cannot attend traditional seminary programs.[3] Such contributions should be received, not as instrumental justifications for the adoption of new technologies, but as distinctively theological rationales for using such technologies discerningly.

---

important and up-to-date treatment, see Diane J. Chandler, *Christian Spiritual Formation: An Integrative Approach to Personal and Relational Wholeness* (Downers Grove: IVP Academic, 2014).

[2] Roger White, "Promoting Spiritual Formation in Distance Education," *Christian Education Journal* 3:2 (2006): 303-15, and Benjamin K. Forrest and Mark A. Lamport, "Modeling Spiritual Formation from a Distance: Paul's Formation Transactions with Roman Christians," *Christian Education Journal* 10:1 (2013): 110-24.

[3] John Gresham, "The Divine Pedagogy as a Model for Online Education," *Teaching Theology and Religion* 9 (2006): 24-28.

The crux of theological education, however, centers on whole-person and spiritual formation. If theological education in the global evangelical context, whether in traditional or online formats, aspires to be Bible-based and Christ-centered, what about the role of the Holy Spirit? This question is motivated in part by the fact that world Christianity is increasingly pentecostalized and charismatized, and in part by the fact that it seems any spiritually formative educational pedagogy ought to attend to these pneumatological dynamics.[4] Put pointedly, then, what difference does the Holy Spirit make in Christian higher education in general and seminary courses more specifically?[5] Further, what difference does the renewing work of the Spirit make when thinking about spiritual formation in the online modality?[6] The remainder of this essay suggests a pneumatologically robust educational theory and pedagogy with special attention to present virtualization trends. It is a pedagogical proposal that builds on but does not necessarily displace more traditional programs, approaches, and gains. Three programmatic theses can be considered.

---

[4] See my "Beyond the Evangelical-Ecumenical Divide for Theological Education in the 21St Century: A Pentecostal Assist," *Theological Education*, forthcoming.

[5] This is a variation of the theme in my forthcoming (with Dale Coulter), *Finding the Holy Spirit at the Christian University: Renewing Christian Higher Education* (Grand Rapids and Cambridge, UK: William B. Eerdmans Publishing Company, 2015), more succinctly elaborated in my "Finding the Holy Spirit at the Christian University: Renewal and the Future of Higher Education in the Pentecostal-Charismatic Tradition," in Vinson Synan, ed., *Spirit-Empowered Christianity in the 21st Century: Insights, Analyses, and Future Trends* (Lake Mary, Fla.: Charisma House, 2011), 455-76 and 577-87.

[6] I will use the nomenclature of Pentecostal, Charismatic, and renewal synonymously in this essay; see my essay, "The Holy Spirit and the Christian University: The Renewal of Evangelical Higher Education," in Gregg ten Elshoff, Thomas Crisp, and Steve L. Porter, eds., *Christian Scholarship in the Twenty-First Century: Prospects and Perils* (Grand Rapids: William B. Eerdmans Publishing Company, 2014), 163-90.

Thesis 1: The many tongues of Pentecost (Acts 2) invite a pluralistic-pedagogical approach to theological education, one that should be facilitated by online technologies. It is by now widely accepted that the Day of Pentecost narrative communicates God's eschatological redemption as involving those from many tongues, tribes, and nations, even to the ends of the earth (Acts 1:8). Insofar as the many tongues are inseparable from their cultural matrices–thus anthropologists talk about cultural-linguistic traditions–so also is it appropriate to conclude that the full declaration of God's wondrous works (Acts 2:11) is possible only through the harmonious blending of the many cultural voices and perspectives.[7] Theological education in a global context therefore is invigorated precisely through such multivocal and polyphonic resounding. Arguably, online modalities of delivery promote such multicultural interactions more than traditional seminary programs do. Where the latter would require a rare convergence of physical bodies from around the world in a specific geographic locale, the former makes possible both asynchronous and synchronous exchanges within virtual arenas that transcend geographic boundaries. What is crucially needed are quality faculty who can provide sufficient pastoral and pedagogical oversight so that the cognitive dissonances introduced by the many tongues lead to amazement and awe (Acts 2:12) rather than to confusion and skepticism ("others sneered and said, 'They are filled with new wine;'" Acts 2:13).

Beyond the multicultural conversation made possible by the virtual classroom, the Day of Pentecost narrative also foregrounds the multiplicity of senses involved in receiving the Spirit's revelation and manifestation. Not only are voices heard, but tongues are also seen and felt: "Divided tongues, as of fire, appeared among them, and a tongue rested on each of them"

---

[7]See my *The Spirit Poured Out on All Flesh: Pentecostalism and the Possibility of Global Theology* (Grand Rapids: Baker Academic, 2005), esp. ch. 4.

(Acts 2:3). The Spirit's appearance thus engages the broad spectrum of human perceiving, highlighting the full range of human ways of knowing and encountering the divine.[8] Contemporary educational theory already presumes that effective teachers interact with their students deploying multiple formats, methods, and approaches, appropriate to the "multiple intelligences" undergirding the variety of learning styles, preferences, and dispositions.[9] Yet while educators are expanding their pedagogical repertoires, the lecture persists as dominant in traditional classrooms. Those who take online teaching and learning seriously, however, consistently insist that the lecture plays only one, perhaps even minor, role in the overall educational experience, and urge a multi-modal pedagogy. Technologies engaging the full range of perceptual engagements are thus emerging as central to contemporary online education. My claim is that the Day of Pentecost narrative provides a theological framework to think about epistemological pluralism and the diversification of online educational media. The richness of Christian educational approaches therefore can proceed because of theological convictions about pedagogical pluralism, not just because such are available technologically, driven by consumer demand or taste, or merely part of the contemporary *zeitgeist* (spirit of the time).

One final point to be noted here, regarding interdisciplinarity, is tangential to the present discussion of online spiritual formation but nevertheless ought to be registered in any broader discussion of theological education. Elsewhere I have argued that the many tongues of Pentecost metaphor invites

---

[8]Elsewhere I make this argument for a pluralistic epistemology vis-à-vis a theology of disability: *The Bible, Disability, and the Church: A New Vision of the People of God* (Grand Rapids and Cambridge, UK: William B. Eerdmans Publishing Company, 2011), ch. 3.

[9]Howard Gardner, *Multiple Intelligences: New Horizons in Theory and Practice*, rev. ed. (New York: Basic Books, 2006).

thinking about the many disciplines–scientific and otherwise–as culturally and educationally formed discursive practices of inquiry that illuminate, in the eyes of faith, that which is true, good, and beautiful.[10] Theological education is already an interdisciplinary undertaking, drawing from the human (scripture study and history), normative (ethics and theology), and professional-practical (counseling, preaching) sciences, at least. All of these already have been activated in the online setting. What is needed is for the formational dimension to be seamlessly integrated across the curriculum. This leads to the second pneumatological hypothesis.

Thesis 2: The many gifts of the Spirit that constitute the diversity of the body of Christ (1 Cor. 12) invite consideration of how we can further develop and expand on a Charismatic-connectivist theory of learning in order to empower theological education and spiritual formation in the present global context. Although the lecture has been and remains, at least in some traditional circles, the dominant form of content delivery, seasoned faculty ensure that there are interactive elements included such as question-and-answer-periods and small group discussion sessions. The asynchronicity predominant in the online sphere, however, invites an alternative conceptualization of such interactivity. More fundamentally, given the dawn of the information age with the World Wide Web, educational goals have expanded from content mediation to cultivation of dispositional aptitudes and development of behavioral competencies. Part of the result of these shifts is that faculties are no longer looked to as the only, or even primary, source of

---

[10]See my "Academic Glossolalia? Pentecostal Scholarship, Multi-disciplinarity, and the Science-Religion Conversation," *Journal of Pentecostal Theology* 14:1 (2005): 61-80; cf. also Yong, *The Spirit of Creation: Modern Science and Divine Action in the Pentecostal-Charismatic Imagination*, Pentecostal Manifestos 4 (Grand Rapids and Cambridge, UK: William B. Eerdmans Publishing Company, 2011), ch. 2.

knowledge. Instead, if content is available anywhere and everywhere, then the educational task involves meeting learners where they are and, as sapiential advisors, helping them to discern their vocational path and directing them toward responsible and constructive engagement with the resources needed to achieve such aspirations. That there are multiple learning pathways for digital learners means that connecting (horizontally) with learning peers and educational resources become just as important as engaging (vertically) with the professor. These facets of virtual education thus presuppose what educational theorists call a connectivist pedagogy that emphasizes the full interactive scope of the learners' experiences, activities, and networks of relations within a decentralized but yet also intentionally communal online milieu, although they do not displace the sagacity that the faculty instructor represents and contributes.[11]

From the perspective of renewal spirituality, the pentecostal outpouring of the Spirit (Acts 2) leads to the Charismatic community of the Spirit (1 Corinthians 12). There are at least three characteristics of such a community or fellowship of the Holy Spirit relevant for our purposes. First, each and every member has spiritual gifts, endowed by the Spirit, for the common good (1 Cor. 12:4-11); no member, therefore, is lacking in potential to make a contribution. Second, there is no hierarchy of gifts, just distinctiveness; no one Charismatic member can minimize the value of others' contributions–instead, "On the contrary, the members of the body that seem to be weaker are indispensable" (1 Cor. 12:22). Last, but not least, not only do all members suffer and rejoice with each other (as appropriate), but

---

[11]For more on the connectivist thesis regarding multi-directional learning, see George Siemens, "Connectivism: A Learning Theory for the Digital Age" (12 December 2004), available at http://www.elearnspace.org/Articles/connectivism.htm [accessed 11 October 2013].

all are urged to use their charisms along the "still more excellent way" (1 Cor. 12:31b) of love; so even as there are no better or worse gifts, there are better and worse manifestations of such within the community of faith for the benefit of others. While it might be thought that the only relevance of this Charismatic ecclesiology for theological education is the incidental reference to the appointment of teachers among other offices (1 Cor. 12:27-29),[12] there are obvious implications for a connectivist approach to theological education.

The following teases out, again only programmatically, application of these pneumatological insights toward what might be called a Charismatically-inflected connectivist pedagogy for online spiritual formation. Here the theological foundations of a Charismatically empowered community provide the framework for a multi-directional, dynamic, and relational learning environment in which the learners' contextual realities are part and parcel of the dialogue between themselves and also with their professors. More palpably, to the degree that online technology can create virtual communities–the shape of which will continue to morph in relationship to changing forms of social media–to that same degree learners will be inspired by, challenged by, and held accountable to a wider range of perspectives than can be generated in many traditional classrooms. The point is that the charisms of the Spirit distributed to each member of the learning community– themselves embedded within multiple networks of shifting relationships–across the global context can be harnessed for instruction and correction.[13]

---

[12]Bert E. Downs, "The Spiritual Gift of Teaching," *Christian Education* 6:1 (1985): 62-67.

[13]For another articulation of these matters, see James T. Flynn, "Scripture as a Catalyst for Effective Online Spiritual Formation," presentation at the North American Professors of Christian Education (NAPCE) (21 October 2011), *Theological Education* (under review).

So far, however, we have focused on charting pneumatological trajectories from central scriptural loci for online theological education and formation. These beg to be situated within a more full-orbed pneumato-theological framework. This leads to *thesis 3: A pneumatological-trinitarian ontology foregrounds the affective-relational dimension of encounter with God and others, which links heads-hearts-hands (from the pietist tradition) and closes the loop of church-academy-world.* Such a proposal ought to be fleshed out in at least three directions: theologically, anthropologically, and contextually.

Theologically, the work of the Spirit is always also the work of Christ and the work of the Father–thus a pneumatological theology is a prelude to and constitutive of a trinitarian theology –even as the person of the Spirit is the divine presence amidst and activity within the world through which creatures live, move, and have their being.[14] As such the Spirit is the horizon of possibility through which human beings encounter God, even in the province of theological education. This goes also for online interfaces: the work of the Spirit is to mediate transformative, sanctifying, and empowering encounters with God in Christ apart from which theological education fails its task.

Yet, anthropologically, the Spirit enables divine encounter and christomorphic transformation through the renewal of human minds, the reformation and renovation of human hearts, and the revitalization and reinvigoration of human hands. Traditional theological education accomplished these goals most formidably through mentorships and apprenticeships–between students and faculty, internship supervisors, and other exemplars –knitted by affective bonds of trust, interpersonal relationships

---

[14]There is a lot going on in this claim that I have to refer readers elsewhere for fuller elaboration–e.g., Yong, *Spirit-Word-Community: Theological Hermeneutics in Trinitarian Perspective* (Burlington, Vt., and Aldershot, UK: Ashgate Publishing Ltd., and Eugene, Ore.: Wipf & Stock Publishers, 2002).

of openness, and mimetic practices that depend on ongoing improvision, innovation, and creativity. In the online environment, such affectivity is nurturable both within and outside of the class "space."[15] A full range of web-available resources, communicative modalities, and social media–i.e., discussion boards, virtual chats, Skype, small group activities, Wimba sessions, wikis, blogs, Facebook–can be deployed to build and nurture online educational communities that activate affective, relational, and imaginative learning. Constitutive here are prayer, meditation, Scripture reading, journaling, and devotional reflection, among other spiritual practices that should be woven into the curriculum. When properly facilitated by an expert, engaged, and virtually present faculty instructor, students are energized by the sense of community and report transformative educational experiences online.[16]

Beyond the virtual arena, theological education bridges academia with the church on the one side and society on the other (spatially and metaphorically speaking). The point is that the classroom–traditional or virtual–is the "space" wherein the real life challenges and opportunities navigated in church and society meet with abstract academic theory. If traditional theological education required students to leave their ministerial contexts and seclude themselves in a seminary for a specified period of time, online courses of study not only allow students to remain engaged in their existing ministerial and social networks but provide a laboratory for the full length of the program for contextual reflection, exploration, and application. Seminary programs are increasingly reconceptualizing the role of field

---

[15] Roger White, "Promoting Spiritual Formation in Distance Education," *Christian Education Journal* 3:2 (2006): 303-15.

[16] Relevant here is the discussion by Kristina L. Stekl-Chalfin, "Evaluation of the Relative Impact of Five Pedagogical Methods of Forming Transformational Community in an Online Spiritual Formation Class" (DMin. thesis, Ashland Theological Seminary, 2008).

mentors and supervisors so that there is a natural feedback loop from instructor-pastor-supervisor that requires ongoing traversal of the hermeneutical spiral between academy-church-society.[17] Curricular designs are also more attentive to including spiritual-formational elements relevant to and engaging with each learner's contextual matrix.[18]

The preceding generalizes almost at a meta-theoretical level and masks the many practical and concrete challenges confronting teachers and learners engaged in theological education across the global context. To be clear, nothing said is intended to supplant the traditional classroom, even as the latter will continue to evolve (oftentimes to include virtual components). However, technological advances will continue to expand the possibilities of online education and further enable the kind of processes central to theological and ministerial formation to unfold across spatial and temporal distances. The main objective of the foregoing, then, is to think through the project of online theological education in general and the task of spiritual formation, especially in light of the increasing pervasiveness of renewal Christianity across the global landscape. More specifically, the goal has been to articulate distinctively pneumatological and trinitarian (i.e., incarnational and pentecostal) rationales for contemporary educational praxis rather than to allow theological educators to be carried by merely pragmatic opportunities or be driven by utilitarian and market factors. If these proposals can in turn inspire more effective spiritual formational pedagogies and widen the online horizons of what is possible and plausible, then it may even contribute in

---

[17]Stephen D. Lowe and Mary E. Lowe, "Spiritual Formation in Theological Distance Education: An Ecosystems Model," *Christian Education Journal* 7:1 (2010): 85-102.

[18]Mary E. Quinn, Laura S. Foote, and Michele L. Williams, "Integrating a Biblical Worldview and Developing Online Courses for the Adult Learner," *Christian Scholar's Review* 41:2 (2011): 163-73.

some small way to the renewal of contemporary theological education itself as it morphs in global context.

Mission Spirituality:
A Pentecostal Contribution
to Spiritual Formation

by Robert P. Menzies

Introduction

The Pentecostal movement is recognized around the world as a powerful and dynamic force impacting the lives of hundreds of millions of people. It is changing the face of the Christian church. And in many cases, such as Korea, it is hard to overestimate its impact on the larger society. Indeed, one scholar has described the modern Pentecostal movement as "the most successful social movement of the past century."[1]

Yet, in spite of this, many Christians still do not see Pentecostals as having much to offer theologically. It is a movement of experience, we are told, not of doctrine. Our cultured friends, who prefer to worship in a more serene and cognitive manner, speak of Pentecostal exuberance in polite but condescending tones. Their negative responses often betray their own oft-unexamined assumptions, primary of which is this—The enthusiasm of the early church was unique to the apostolic era and is no longer appropriate for Christians today. "Visions and dreams, prophecy and tongues, loud and joyful praise are all anachronisms," they maintain, "and should not be viewed as contemporary models." Implicit in this friendly critique is the presumption that Pentecostals are driven by emotion and need

---

[1] Philip Jenkins, *The Next Christendom: The Coming of Global Christianity* (Oxford: Oxford University Press, 2002), 8.

to spend more time studying the Word. Or to put it another way, many Christian brothers and sisters view the Pentecostal contribution to the larger church (if there is one) in experiential rather than theological terms.

This judgment, I would suggest, misses something important. Pentecostals have always been 'people of the Book' and committed to it. In fact, the origins of the Pentecostal movement may be traced to a Bible college and to serious study of the Scriptures. Pentecostal experience flows from a desire to embrace the biblical record and encounter God in Christ through the Holy Spirit like the apostolic church did.[2] Indeed, a Pentecostal approach to the Bible may be summed up with the simple statement, "Their stories are our stories."[3] This approach has enabled the Pentecostal movement, at least in modern times, to bring together an emphasis on experience and a commitment to the authority of the Bible. Rather than competing with one another, most Pentecostals see these twin themes as complimentary.

This blending of a desire for authentic apostolic experience with a commitment to the Bible has uniquely marked the Pentecostal movement. It has encouraged Pentecostals to re-examine the New Testament (particularly the book of Acts) in an attempt to recover the calling and experience of the apostolic church. This approach, I would suggest, has led to fresh and important insights into the Luke's theological perspective and his missiological purpose. I believe these insights have profound implications for the life of the church.

---

[2]As Keith Warrington notes, Pentecostal theology is, at its heart, a theology of encounter. See Warrington, *Pentecostal Theology: A Theology of Encounter* (London: T&T Clark, 2008), 21.

[3]For more on the theological contribution of the Pentecostal movement to the larger church world, see Robert P. Menzies, *Pentecost: This Story Is Our Story* (Springfield, MO: Gospel Publishing House, 2013).

In this essay, then, I will argue that Pentecostals have an important theological contribution to make to the larger church world, one that directly impacts a topic of vital importance to every Christian, that being the Holy Spirit's contribution to spiritual formation. I will attempt to accomplish this task by outlining what I would describe as a uniquely Pentecostal contribution to spiritual formation then by showing that this contribution is rooted in a reading of Luke-Acts that captures well Luke's intent.

Missional Spirituality

Pentecostal experience and praxis are shaped, in large measure, by the stories contained in the book of Acts. The central texts that Pentecostals around the world memorize and feature are Acts 1:8 ("But you will receive power when the Holy Spirit comes on you; and you will be my witnesses in Jerusalem, and in all Judea and Samaria, and to the ends of the earth") and Acts 2:4 ("All of them were filled with the Holy Spirit and began to speak in other tongues as the Spirit enabled them"). These verses and the related stories of bold missionary endeavor that follow in Acts provide the templates for our understanding of the Baptism in the Spirit. They shape Pentecostal experience and give direction to our mission.

Within the larger Christian family, this emphasis is unique and gives the Pentecostal movement a profoundly missional ethos. In my opinion, this is one of the key reasons why Pentecostal churches around the world have grown at such an amazing rate. And it was certainly a central reason why scores of missionaries (most with meager financial backing) left the Azusa Street Revival and traveled to diverse points of the globe to proclaim the apostolic faith. I would further suggest it is why Pentecostals today constantly share their faith with others. Bold witness for Jesus is recognized as their primary calling and the core purpose of their experience of the Spirit's power. Missions is woven into the fabric of their DNA.

This missiological emphasis gleaned from Luke's writing and the book of Acts is unique to Pentecostals. While they have featured Luke-Acts, other Protestant churches have highlighted the Pauline epistles. The great truths of the Reformation were largely gleaned from the writings of Paul, particularly Romans and Galatians. The terminology 'justification by faith' echoes Paul. So following the lead of Luther, Calvin, and the other reformers, the Protestant churches have largely emphasized the Pauline epistles as their core texts.

This emphasis has, to a large extent, shaped the Evangelical movement. Elsewhere I have outlined how Evangelical theologians of the past century over-reacted to liberal scholarship that challenged the historical reliability of Luke's writings.[4] As a result, they rejected the notion that Luke as well as the other gospel writers were *not* historians, but rather theologians. In Evangelical circles, any discussion of the theological purpose of Luke and his narrative was muted. The Gospels and the book of Acts were viewed as historical records, not accounts reflecting self-conscious theological concerns. Of course, this approach essentially created a canon within the cannon and, by giving Paul pride of place as *the* theologian of the New Testament, had a significant Paulinizing effect on Evangelical theology. Many Evangelicals are just now beginning to come to terms with the theological significance of the biblical narratives.

Certainly, Evangelical scholars have, in their own way, highlighted the missionary call. Generally, this has come by way of the Great Commission in Matthew 28:18-20. That text has

---

[4]See William W. Menzies and Robert P. Menzies, *Spirit and Power: Foundations of Pentecostal Experience* (Grand Rapids: Zondervan, 2000), 37-45.

perhaps been more acceptable to them than the commissioning material found in Acts, since Jesus is the one who has "all authority" and there is no overt commission for his disciples to work "signs and wonders." Yet even here, tensions persist. Is this commission valid for everyone in the church? And how does Jesus' authority relate to the disciples whom he sends out? The Pentecostal reading of Acts provides clear and ready answers. On the basis of that reading, Pentecostals affirm that every disciple is called and empowered and every disciple encouraged to expect that signs and wonders will accompany their witness. Evangelicals tend to be, at best, less clear on these matters.

More recently, Third-Wave Evangelicals have highlighted the role of spiritual gifts in evangelism.[5] But as I have pointed out elsewhere, this perspective (rooted as it is in Paul's gift language) fails to offer a solid rationale for a high sense of expectancy with respect to divine enabling.[6] When it comes to spiritual gifts, the attitude of many is quite passive, saying "Perhaps verbal witness is not our gift." What is lacking here is a clear promise of empowering that extends to every believer. Pentecostals find this in the narrative of Acts (e.g., 1:8, 2:19). Furthermore, Luke highlights more than simply 'signs and wonders.' His narrative is also filled with examples of bold, Spirit-inspired witness in the face of opposition and persecution (e.g., Luke 12:11-12, Acts 4:31). This staying power is an indisputable focus, and it has been central to Pentecostal missions as well. Here again, we need to hear Luke's unique contribution.

I do not wish to minimize the significance of the great doctrinal truths of Paul's writings. I merely point out that, since Paul was, for the most part, addressing specific needs in various churches, his letters tend to focus on the inner life of the

---

[5]See John Wimber and Kevin Springer, *Power Evangelism* (San Francisco: Harper & Row, 1991).
[6]Menzies, *Spirit and Power*, 145-58.

Christian community rather than on the mission of the church to the world. For example, he has much to say about spiritual gifts and how they should be exercised in corporate worship (1 Cor. 12-14) but is relatively silent went it comes to the Pentecostal outpouring of the Holy Spirit. It is probably fair to say that, while Paul features the Spirit's *interior* work, such as the fruit (Gal. 5:22-23), Luke features the Spirit's *expressive* work (Acts 1:8). Thus, by appropriating in a unique way the significant contributions of Luke-Acts, Pentecostals have developed a piety with a uniquely outward or missiological thrust; thus, Pentecostal spirituality is missional spirituality.

This Lukan and missiological emphasis, transmitted largely through the stories in the book of Acts, also points to a significant difference that distinguishes the Pentecostal movement from the Charismatic movement. Whereas the Pentecostal movement from the very beginning has been a missionary movement, the Charismatic movement has largely been one of spiritual renewal within existing, mainline churches. Here, the nomenclature is instructive. The term "Pentecostal" points us to Pentecost and the missionary call and power that is given to the church (Acts 1-2). In contrast, the term 'Charismatic' points to the spiritual gifts that serve to edify the church, particularly as it gathers together for corporate worship (1 Cor. 12-14). Both movements have blessed the wider church and brought fresh insights and much-needed spiritual energy. However, the missiological legacy of the Pentecostal movement is conspicuous, while the same cannot be said for the Charismatic movement.

Our unique appropriation of Luke-Acts not only distinguishes Pentecostals from our Evangelical and Charismatic brothers and sisters, it also highlights a significant difference that separates us from the liberal wing of the Protestant church. It should be noted that many liberals, unlike their Evangelical counterparts, have given more attention to the Gospels, and particularly Jesus, than to Paul. In fact, some go so far as to claim that Paul distorted or obscured the pure teachings of Jesus. It would appear, at least with this emphasis on the Gospel narratives, that liberals and Pentecostals might find some common ground. But here again, we encounter a major difference. Whereas liberals seek to understand Jesus in the light of a critical scholarship that discounts the possibility of the miraculous, Pentecostals embrace the miracle-working Jesus of the New Testament who is both fully human and fully divine. That difference is profound. One has an apostolic faith to proclaim, the other left with little but pious platitudes. Again, it is not difficult to see why one is a missionary movement and the other not.

All of this suggests that, with their simple approach to the book of Acts ("their stories are our stories"), Pentecostals have uniquely highlighted an important aspect of the work of the Holy Spirit and Christian discipleship. They assert that every Christian is called and empowered (at least potentially) to be a bold, Spirit-inspired witness for Jesus. As Peter declared in his Pentecost sermon (Act 2:14-36), the church is nothing less than a community of end-time prophets.[7] Thus, from a Pentecostal perspective, one cannot separate missions from discipleship or bold witness from Christian character. The call comes to every believer, and the enabling of the Spirit is promised to all.

Missional Spirituality and Luke's Purpose

While all this may sounds very inspiring, the question must

---

[7] For more on this theme see Robert Menzies, *The Development of Early Christian Pneumatology with special reference to Luke-Acts* (JSNTSS 54; Sheffield: JSOT Press, 1991), especially pp. 198-229 and Roger Stronstad, *The Prophethood of All Believers: A Study in Luke's Charismatic Theology* (JPTSS 16; Sheffield: Sheffield Academic Press, 1999), *passim*.

be asked, Is this really the message Luke intended to communicate? In other words, how did Luke expect his story to be read? As we have noted, many Christians have not read Luke-Acts as presented here. Non-Pentecostal Evangelicals generally maintain that Luke wrote to provide an historical account of the beginnings of the church so that subsequent readers might have an accurate account of the gospel message and be assured of the historical basis upon which its stands. Many of these Evangelicals also insist that, since Luke's historical narrative treats a unique era in the life of the church, the events he describes are not presented as models for the missionary praxis of subsequent generations of Christians.[8] In short, they generally assume that Luke the historian wrote to provide the church with its message, not its methods.

This assumption has produced a choir of Evangelical scholars who constantly tell us that Pentecost is a unique and unrepeatable event.[9] As a young student, I was puzzled by such statements. In what sense is Pentecost unique? Any event in history cannot be repeated, but many events in the narrative of Acts are clearly presented as models for Luke's church. They are

---

[8]See Ben Witherington III, *The Acts of the Apostles: A Socio-Rhetorical Commentary* (Grand Rapids: Eerdmans, 1998), p. 132; Darrell Bock, *Acts* (Baker Exegetical Commentary on the New Testament; Grand Rapids: Baker, 2007), *passim* (cf. Darrell Bock, *Luke* [The IVP Commentary Series; Downers Grove: InterVarsity Press, 1994], 189-90); and Keith J. Hacking, *Signs and Wonders, Then and Now: Miracle-Working, Commissioning and Discipleship* (Nottingham: Apollos/IVP, 2006), *passim*. Witherington highlights the 'unique' nature of Pentecost. Bock also fails to develop the theological implications of Acts 1-2 for the missionary praxis of the contemporary church (see my review of Bock's Acts commentary in *Pneuma* 30 [2008]: 349-50). Hacking argues that the miracles of Jesus and the apostles were not intended to serve as models for the post-apostolic church and that the commissioning accounts are relevant only to a select few (see my review of Hacking's book in *EQ* 79 [2007]: 261-65).

[9]Dunn, *Baptism*, p. 53: "Pentecost can never be repeated—for the new age is here and cannot be ushered in again." Note also Witherington, *Acts*, 132: "[of Pentecost] . . . in crucial ways it is unique."

recorded by Luke precisely so that they will be repeated in the lives of his readers. Why do Evangelical scholars, then, insist that Pentecost is unique and unrepeatable? This response seems to be connected to their view of Luke's purpose.

Although I would acknowledge that Luke does stress the reliability of the apostolic witness and remarkable nature of the origins of the Christian movement, his purposes go beyond simply 'confirming the gospel.'[10] Luke's narrative is far more than a nostalgic review of how it all began. For him, the story does not end with the apostles and their witness, but rather continues (as the ending of Acts anticipates) with the readers taking up the mantle of ministry modeled by Jesus and his disciples. Luke narrates the story of Jesus and the early church in order to challenge his church (and every church in "these last days") to assume its prophetic calling by listening to the voice of the Spirit and bearing bold witness for Jesus.

Luke's two-volume work is a missions manifesto. Through it, he seeks to remind his Christian readers of their true identity (i.e., they are a community of prophets called to be a "light to the nations") and to encourage them, even in the face of opposition and persecution,[11] to listen to the voice of the Spirit and, through his power, to bear witness to Jesus. Of course, Luke accomplishes this by providing various models–above all, Jesus, but also Peter, Stephen, Philip, Paul, and others. With great literary skill and artistry, he provides his intended readers (the persecuted Christians of his church) with theological and methodological

---

[10]Robert Maddox, *The Purpose of Luke-Acts* (Edinburgh: T.&T. Clark, 1982). He argues that Luke writes to reassure his largely Gentile church of the reliability of the gospel despite Jewish hostility and rejection.

[11]Martin W. Mittelstadt, *The Spirit and Suffering in Luke-Acts: Implications for a Pentecostal Pneuma--tology* (JPTSS 26; London: T&T Clark International, 2004) and Scott Cunningham, *"Through Many Tribulations:" The Theology of Persecution in Luke-Acts* (JSNTSS 142; Sheffield: Sheffield Academic Press, 1997) argue convincingly that Luke wrote to a church that was experiencing persecution. See especially Cunningham, *Persecution*, 328–36.

guidance for their mission.[12] If this summary of one of Luke's purposes is correct, then Pentecostals read Luke-Acts as he hoped they would–as providing models for life and action for the mission every believer is called to embrace.[13]

Here I would like to focus on a particular text–Acts 2:17-21–that I believe offers considerable support for this Pentecostal reading of Luke-Acts. It is a classic one that calls us back to the missional spirituality of the apostolic church.

Pentecost as a Paradigm (Acts 2:17-21)

Most New Testament scholars would likely concur that Luke 4:16-30 (Jesus' dramatic sermon at Nazareth) is paradigmatic for Luke's Gospel. All of the major themes that will appear in his Gospel are foreshadowed here–i.e., the work of the Spirit, the universality of the gospel, the grace of God, and the rejection of Jesus. This is the one significant point where the chronology of Luke's Gospel differs from that of Mark. Luke takes an event from the middle of Jesus' ministry and brings it right up front to inaugurate that ministry. He does this because he understands that this event, particularly Jesus' recitation of Isaiah 61:1-2 and declaration that this prophecy is now being fulfilled in his ministry, provides important insights into the nature of Jesus and his mission. This passage, then, provides us with a model for Jesus' subsequent ministry.

It is interesting to note that Luke provides a similar sort of

---

[12] I am in agreement with Karris, who posits that Luke wrote shortly after the destruction of Jerusalem and its temple (around 75 A.D.) and that he wrote to "communities whose missionary work and daily existence are prone to danger and suffering—both from Jew and Gentile, but primarily from the Jewish synagogal authorities" (Karris, "Missionary Communities," 96).

[13] Green, "Learning Theological Interpretation from Luke," 66: "Luke's model readers will embrace this narrative as their own and seek to continue it in their lives."

paradigmatic introduction for his second volume–the book of Acts. After the coming of the Holy Spirit at Pentecost, Peter delivers a sermon (Acts 2:14-41) that, in many ways, parallels that of Jesus in Luke 4. Peter also refers to an Old Testament prophecy concerning the coming of the Spirit–Joel 2:28-32–and declares that it too is now being fulfilled (Acts 2:17-21). The message is clear. Just as Jesus was anointed by the Spirit to fulfill his prophetic vocation, so also Jesus' disciples have been anointed as end-time prophets to proclaim the word of God. The text of Joel 2:28-32 that is cited here, like the paradigmatic passage in Luke 4, also shows signs of careful editing on the part of Luke. Acts 2:17-21 reads thusly *(modification of Joel 2:28-32 italicized)*:

> **v. 17** *In the last days, God says,* [Joel: "after these things"]
> I will pour out my Spirit on all people.
> Your sons and daughters will prophesy.
> *Your young men will see visions,* [Joel: these lines are inverted]
> *Your old men will dream dreams.*
> **v. 18** *Even* on *my* servants, both men and women, [additions to Joel]
> I will pour out my Spirit in those days,
> *And they will prophesy.*
> **v. 19** I will show wonders in the heaven *above*
> And *signs* on the earth *below,*
> Blood and fire and billows of smoke.
> **v. 20** The sun will be turned to darkness and the moon to blood Before the coming of the great and glorious day of the Lord.
> **v. 21** And everyone who calls on the name of the Lord will be saved.

Luke carefully shapes this quotation from the Septuagint

(LXX) in order to highlight important theological themes. The following three modifications are particularly striking.

Modification 1. In v. 17, Luke alters the order of the two lines that refer to young men having visions and old men dreaming dreams. In Joel, the old men dreaming dreams comes first; but Luke rearranges these two lines so the reference to visions precedes the comment about dreams. A survey of Acts reveals that this alteration is not simply an insignificant stylistic change, a whim, or a slip of the eye; it is intentional. Luke gives the reference to visions pride of place in order to emphasize its importance. With this modification, he highlights a theme that he sees as vitally important, one that recurs throughout his narrative.[14]

A survey of the key terms is instructive. First, we find that those associated with dreams and dreaming occur only in the book of Acts. The term translated "shall dream" is a future passive of ενυπνιάζω. In the entire New Testament, this verb occurs only here and in Jude 8. The noun, ενύπνιον ("dream"), is found nowhere else in Acts or the rest of the New Testament. Clearly, Luke is not big on dreaming.[15]

He does, however, love to recount stories that reference guidance through visions; although at first glance, this may not appear to be the case. The noun translated "visions" in v. 17, ὅρασις, occurs four times in the New Testament–once in Acts, the other three in Revelation. But appearances are often misleading, and such is the case here. Luke uses another term often and at decisive points in his narrative to refer to visions– the neuter noun ὅραμα (a close cousin to ὅρασις). The noun

---

[14]This insight into Luke's special use of 'vision' was inspired by a conversation with Dr. David Yonggi Cho during my visit to Seoul, Korea, in 2007.
[15]Note how Luke describes revelatory experiences at night, which might have taken place during sleep, as 'visions' and not 'dreams' (e.g., Acts 16:9-10).

ὅραμα occurs 12 times in the New Testament, 11 of them in the book of Acts.[16] Luke is, indeed, fond of visions. Although in Acts 2:17 he retains the language of the LXX, elsewhere in his narrative he employs his preferred and very similar term to speak of visions.

As already noted, references to visions are not only plentiful in Luke's narrative, they also come at strategic moments.[17] Thus, his alteration at this point appears to be theologically motivated. Of course, visions are not the only way that God guides the church in the book of Acts, yet Luke's point is hard to miss. By linking the visions of Joel's prophecy (Acts 2:17) with the visions of the early church, he is saying, in effect, that in "these last days" (i.e., the period from Jesus' birth up to the Day of the Lord) the mission of the church must be directed by God, who will lead his end-time prophets in special and personal ways, including visions, angelic visitations, and Holy Spirit prompting, so that we might fulfill our calling to take the gospel to "the ends of the earth." In short, for Luke, the experience of the early church, one that is supernaturally led by God, serves as a model for his church (and ours).

Modification 2. With the addition of a few words in v. 19, Luke transforms Joel's text to read: "I will show wonders in the heaven *above*, and *signs* on the earth *below*." In this way, Luke consciously links the miracles associated with Jesus (see v. 22, "Jesus...was a man accredited by God to you by miracles, wonders and signs,") and the early church (e.g., 2:43) together with the cosmic portents listed by Joel (vs. 19-20). All are signs and wonders that mark the end of the age. For Luke, "these last days" (remember that Luke's church and ours are firmly rooted

---

[16]Acts 7:31; 9:10, 12; 10: 3, 17, 19; 11:5; 12:9; 16:9, 10; 18:9; and then also in Mt. 17:9.

[17]For the strategic role of visions in the book of Acts, see 9:10-12; 10:3, 17, 19; 11:5; 16:9-10; 18:9-10.

in this period) represents an epoch marked by signs and wonders. Luke, then, is not only conscious of the significant role that miracles have played in the growth of the early church, he also anticipates that these signs and wonders will continue to characterize the ministry of the church to whom he writes.

Modification 3. Luke inserts the phrase "And they will prophesy" into the quotation in v. 18. This insertion simply emphasizes what is already present in the text of Joel. The previous verse has already reminded us that this end-time outpouring of the Holy Spirit of which Joel prophesies is nothing less than a fulfillment of Moses' wish "that all the Lord's people were prophets" (Num. 11:29). Acts 2:17 quotes Joel 2:28 verbatim: "I will pour out my Spirit on all people. Your sons and daughters will prophesy." Now, in v. 18, Luke echoes this refrain to highlight the fact that the Spirit comes as the source of prophetic inspiration because this theme will dominate his narrative. It is a message he does not want his readers to miss. The church in "these last days," Luke declares, is to be a community of prophets who are called to bring the message of "salvation to the ends of the earth" (Isa. 49:6). And now Luke reminds his readers that they also have been promised power to fulfill this calling. The Spirit will come and enable the church–Luke's and ours–to bear bold witness for Jesus in the face of opposition and persecution.

This theme of bold, prophetic witness was anticipated in Luke's Gospel. Jesus is anointed with the Spirit so that he might preach the good news to the poor, proclaim freedom for the prisoners and proclaim the year of the Lord's favor (Lk 4:18-19). The parallels between Jesus' experience at the Jordan and that of the disciples at Pentecost are striking and should not be missed. Both occurred at the beginning of the respective missions of Jesus and the early church, both centered on the coming of the

Spirit, and both are described as a prophetic anointing in the context of a sermon that cites Old Testament prophecy. Through his careful shaping of the narrative, Luke presents Jesus, the ultimate prophet, as a model for all of his followers from Pentecost onward. Luke's church has a mission to carry out, a message to proclaim.

This motif of bold, Spirit-inspired witness is also highlighted in Jesus' teaching. Luke foreshadowed events that will follow in his second volume by relating the important promise of Jesus recorded in Luke 12:11-12: "When you are brought before synagogues, rulers and authorities, do not worry about how you will defend yourselves or what you will say, for the Holy Spirit will teach you at that time what you should say."

Immediately after Pentecost, in the first story Luke recounts, we begin to see how relevant and important this promise of Jesus is for the mission of the church. Luke describes Peter and John's encounter with a crippled beggar and his miraculous healing. A large crowd gathers, gaping at this marvelous event. The story builds to a climax as the Jewish leaders, upset with this turn of events, arrest Peter and John for preaching about the resurrection of Jesus. "You killed the author of life," Peter declares, "but God raised him from the dead. We are witnesses of this" (Acts 3:15). After spending the night in prison, the two are called before the leaders and questioned. Peter, filled with the Holy Spirit, begins to bear bold witness for Jesus (Acts 4:8). Their courage is so striking that it leaves the leaders astonished and amazed. Finally, after deliberation, they are commanded to stop preaching about Jesus, but reply with incredible boldness: "Judge for yourselves whether it is right in God's sight to obey you rather than God. We cannot help speaking about what we have seen and heard" (Acts 4:19-20).

This is merely the beginning of the persecution the end-time prophets must face. Very soon, the apostles are again arrested, interrogated, angrily told, "We gave you strict orders not to teach in this name . . . Yet you have filled Jerusalem with your teaching" (Acts 5:28). To which again Peter responds, "We must obey God rather than men! The God of our fathers raised Jesus from the dead . . . We are witnesses of these things, and so is the Holy Spirit" (Acts 5:29-32). After being are flogged, warned not to speak about Jesus, then released, the apostles rejoice that they have been "counted worthy of suffering" for Jesus and continue to proclaim "the good news that Jesus is the Messiah" (Acts 5:41-42).

The persecution intensifies. What began with warnings in Acts 4 and led to beatings in Acts 5 now extends to Stephen's martyrdom in Acts 7. In the same way the apostles were strengthened by the Spirit to bear bold witness for Jesus so also is Stephen (Acts 6:10). In the midst of his sermon to his persecutors, Stephen declares, "You always resist the Holy Spirit! Was there ever a prophet your fathers did not persecute?" (vs. 51-52). The powerful irony should not be missed, for this same crowd moves in to kill Stephen, a man "full of the Holy Spirit" (vs. 55).[18] The witness of another prophet is rejected.

This pattern of bold, Spirit-inspired witness in the face of opposition continues with Paul, the dominant character in the latter portion of Acts. Chosen by the Lord to take the gospel to the Gentiles, we are told that his journey will not be easy. The Lord, speaking to Ananias, declares, "I will show him how much he must suffer for my name" (Acts 9:16). And suffer he does. Yet in the face of mind-numbing opposition, Paul is guided and strengthened by the Holy Spirit—and a trail of churches filled with believers who worship Jesus are left in his wake. The

---

[18]Karris notes that in Acts 7:55-56 the promises of Luke 6:22-23 and 12:8 are fulfilled and concludes: "Luke 6:22-23 and 12:8 are meant for the edification of Luke's persecuted and harassed readers" (Karris, "Missionary Communities," 95).

narrative of Acts ends with Paul in prison in Rome, where he "boldly and without hindrance" preached about Jesus (Acts 28:31).

Luke's motive in presenting these models of Spirit-inspired ministry–Peter, John, Stephen, Paul, and others–should not be missed. For he has more in mind than simply declaring to his church, "This is how it all began!" Certainly, Luke highlights the reliability of the apostolic witness to the resurrection of Jesus; and he wants to be sure that all of us are clear about their message, which is to be passed on from generation to generation, people group to people group, until it reaches "the ends of the earth." Yet Luke also narrates the ministry of these end-time prophets because he sees them as important models of missionary praxis that his church needs to emulate. These characters in Acts demonstrate what it truly means to be a part of Joel's end-time prophetic band and thus challenge Luke's readers to fulfill their calling to be a "light to the nations."[19] As they face opposition by relying on the Holy Spirit, who enables them to bear bold witness for Jesus no matter what the cost, these end-time prophets call Luke's church to courageously follow the path first traveled by our Lord.

---

[19]This conclusion is supported by Stronstad, *The Prophethood of All Believers: A Study in Luke's Charismatic Theology*. For a dissenting perspective, see Max Turner's two articles, "Does Luke Believe Reception of the 'Spirit of Prophecy' Make All 'Prophets'?—in Inviting Dialogue with Roger Stronstad," *Journal of the European Pentecostal Theological Association* 20 (2000): 3-24, and "Every Believer As a Witness in Acts?—in Dialogue with John Michael Penney," *Ashland Theological Journal* 30 (1998): 57-71. Turner argues that only a select group is empowered for prophetic witness. Yet I would suggest that his discussion fails to adequately account for the Lukan texts cited above.

Conclusion

I hope that this analysis of Acts 2:17-21 has shed significant light on Luke's larger purpose. Luke is a missiologist who, with his two-volume work, has produced a manifesto for the Christian mission.[20] Through this manifesto, he seeks to remind his readers of their true identity–i.e., they are a community of prophets called to be a "light to the nations." He also seeks to encourage these Christians, even as they face opposition and persecution, to listen to the voice of the Holy Spirit and, through his power, to bear bold witness for Jesus. Luke accomplishes these objectives by providing various models—above all, Jesus, but also the Twelve, the Seventy, Stephen, Philip, Paul, and others. With great literary skill, Luke provides his intended readers (the persecuted Christians of his church) with encouragement and guidance for their mission.

This conclusion also indicates that Pentecostals, with their simple narrative approach to Acts—"their stories are our stories"—actually read Luke-Acts as Luke hoped they would—i.e., providing models for life and action, models for the mission every believer is called to embrace. Such an approach has enabled Pentecostals to highlight, in a unique way, an important aspect of the work of the Holy Spirit and Christian spirituality. They affirm that every Christian has been called and promised the power needed to become bold, Spirit-inspired witnesses for Jesus. The church is nothing less than a community of end-time prophets. By appropriating Luke's dynamic message, Pentecostals have developed a piety with a uniquely outward thrust. This is missional spirituality, and it flows from the apostolic church.

---

[20]Matson, *Household Conversion Narratives*, 184: "Luke is a missiologist."

Theological Education in a Pluralistic World: *Theological* Reflections

by *Veli-Matti Kärkkäinen*

Among several other legacies Doctors Julie and Wonsuk Ma are highly respected for–which include published and edited scholarly works and missiological and intercultural research–none will surpass their untiring and continuing work in the area of missiological and theological education. This legacy is not limited to one continent, as vast and diverse as Asia is, but includes also the international and ecumenical work in their current appointment at Oxford Center for Mission Studies–and beyond!

This brief essay seeks to offer some theological (rather than pedagogical) reflections on international theological education with a focus on one particular issue that I find increasingly challenging, namely training ministers in and for a religiously pluralistic world.[1] The theme of interfaith engagement is well-known to the Mas and their contributions on the theology of religions–particularly in the widely-acclaimed *magnum opus*, *Mission in the Spirit: Towards a Pentecostal/Charismatic Missiology* (2010)–are important.[2] Indeed, unlike many

---

[1] Simultaneously with the preparation of this essay, I was also finishing up with another related writing, entitled "Seeking to Discern the Mind of Christ in a Pluralistic World: Theological Reflections on Theological Education in a New Environment" (to be published in *Theology News & Notes* Fall 2013 issue). Both essays borrow from and depend on each other.

[2] Julie C. Ma and Wonsuk Ma, *Mission in the Spirit: Towards a Pentecostal/Charismatic Missiology* (Oxford, UK: Regnum Books, 2010).

theological educators who speak much of the interfaith challenge but lack grass-roots level experience, Julie and Wonsuk have lived out that experience for decades.

Thinking of the interfaith challenge, I am often reminded of the well-known confession of Paul Tillich, the great Lutheran theologian of the past generation, made just a few days before his death. He is reported to have admitted that if he had the opportunity to rewrite his three-volume *Systematic Theology*, he would widely engage world religions in that project.[3] This was due to his brief exposure at the end of his life to the forms of Japanese Buddhism as well as the influence from his famed Romanian religious studies colleague, Mircea Eliade. The recent ecumenical document-in-the-making, "Religious Plurality and Christian Self-Understanding," reminds us of the most prominent challenge the Christian church faces in the beginning of the third millennium:

> Today Christians in almost all parts of the world live in religiously plural societies. Persistent plurality and its impact on their daily lives are forcing them to seek new and adequate ways of understanding and relating to peoples of other religious traditions.... All religious communities are being reshaped by new encounters and relationships.... There is greater awareness of the interdependence of human life, and of the need to collaborate across religious barriers in dealing with the pressing problems of the world. All religious traditions, therefore, are challenged to contribute to the emergence of a global community that would live in mutual respect and peace.[4]

---

[3]Paul Tillich, *Future of Religions*, ed. Jerald Brauer (New York: Harper & Row, 1966), 91.
[4]"Religious Plurality and Christian Self-Understanding," #2, 3, World Council of Churches Ninth Assembly (Porto Alegre, Brazil, 206, February 14-

It is a recognized fact that Christian ministers and even missionaries at large are not well-prepared for the religiously diverse world. What Timothy C. Tennent, the President of Asbury Theological Seminary, says is a timely reminder to all theological and missiological educators. Rightly he notes, "In the West, it is rare to find someone who has more than a cursory knowledge of the sacred texts of other religions. In contrast, because Christians in the Majority World are often in settings dominated by other religions, it is not uncommon to meet a Christian with a Muslim, Hindu or Buddhist background who has an intimate knowledge of another sacred text."[5] What I would like to revise in Tennent's observation is that not only in the West is there a lack of knowledge of other religions among the theologically trained, but also in the Global South, particularly among Pentecostals and other Evangelicals. Where Asian students are ahead of the rest is that for them it has been obvious for a long time that the Christian faith cannot be taken as the "religion of the land." Indeed, in most Asian contexts, it never was the dominant one–and now even American and European Christians are waking up to a new situation. According to recent polls, more than one-quarter of Americans have changed their faith allegiance or confess no faith. Both religious diversity and pervasive secularism have transformed American and European cultures in dramatic ways. Consequently, "We do our theology from now on in the midst of many others 'who are not ... of this fold.' Our own faith, if only

---

23), http://www.oikoumene.org/en/resources/documents/assembly/porto-alegre-2006/3-preparatory-and-background-documents/religious-plurality-and-christian-self-understanding.html.

[5]Timothy C. Tennent, *Theology in the Context of World Christianity: How the Global Church Is Influencing the Way We Think about and Discuss Theology* (Grand Rapids: Zondervan, 2007), 55.

we are aware of it, is a constantly renewed decision, taken in the knowledge that other faiths are readily available to us."[6]

What kind of theological education would best prepare men and women to discern the mind of Christ in this kind of diverse, pluralistic, heterogeneous environment? What are the virtues, attitudes, and practices that would facilitate the vision of those who wish to engage the manifold ministries of Christ in the third millennium? Are there any theological hints about how to best think of the pedagogical task in the ministerial setting?

In a highly acclaimed and programmatic work titled *Between Athens and Berlin: The Theological Debate*,[7] the premier American theological educator, Professor David H. Kelsey of Yale University, outlines the underlying epistemology and theology of theological education using two cities as paradigms. "Athens" refers to the goals and methods of theological education that are derived from classical Greek philosophical educational methodology, *paideia* (training). The early church adopted and adapted this model. The primary goal of this form of education is the transformation of the individual. It is about character formation and learning–the ultimate goal of which is the knowledge *of* God rather than merely knowledge about God. Being crafted as it were into daily followers of Christ, rather than having mere book wisdom, was the goal of Christian adaptation of the originally secular "Athens" pedagogical vision. Personal development and spiritual formation stood at the forefront. The second pole of Kelsey's typology, "Berlin," is based on the Enlightenment epistemology and ideals, which of course remind us of the German Enlightenment's radically different vision. Whereas the classical model of "Athens" accepted the sacred

---

[6]Douglas John Hall, *Thinking the Faith* (Minneapolis: Fortress, 1991), 209.

[7]David H. Kelsey, *Between Athens and Berlin: The Theological Debate* (Eugene, OR: Wipf and Stock, 2011).

texts as revelation containing the wisdom of God and not simply knowledge about God, in the "Berlin" model, critical reasoning and rational enquiry reign. The ultimate goal of theological training is no longer personal formation based on the study of authoritative texts. Rather, it aims to train people in intellectual affairs.

Are we left with only these two models of *paideia*? Are they enough to equip theological students for the pluralistic world? Hardly. Elsewhere I have suggested that two other models could be added to the menu.[8] The former faculty member of Fuller Theological Seminary (*alma mater* for the Mas, and myself in my current teaching location), Robert Banks, proposed the "Jerusalem" model. This refers to the missionary impulse of the Christian church in its desire to spread the gospel from Jerusalem to the ends of the earth (Acts 1:8). In an important work titled *Revisioning Theological Education*, Banks argues that if Martin Kähler's classic dictum "Mission is the Mother of Theology" is true, it means theology should be missional in orientation. The ultimate goal and context of theological education should thus be missional, which at the end of the day fosters and energizes the church's mission. It is, however, more than what is usually taken as "missiological" education–as in the training of foreign missionaries: It is about theological education building the "foundation," which is the mission of the church in all aspects of the church's life and work. It is nothing less than "mission beyond the mission" to cite our own community's motto. This missional orientation is in keeping with the current ecclesiological conviction that declares mission is not just one task given to the church among other tasks such as teaching or children's work, but that the church is missional by its very nature. Thus, everything the church does derives from its

---

[8]See my "Epistemology, Ethos, and Environment: In Search of A Theology of Pentecostal Theological Education," *Pneuma* 34 (2012): 1-17.

missional nature. In this missional orientation of all theological education, Julie and Wonsuk have done an awesome work. Part of that pioneering long-term work is their unbelievably wide and deep editorial work (on top of their own writings) in Pentecostal theological and missiological literature, including books and scholarly periodicals. Those literary resources have given the worldwide Pentecostal and Evangelical guild of ministerial educators an indispensable tool and inspiration.

Yet one further model can be added to complement, enrich, and challenge the theology of theological education. Named "Geneva" after the great center of the Reformation, this approach to theological education cherishes a confessional approach. It seeks to help students know God through the study of the creeds and the confessions, as well as the means of grace. Formation is focused on the living traditions of the community. "Formation occurs through *in-formation* about the tradition and *en-culturation* within it."[9] For Pentecostal theological education, the question of confessional identity is of course a great challenge and in many ways a new and unprecedented one. Pentecostalism does not have a centuries-long historical tradition and in most cases not even well-developed confessional formulae! How to discern and affirm Pentecostal identity has been a life-long pursuit of the Mas. In their current location at the center of international and intercultural missiological-theological training, the question of identities and confessions becomes even more pertinent.

But what about the confessional model with regard to the pluralistic world, the focus of this essay? Shouldn't one rather downplay any particular confessional standpoint in order to make room for diversity? Not necessarily–unless one wishes to

---

[9]Brian Edgar, "The Theology of Theological Education," *Evangelical Review of Theology* 29, no. 3 (2005): 211.

go with what I call the "first-generation pluralism"[10] that presupposes the similarity of all traditions as the condition for dialogue. Aiming at dialogue from that kind of modernist standpoint, however, is a contradiction in terms. Why dialogue when it has been established beforehand that differences and distinctive features do not matter? A dialogue only matters if it not only bears with but also facilitates genuine differences of convictions and unique testimonies. As the German Reformed theologian Jürgen Moltmann aptly puts it, a theologian only "merits dialogue" when he is convinced of the truthfulness of a certain belief and deems it worth sharing with others. This has nothing to do with militant defeat of the Other but rather with the desire to share a gift–a treasure! That kind of confessionally based, truthful dialogue also makes room for the Other to be Other. A powerful metaphor used of this kind of encounter is that of "hospitality," a concept well represented in the biblical canon as well as in various cultures. The above-cited ecumenical document "Religious Plurality and Christian Self-Understanding" reminds us that "in the New Testament, the incarnation of the Word of God is spoken of by St. Paul in terms of hospitality and of a life turned towards the 'other' [Phil. 2:6–8]."[11] Borrowing from the biblical scholar Walter Brueggemann, we can make the term *other* a verb to remind us of the importance of not engaging the religious Other as a counter-object but rather entering into "the risky, demanding, dynamic process of relating to one that is not us."[12]

Only the minister who is well established in his or her own tradition can learn how best to navigate a religiously plural and

---

[10] See ch.14 in my *Trinity and Revelation. Constructive Christian Theology for the Church in the Pluralistic World,* vol. 2 (Grand Rapids: Eerdmans, 2014, forthcoming).

[11] "Religious Plurality and Christian Self-Understanding," #27.

[12] Walter Brueggemann, *The Covenanted Self: Explorations in Law and Covenant* (Minneapolis: Augsburg Fortress, 1999), 1.

diverse environment–particularly when the rootage in tradition takes place in a community of faith that embraces the tradition and also gracefully critiques and revisions it. Personal development, character formation and Christ like attitudes, cultivated by the patristic Athens model, offer great aid in that life-long process. It is significant that for the first millennia or so the theologians of the church were bishops, evangelists, pastors, and other church leaders. Their theology emerged from and was shaped by daily practices of the community. To those theologians, the Jerusalem model's missional orientation was taken for granted. Liturgy, worship, prayer life, and sharing in spiritual exercises was missionally oriented, particularly before the Christendom establishment arose, but to various degrees also thereafter.

However, we live in a different kind of world in the post-Enlightenment pluralistic society. There is no harking back to homogenous culture, shared values, and shared presuppositions. As a result, the Berlin model's robust emphasis on critical thinking, analytic assessment, and questioning of all "foundations"–as unsatisfactory and reductionist as it is in itself when made the sole source of theological training of ministers, as it tends to be in too many "secular" university-based theological faculties–provides a necessary asset to ministerial cultivation. The highest-level theological education for the third millennium has to be mature enough to live in the sometimes-painful dynamic tension between affirming tradition and questioning its presuppositions, embracing the biblical authority and challenging our deepest hermeneutical assumptions, as well as retrieving the ancient sources and applying to their study the most recent critical tools. Religious plurality, along with philosophical, cultural, and ethnic diversity, is a highly complex and complicated phenomenon. To penetrate its intricacies in order to discern the mind of Christ takes the best intellectual, spiritual, and theological powers. Theological education for the pluralistic world better draw its resources from all of these cities—and beyond. Perhaps then our students will be ready for a deeply missional dialogue/dialogical mission in this complex world of ours:

> Dialogue is *a basic way of life* because Christians share life and contexts with neighbours of other faiths. This implies that they establish dialogical relations so that there is hope of mutual understanding and fruitful coexistence in multi-religious and pluralistic societies. . . . Dialogue is no [sic] a substitute for mission or a hidden form of mission. Mission and dialogue are not identical, neither are they so opposed to one another. One can be committed to dialogue and to Christian witness at the same time.[13]

---

[13] "Theme Two: Christian Mission among Other Faiths," in *Edinburgh 2010*, vol. 2: *Witnessing to Christ Today*, ed. Daryl Balia and Kirsteen Kim (Oxford, UK: Regnum, 2010), 47.

Contextualization and Pentecostal-Charismatic Education in a Global Village

by Allan Heaton Anderson

Professor of Mission and Pentecostal Studies
University of Birmingham, England

The Challenge of Contextualization

I have been privileged to know and work with Wonsuk and Julie Ma, not only professionally but also as personal friends, particularly since they moved to the UK. They invited me to speak at a conference at the Asia Pacific Theological Seminary in Baguio, Philippines in 2003, although I was prevented from attending due to a medical emergency in Manila before I could make the journey north. Three years later, I was invited to give the annual William Menzies lectures in Baguio at their instigation and towards the end of their time there. I have worked with them on several writing projects, and their zeal for good quality publications in mission and Pentecostal studies knows no bounds. The world of Pentecostal Studies is enormously indebted to them for their gracious and humble academic leadership, their concern for mission studies to be relevant, their generous ecumenism and participation in ecumenical events, and not least for their numerous publications and edited works that have made a substantial contribution to understanding Pentecostalism and mission from an Asian perspective. They have truly made a global impact.

Contemporary Christianity in general and Pentecostalism in particular are not predominantly North American and European today, but Asian, African, and Latin American. Here, the experience of the Spirit working actively in the world is often more important than adherence to creed. That is why the work of the Mas is so significant in placing their theological writings within their own Asian (Korean and Filipino) contexts. Whether writing about the Kankana-Ey and Igorot tribal peoples in the northern Philippines and their encounter with Pentecostalism in their own mission work,[1] Asian Pentecostal women leaders, [2] or Pentecostal theology,[3] Julie and Wonsuk Ma have stressed the importance of taking context seriously when engaging in Pentecostal scholarship. This has not only been significant, but also refreshing. Their academic writing has opened up Pentecostal Studies to a perspective that is seldom heard in the English language academia.

Those familiar with theological and religious studies in Europe, and increasingly in North America, know that this is a very difficult environment.[4] Educators working in universities

---

[1] Julie Ma, "A Comparison of Two Worldviews: Kankana-Ey and Pentecostal;" Wonsuk Ma, "The Spirit of God upon Leaders in Israelite Society and Igorot Tribal Churches," in Wonsuk Ma & Robert P. Menzies (eds.), *Pentecostalism in Context: Essays in Honor of William W. Menzies* (Sheffield Academic Press, 1997), 265-316.

[2] Julie Ma, "Korean Pentecostal Spirituality: A Case Study of Jashil Choi," in Wonsuk Ma & Robert P. Menzies (eds.), *The Spirit and Spirituality: Essays in Honour of Russell P. Spittler* (T&T Clark, 2004), 298-313; Julie Ma, "Asian Women and Pentecostal Ministry," in Allan H. Anderson & Edmond Tang (eds.), *Asian and Pentecostal: The Charismatic Face of Christianity in Asia* (Regnum, 2011), 103-24.

[3] Wonsuk Ma, "Asian (Classical) Pentecostal Theology in Context," in Anderson & Tang, *Asian and Pentecostal,* 48-76; Wonsuk Ma, "Toward the Future of David Yonggi Cho's Theological Tradition" in Wonsuk Ma, William W. Menzies & Hyeon-sung Bae (eds.), *David Yonggi Cho: A Close Look at his Theology and Ministry* (APTS/Hansei University, 2004), 255-72.

[4] Much of the rest of this paper is abridged and adapted from Allan H. Anderson, "The 'Fury and Wonder?' Pentecostal-Charismatic Spirituality in Theological Education,"*Pneuma* 23:2 (Fall 2001): 287-302.

have to deal with a liberal, pluralistic theological agenda that often seems to diametrically oppose Pentecostal/Charismatic spirituality and evangelical theology. A certain tension exists between academic integrity and spirituality, especially when education does not seem to further Christian spirituality and formation.[5] Pentecostalism has a tenuous relationship with theological training and there is always the danger that intellectualism may result in a suppression or even a rejection of the supernatural.[6] The Mas have certainly not been guilty of this and have stressed the importance of the supernatural signs that accompany preaching in the non-western world. This stress comes from their practical experience in the "mission field" in Asia. Wonsuk Ma warns of the danger of "extreme Pentecostal scholasticism" that can "easily suffocate spiritual dynamics if not carefully guarded."[7] That the Mas have been able to remain true to the holistic and dynamic world of Asian Pentecostal spirituality in their involvement in theological education speaks volumes. Most people in the West might not have thought of theological education in any terms other than that which they are accustomed to–a particularly western, conservative model that divides the subject into clearly defined disciplines and processes self-selected (and sometimes denomination-selected) people through an information-supplying institution into "ministry." The end result is like a sausage factory when the end product is almost identical to everyone else who has been through the same process.

---

[5] Allan H. Anderson, *An Introduction to Pentecostalism* (Cambridge, 2014), 242-48; Everett L. McKinney, "Some Spiritual Aspects of Pentecostal Education: A Personal Journey,"*Asian Journal of Pentecostal Studies* 3:2 (June 2000): 253.
[6] Byron D. Klaus and Loren O. Triplett, "National Leadership in Pentecostal Missions," Murray A. Dempster, Byron D. Klaus, and Douglas Petersen (eds), *Called and Empowered: Global Mission in Pentecostal Perspective* (Peabody: Hendrickson, 1991), 226.
[7] Wonsuk Ma, "Asian (Classical) Pentecostal Theology," 75.

Pentecostal theology in the twenty-first century needs to be "contextual" more than ever before. Voices from Asia like the Mas, accompanied by similar voices from other parts of the Global South are heard through their academic writing to strengthen and critique the global Pentecostal and Charismatic community.[8] This is also very difficult to achieve when English is the dominant language of communication in this sphere. The earlier focus on "indigenization" of evangelical and Pentecostal missionary scholars like Alice Luce and Melvin Hodges,[9] often assumed that the gospel message and Christian theology are the same in all cultures and contexts. They also tended to relate the Christian message to traditional, "indigenous" cultures, often set in confrontation with each other. Pentecostal missionaries have supported the idea of a "three-self" (self-supporting, self-governing and self-propagating) church. But, the church must also be "self-contextualizing," because every theology is influenced by its particular context, and must be so to be relevant. Contextualization relates the Christian message to all contexts and cultures, especially including those undergoing rapid change.

The rise of particular contextual theologies like liberation theology, Black theology, Dalit theology in India, and *Minjung* theology in Korea increased evangelical concerns that this new trend in theology would lead to "syncretism" and a placing of culture above God's revelation in the Bible. Evangelical scholars, however, gradually began giving prominence to the importance

---

[8] John Christopher Thomas, "Pentecostal Theology in the Twenty-First Century," *Pneuma* 20:1 (Spring 1998): 10-11.
[9] Melvin L. Hodges: *The Indigenous Church* (Springfield, MO: Gospel Publishing House, 1953) Allan H. Anderson, *To the Ends of the Earth: Pentecostalism and the Transformation of World Christianity* (Oxford, 2013), 88-90.

of culture in the seventies and eighties.[10] Charles Kraft spoke of "the constant message in alternative forms," and of "dynamic-equivalence theologizing," and that "all theologizing is culture-bound interpretation and communication of God's revelation."[11] David Bosch declared that all theologies were contextual theologies, but that we should not confuse the essential and universal aspects of the Christian message from the local, contextual ones.[12] Lesslie Newbigin wrote that "every communication of the gospel is already culturally conditioned," but that the gospel was "not an empty form into which everyone is free to pour his or her own content," but that the content of the gospel is "Jesus Christ in the fullness of his ministry, death, and resurrection."[13]

The importance of contextualization is now readily accepted by evangelical scholars. Dean Gilliland defined the goal of "contextualization" as "to enable, insofar as it is humanly possible, an understanding of what it means that Jesus Christ, the Word, is authentically experienced in each and every human situation."[14] The Christian message must be proclaimed in the framework of the context of the particular people to whom it is addressed, it must emphasize those parts of the message that answer the questions and needs of those people, and it must be expressed through the medium of the cultural gifts of those people. Nigerian Catholic theologian Justin Ukpong wrote that "in the process of evangelization each new culture with which

---

[10]Charles H. Kraft, *Christianity in Culture* (Maryknoll, NY: Orbis Books, 1979); David J. Hesselgrave, *Communicating Christ Cross-Culturally: An Introduction to Missionary Communication* (Grand Rapids: Zondervan, 1978)

[11]Kraft, *Christianity in Culture,* 257, 291.

[12]David J. Bosch, *Transforming Mission: Paradigm Shifts in Theology of Mission* (Maryknoll, NY: Orbis, 1991), 423.

[13]Lesslie Newbigin, *The Gospel in a Pluralist Society* (London: SPCK, 1989), 142, 152-153.

[14]Dean Gilliland, "Contextualization," in A. Scott Moreau, Harold Netland & Charles Van Engen (eds.), *Evangelical Dictionary of World Missions* (Grand Rapids, MI & Carlisle, UK: Baker Books & Paternoster, 2000), 225.

Christianity comes into contact should be respected and given the chance to give its own expression to the Christian message."[15] The Mas in their academic reflections on their work in the Philippines did just this.

Theological education is usually strongly influenced by its cultural and political context, often with disastrous consequences, as my own experience has illustrated.[16] American Pentecostal theological education, as used in the ICI degree program with which I was familiar, used four distinct ingredients of a "Bible/Theology" degree (Bible, Theology, Church Ministries, and General Education) influenced by the "liberal arts" model.[17] Theological education in North America is often based on the classical fourfold educational model of Bible, theology, history (education) and praxis.[18] Here I indulge in some personal reflection.[19] Over thirty years ago, I went through a personal paradigm shift as a Pentecostal missionary in South Africa and began to work towards reconciliation in our deeply divided and traumatized society. Other white South Africans considered me a "liberal," but I began to realize that theological colleges in South Africa and in many other countries were answering questions that no one was asking—and worse, not answering questions that most people *were* asking. I had begun to think about contextual theology, but up until that time most of my academic work was exploring African independent churches with Pentecostal connections, and the role of African religions

---

[15]Justin Ukpong, "What is Contextualization," in Norman Thomas (ed.), *Readings in World Mission* (London: SPCK, 1995), 179.

[16]Anderson, "The 'Fury and Wonder,'" 288-91.

[17]Michael Palmer, "Orienting Our Lives: The Importance of a Liberal Education for Pentecostals in the Twenty-First Century,"*Pneuma* 23:2 (Fall 2001): 197-216.

[18]Robert K. Johnston, "Becoming Theologically Mature: the Task of Theological Education Today for American Evangelical Seminaries,"*Ministerial Formation* 73 (April 1996), 43.

[19]Anderson, "The 'Fury and Wonder'."

and cultures in formulating a relevant Christian theology. I devised two courses at the college I ran that tried to be more "contextual" and used two books I had written by then.[20] There was a dearth of materials on these subjects for theology students. But, I had neither thought much about the socio-political implications of theology, nor about God's concerns for the poor and oppressed in this world, even though the Bible was full of these issues.

Shifting Perspectives

The issues of the religious righting North America that influence "conservative evangelicals" are quite peripheral to the concerns of people in the rest of the world, including most of Europe. The old, characteristic battles against "Communism" and abortion, supporting the state of Israel, retaining the death penalty, and so on, were not major concerns for people who lived under oppressive governments that sometimes used "Christianity" to maintain that oppression, as was the case in apartheid South Africa. Issues of rampant poverty, unemployment, institutional corruption, housing shortages, the HIV/AIDS pandemic (an estimated 30% of pregnant women in South Africa are infected),[21] poor educational and medical facilities, the exploitation of women and ethnic minorities, and the redistribution of land, were some of the much more pressing needs. Furthermore, Pentecostals in the Global South have a spirituality influenced by the popular religions of the regions in which they live, which often led to sharp differences with the rather cerebral Christianity of western missionaries and their

---

[20]Allan Anderson, *Moya: The Holy Spirit in an African Context* (Pretoria: University of South Africa Press, 1991); id, *Bazalwane: African Pentecostals in South Africa* (Pretoria: University of South Africa Press, 1992).

[21]http://www.avert.org/south-africa-hiv-aids-statistics.htm, Accessed 11 July 2014.

theological colleges. The context of theological education is often not the Bible college, the seminary or the university, but the community in which God's people are found. Only when the context is clear in our minds can we begin to adjust the content of our education. Pentecostals and Charismatics are often viewed by the outside Christian world as those who are "otherworldly" and unconcerned about the pressing needs of society, but this is not true, as the work of Wonsuk and Julie Ma reveals.

The missiological maxim of the southward swing of the Christian centre of gravity has made Christianity more African, Latin American and Asian than North American or European.[22] The leading missionary sending nations are no longer Britain or Germany, but include South Korea, India, Brazil and Nigeria.[23] In the Global South, there are very large numbers of Christians for whom theology can only be studied within their own context. The largest number of evangelical Christians in any continent of the world live in Asia, most of whom are of a Pentecostal and Charismatic type; Africa has many millions of Pentecostals and Charismatics; and the largest number of Pentecostals in any continent live in Latin America. Barrett and Johnson's statistics give dramatic evidence of how rapidly the Northern share of world Christianity has decreased in the century of Pentecostalism. In 1900, 77% of the world's Christian population was in Europe and North America. By 2000, only 37% of the two billion Christians in the world were from the northern continents, while 63% were from Asia, Oceania, Africa, and Latin America. Furthermore, 26% of the world's Christians were "Pentecostal/ Charismatics" (as defined by them), expected to

---

[22]Andrew F. Walls, "Of Ivory Towers and Ashrams: Some reflections on theological scholarship in Africa,"*Journal of African Christian Thought* 3:1 (June 2000): 1.

[23]Larry D. Pate, "The Dramatic Growth of Two-Thirds World Missions," William D Taylor (ed), *Internationalising Missionary Training* (Exeter: The Paternoster Press, 1991): 35.

rise to 31% by 2025.[24] The "southward swing" is more evident in Pentecostalism than in other forms of Christianity. Most of the dramatic church growth in the 20th Century in Asia, Africa and Latin America has taken place in Pentecostal and independent Pentecostal-like churches, and I would guess that at least three-quarters of Pentecostalism today is found in the Global South. Classical Pentecostal churches with roots in North America like the Assemblies of God, have probably only some 8% of their world associate membership in North America, with at least 80% in the Third World.[25]

But, this drastic transformation in Christian demographics has made little impact on western theological education, which continues to be the leading model in seminaries across the globe. Africans and Asians do not become either Pentecostals or Presbyterians for the same reasons that North Americans do, and neither do Europeans. Academic appointments of scholars from the Global South in western institutions often serve as smokescreens to camouflage the reality of or further marginalize the "voices from the margin,"[26] whereas actually little has changed in the way most educators think of and teach theology. We must applaud the efforts of Pentecostal colleges in Europe to forge alliances with secular universities and seek validation for degrees including masters' programs in Pentecostal studies, while Pentecostal educators attain doctoral degrees in theology. In Britain, these validation agreements have been seriously

---

[24]David B. Barrett & Todd M. Johnson, "Annual Statistical Table on Global Mission: 2001,"*International Bulletin of Missionary Research* 25:1 (January 2001): 25; Todd M. Johnson & Peter F. Crossing, "Christianity 2014,"*International Bulletin of Missionary Research* 25:1 (January 2014), 29. See my critique of these statistics in Allan H. Anderson, *Introduction to Pentecostalism* (Cambridge, 2014): 3-6.

[25]Everett A. Wilson, *Strategy of the Spirit: J Philip Hogan and the Growth of the Assemblies of God Worldwide 1960-1990* (Carlisle: Regnum, 1997), 3, 107, 183.

[26]R.S. Sugirtharajah (ed.) *Voices from the Margin: Interpreting the Bible in the Third World* (Maryknoll/ London: Orbis/ SPCK, 1995).

threatened, but there are other dangers here. Although western theology has adjusted to the particular challenges of post-modernism, feminism and religious pluralism, the presuppositions remain. The rise of post-modernism has profoundly challenged the autonomous rationalism and empirical scepticism of western theology, but it has not yet shaken the foundations of the theology taught in Pentecostal and Evangelical seminaries. According to Andrew Walls, this theology exported to the rest of the world is a "heavily indigenised, highly contextual theology . . . a way of making peace between Christianity and the European Enlightenment, of translating Christian affirmations into Enlightenment categories."[27] Characteristic of this is the literary-historical method of approach to Scripture that is almost universal in the North. Such theological methods were foreign to the European church for centuries. No less so in the Global South. The African Theological Conference in Nairobi, Kenya, meeting in August 2000, affirmed that a "reader-centred approach to biblical hermeneutics" was "more appropriate than the dominant historical-critical approach."[28] Walls shows how all theological disciplines are affected, actually representing "a series of choices related to the cultural and religious history of the Western world."[29] However, the "southward movement" of world Christianity has both "opened up untold fresh possibilities for theology" and "vastly multiplied the resources available,"[30] but the western hegemony remains in theological institutions and their curricula. If the "non-western" world is given any attention, it is usually placed in the context of western churches and missions.

---

[27]Walls, "Of Ivory Towers," 2.
[28]African Theological Conference, "Final Communiqué," *Ministerial Formation* 91 (October 2000), 65.
[29]Walls, "Of Ivory Towers,"1-2.
[30]Ibid., 3.

North American Pentecostal missions, particularly those of the Assemblies of God, contributed generously towards the establishment of Bible schools and in-service training structures throughout the world, resulting in the more rapid growth of Pentecostal churches.[31] However, the fundamental flaws in these structures exist particularly because they are western models exported to the rest of the world, albeit unconsciously. This is part of the legacy of the colonial past with its cultural imperialism and ethnocentrism. Somewhat paternalistically, western missionaries thought they knew what sort of training people needed in Africa, Asia and Latin America, in order to become ministers after their own model and experience. It is clear that the alliance between Evangelicalism and white classical Pentecostalism in the USA from 1943 onwards had a profound effect on Pentecostal theological education. Pentecostals found themselves being drawn into the evangelical-ecumenical dichotomy pervading evangelical Christianity.[32] They became vulnerable to losing their distinctive experience-oriented spirituality as Evangelical and fundamentalist models of education were bought into wholesale and uncritically. Reformed theologian Henry Lederle points out the irony of "recent ecclesiastical history" that: "...much of Pentecostal scholarship has sought to align itself so closely with the rationalistic heritage of American Fundamentalism . . . without fully recognizing how hostile these theological views are to Pentecostal and Charismatic convictions about present-day prophecy, healing miracles and other spiritual charisms."[33] Pentecostal Bible colleges became

---

[31]Klaus & Triplett, "National Leadership,"227-29.
[32]Harvey Cox, *Fire from Heaven: The Rise of Pentecostal Spirituality and the Reshaping of Religion in the Twenty-first Century* (London: Cassell, 1996), 303, suggests that fundamentalism was "a desperate effort to fend off modernity by using modernity's weapons."
[33]Henry I. Lederle, "Pentecostals and Ecumenical Theological Education,"*Ministerial Formation* 80 (January 1998): 46.

generators of this new Pentecostal fundamentalism,[34] and western Pentecostal denominations gave priority to exporting this theological education to the Global South. The American Assemblies of God was in the vanguard of this trend, being particularly influential in Africa and Asia. A survey conducted in 1959 by the AG revealed that half of its missionaries and half the budget of the Missions Department were committed to theological institutions.[35] The question is whether this new emphasis was at the expense of spirituality. After noting that theological education had been dominated by the West, Lee Wanak observed how this had affected its basic nature: ". . . its theological categories shaped by Greek culture; its educational patterns shaped by the university model; its attitudes influenced by modernity, industrialism, colonialism, and individualism. In the past its spirituality was marked by pietism, in the present it bears a faith of affluence and superficial commitment. . . ."[36]

The rest of the world suffered from this great malaise in theological education, as western-influenced missionary educators unconsciously shared their presuppositions, paradigms and theological prejudices in Asia, Africa, Latin America and the Pacific. Malaysian Chinese Methodist scholar Hwa Yung points out that the many theological institutions that have sprung up all over Asia have been "conditioned by the methodologies, agenda, and content of western theology." He pleads for a complete change in approach before the Asian church can "come to terms more adequately with its own

---

[34] D. William Faupel, "Whither Pentecostalism," *Pneuma* 15:1 (Spring 1993): 24.

[35] Quoted in Benjamin Sun, "Assemblies of God Theological Education in Asia Pacific: A Reflection," *Asian Journal of Pentecostal Studies* 3:2 (July 2000): 230.

[36] Lee C. Wanak, "Theological Education and the Role of Teachers in the 21st Century: A Look at the Asia Pacific Region," *Journal of Asian Mission* 2:1 (January 2000): 3.

identity, context, and mission."³⁷ But, this conditioning has not only disturbed the Global South; western Pentecostalism itself has lost something as a result. Del Tarr writes of "the erosion of the sense of the supernatural" and "the eclipse of the experiential dimension of the Christian faith." The emphasis on rationalism in western theology led to an "indifferent attitude towards spiritual experience and power."³⁸ This all had a profound effect upon Christians in the Global South for whom this dimension was vital. Historical and political factors also play a role. The independence of India in 1949 began a domino-like fall of colonies culminating with the first democratic government in South Africa in 1994. The end of colonialism gave rise to a new and strident nationalism and there has emerged a continentalism that emphasizes human dignity, such as former South African President Thabo Mbeki's ideology of an "African renaissance." The emerging of an "Asian Pentecostal theology" in which the Mas have been the driving force is one example of the changing scenario. Pentecostal/ Charismatic churches are beginning to develop their own theological paradigms that challenge and transform Christianity throughout the world.

It is all the more sobering for us to remember that many of the Pentecostal leaders in many parts of the world have been those with little or no theological education. In the 1960s, Swiss sociologist Lalive d'Épinay contrasted the remarkably successful Pentecostal pastors in Chile who had little or no education and the "complete stagnation" of the Methodists and Presbyterians whose pastors had high educational levels. This made him "less confident of the benefits of theological education, and even of the

---

³⁷Hwa Yung, "Critical Issues Facing Theological Education in Asia," *Transformation* (October-December 1995): 1.
³⁸Del Tarr, "Transcendence, Immanence, and the Emerging Pentecostal Academy," Wonsuk Ma & Robert P. Menzies (eds) *Pentecostalism in Context: Essays in Honor of William W Menzies* (Sheffield: Sheffield Academic Press, 1997), 195-222, 206-7.

method of training in the developed countries which we impose on Protestants in the developing nations." He wrote that the educational methods of Europe and the USA were simply "not suitable for the needs in Chile."[39] There, because North American missionaries had instituted theological education to avoid the "excesses" and "ignorant fanaticism" of Pentecostalism, Chilean Pentecostalism now has a "strong anti-theological, anti-academic prejudice."[40] The emphasis in Pentecostal and Charismatic leadership usually has been on the spirituality of the leader rather than on intellectual abilities or even ministerial skills. The first European training college was run by the Pentecostal Missionary Union in London. It provided rudimentary training for missionary candidates, but stated that their qualifications had simply to be "a fair knowledge of every Book in the Bible, and an accurate knowledge of the Doctrines of Salvation and Sanctification," to which was added that candidates "must be from those who have received the Baptism of the Holy Ghost themselves." There was no shortage of applications, and entrance requirements subsequently became more difficult, including a required two-year training period.[41]

Pentecostals probably did not exhibit the same enslavement to rationalistic theological correctness and cerebral Christianity that plagued many of their contemporary Protestant missionaries. They were not as thoroughly immersed in western theology and ideology as their counterparts were. Most early Pentecostals, who suffered from a siege mentality because they were such a small minority, shunned universities. No wonder: the university model that pervades education in western cultures

---

[39] Christian Lalive d'"Epinay, "The Training of Pastors and Theological Education: The case of Chile," *International Review of Missions* LVI: 222 (April 1967): 185, 191.

[40] Juan Sepúlveda, "The Challenge for Theological Education from a Pentecostal Standpoint," *Ministerial Formation* 87 (October 1999): 29-30.

[41] *Confidence*, 2:6 (June 1909): 129.

created an educated elite that often lost touch with ordinary people. Robert Schreiter wrote of the "separation of the theologian from the experience of living communities."[42] The doctrine of the priesthood of believers that spurred on early Pentecostals to great heights of mission and ministry has eroded and the clergy/ laity dichotomy has been recreated through an emphasis on the need for a paper qualification before recognizing a calling and gifting for ministry. Edgar Elliston wrote of the "inflationary professionalization of the ministry" that posed serious questions for the church, exerting "pressure for ever higher entrance and exit requirements for our training programs." The "requirements for accreditation and certification (ordination) move ever higher in terms of academic achievement and away from effective ministry experience."[43]

Western models of theological education often do not take enough notice of the specific, local, religious, social, and cultural contexts that dominate people throughout the rest of the world. Paul Pierson points out that because theology was perceived to be "a list of timeless doctrines, the theological training of missionaries did not prepare them to recognize the theological issues arising in their host countries." Consequently, it was also assumed that leadership would be trained using western methodologies, and little thought was given "to understanding how the gospel might be communicated appropriately in the receptor cultures."[44] The world is becoming increasingly globalized, multi-ethnic, pluralistic, and urbanized. In addition, a polemical and confrontational approach to Christian theology

---

[42]Robert J. Schreiter, *Constructing Local Theologies* (Maryknoll: Orbis, 1995), 18.

[43]Edgar J. Elliston, "Designing Leadership Education,"*Missiology* 16:2 (April 1988): 204.

[44]Paul E. Pierson, "A North American Missionary Trainer Responds to Two-Thirds World Concerns," in William D. Taylor (ed), *Internationalising Missionary Training* (Exeter: The Paternoster Press, 1991), 193-202, 194.

seeking to preserve a "Pentecostal spirituality" often unrelated to the majority world contexts and overly reliant upon foreign personnel has been nurtured. This in turn creates a vicious circle where "religious right" ideology and premillenial eschatological pessimism become "orthodoxy" in Pentecostal institutions throughout the world. Pentecostal and Charismatic quietism in the face of oppressive regimes, racism and "ethnic cleansing" is a disturbing feature of its recent history. Sometimes, insensitive and paternalistic attitudes on the part of dominant foreign missionaries have tended to stifle protest and constructive change. The problem is exacerbated by the fact that in some Pentecostal and Charismatic churches in the Global South, a new, educated elite in the ministry have sometimes become clones of western forms of theologizing, and new initiatives in providing relevant theological education for majority world contexts are very few and far between.[45]

In spite of this, fundamental questions are now being asked about the nature of theological education in the Global South. Hwa Yung says that "there is even less reason today for non-western Christians today to allow their theologies to be domesticated by Enlightenment thinking, something which western Christians themselves find increasingly dissatisfying."[46] From Ghana, the Presbyterian theologian Kwame Bediako wrote of the "hard-line and historically imported categories" from the West that are "now found to be not always helpful, as they do not describe adequately the actual experience of the majority of African Christians."[47] In addition, Latin American Methodist José Miguez Bonino thought that Pentecostalism had been "too limited by some current theological formulations adopted from

---

[45]Wanak, "Theological Education,"12.
[46]Hwa Yung, "Critical Issues,"2.
[47]Kwame Bediako, "A Half Century of African Christian Thought: Pointers to Theology and Theological Education in the Next Half Century,"*Journal of African Christian Thought* 3:1 (June 2000): 7.

Anglo-Saxon Evangelical circles" and that "the spiritual experience and the evangelical praxis of the Pentecostal/ Charismatic Renewal is much larger and richer than those formulations." He drew particular attention to the Pentecostal emphasis on experience as the grid by which to interpret the Bible.[48] These challenges by outside observers do need to be taken seriously by Pentecostal and Charismatic educators.

The Needs of our Global Village

The way forward might be first, to acknowledge that for Pentecostal theological education to be truly *contextual,* its *content* must change. This means, for example, that European and North American theological institutions could focus more on the "Rest of the World" in their education, which will often require re-educating on the part of educators themselves. Culture, global ideologies, local theologies, religions and new religious movements (for example) should be given more priority. Attention could be paid to insights from local anthropology, sociology, history, strategic and political studies, communication theory and cultural studies—not as exotic studies of "the other," but as part of a comprehensive attempt to learn more about the context in which global Pentecostal and Charismatic communities are found. Africa, Asia and Latin America have their own Christian heroes, who are not just the western missionaries that went there long ago! More work should be done on the pioneers of Pentecostalism, so that their voices are heard in the study of church history and theology. So for example, African writers have often pointed out that in the western world, information on western missionaries to Africa "is many times disproportionate to their role and contribution,"

---

[48]José Míguez Bonino, "Pentecostal missions is more than what it claims."*Pneuma* 16:2 (Fall 1997): 288.

mainly because of the scarcity of written information on African Christians.[49] A serious and extensive revision of Pentecostal history needs to be done, in which the enormous contributions of the as yet unnamed local pioneers is properly recognized, so that North American classical Pentecostals in particular shed their often-heard assumption that Pentecostalism is a "made in the USA" product that has been exported to the world. Walter Hollenweger wrote that the challenging issues of today are the emergence of majority world Pentecostal churches with their own theologies, Pentecostal missionaries who "are prisoners of their own western culture due to their monocultural education," and the burgeoning numbers of majority world missionaries. He pleads for an "intercultural" theology and education that "does not transform vital and spontaneous Christians into detached intellectuals" and says we must "break out of the monocultural methodologies and topics of the past" and allow the theologies of the Global South to be heard. The Holy Spirit often works without western missionaries; and theologies, liturgies and ethics that are a result cause tensions with western Pentecostal missions. The "bewildering pluralism within Pentecostalism worldwide" and "the theological contributions of Third World Pentecostalism" must be fully acknowledged and given due recognition.[50]

The "voices from the margin" of Pentecostal contextual theology should be given attention, particularly as Pentecostalism encounters very different contexts outside the western world. Although the sources of these local voices are more difficult to come by, academic theses and publications on Pentecostalism in Africa, Asia and (especially) Latin America

---

[49]Watson A.O. Omulokoli, "Researching and Writing Christian Biography in Africa: A Challenge to Evangelical Studies in Global Context," *Journal of African Christian Thought* 3:1 (June 2000): 41.
[50]Walter J. Hollenweger, *Pentecostalism: Origins and Developments Worldwide* (Peabody: Hendrickson, 1997), 301-2.

continue to multiply, and the information highway has opened up new vistas of knowledge for those who are genuinely concerned to change and challenge the status quo. This also means that educators from the majority world could participate fully in western institutions, and not serve as mere tokenism. Julie and Wonsuk Ma have been exemplars of this trend. Wonsuk Ma writes of the "unique struggles of the Pentecostal movement as it engages the Asian context."[51] As Wesley Ariarajah observes, "Third World" theologies are not just optional extras, but they "provide fundamental challenges to what has been going on within the dominant tradition in the name of 'theology.'"[52] Western theological educators should themselves be given thorough exposure to the contexts in which they work, in which the agenda is set by local people. They should first and foremost be learners, where they can listen to local concerns before presuming to teach and preach. This probably means that before educators or "missionaries" from North America and Europe in other continents begin their work, they should first be apprenticed to local ministers and be thoroughly exposed to the local context. This may sound radical to some readers, but it is something that I have practiced myself in Africa. Through serving people in humility over an extended period of time, intercultural workers will learn many vital lessons that several years in theological seminaries back home did not teach, and thus will be much more effective.

Second, our theological education should be more *holistic* and *functional*. The curricula we develop are usually photocopies of our own curricula and reflect our own worldview. We can no longer assume that a "liberal arts" or a classical European education followed by specialized seminary training will make a

---

[51] Wonsuk Ma, "Asian (Classical) Pentecostal Theology," 49.
[52] S. Wesley Ariarajah, "Changing Frontiers of Ecumenical Theology: A Challenge to Ecumenical Formation," *Ministerial Formation* 89 (April 2000): 10.

person fit for ministry anywhere in the world. This does not mean that we should simply expand our curricula to add more knowledge. Theological education must become "training in diversity to build tolerance and understanding, without which evangelization will be fruitless."[53] Evangelical Anglican bishop John V. Taylor, after many years of missionary service in East Africa, lamented that the churches' training curricula were "largely a hangover from the past" and were not "functionally related to the tasks" for which people are being trained. He suggests that the only way forward is "to abandon the ideal of a comprehensive theology" and to train people "for different functions of ministry in the same way that all other professions have adopted long ago"–what he calls "a functional approach to theology."[54] Lalive d'Épinay observed that Chilean Pentecostals were trained "by the street," that any convert could become a minister after a long time of testing of calling and capabilities in leadership and preaching, to the extent that this person must have actually "gathered a flock" before appointment as a pastor.[55] Sepúlveda speaks of "the inadequate nature of a model of theological education that takes for granted a professionalized ministry with independent means," and says that the Chilean "practical apprenticeship" model is well suited to their own needs.

The dichotomy between training for the ministry and academic theology must be overcome.[56] Elliston recommends a "non-formal" education that is "usually functionally oriented, democratic, and the entry requirements are set by the community being served." This "task-oriented" education has clear goals to be achieved, and is labour-intensive rather than

---

[53] Wanak, "Theological Education," 6.
[54] John V. Taylor, "Preparing the Ordinand for Mission," *International Review of Missions* LVI:222 (April 1967): 147-49.
[55] Lalive d'Épinay, "The Training of Pastors," 188-89.
[56] Sepúlveda, "The Challenge," 32, 34.

resource-intensive.[57] Theological education has certainly departed from the biblical model of in-service leadership training by apprenticeship, but then we do live in a very different context where formal university education is essential for progress.[58] Jesus and the apostle Paul both took "education for spirituality" very seriously, but the methods they used were very different from ours. They were also very different from the rabbinic method of education that Jesus vigorously rejected, an academic and residential method that was not unlike the models we use in theological education today.[59] The Holy Spirit did not come on "empty heads" on the Day of Pentecost. He empowered those who had been through a three-year intensive process of training on the job. This is not to suggest that we take a first century model (or even an early twentieth century one) and make it normative for the twenty-first century. But, if more recognition or accreditation were given to the experiences of ministry and the developing spirituality that these experiences bring, we would be educating people in Pentecostal/Charismatic spirituality more effectively. We must find ways and means to quantify and realize this, and to integrate cognitive learning with concrete, active learning.

Third, and most importantly, Wonsuk and Julie Ma show us by their example that Pentecostal and Charismatic spirituality leads to total dependency on the Spirit of God in teaching and practice. The Spirit is the one who makes and equips teachers–the active participant in our development, and the one who enables us to change in a changing world. The western Church in

---

[57] Elliston, "Designing Leadership Education," 212.

[58] Jon Ruthven, "'Between Two Worlds': Theological Education vs. Christian Discipleship," 30th Annual Meeting of the Society for Pentecostal Studies, March 2001, Oral Roberts University, Tulsa, Oklahoma, Collected Papers, 731-748.

[59] Paul M. Zehr and Jim Egli, *Alternative Models of Mennonite Pastoral Formation*, Occasional Papers No. 15 (Elkhart: Institute of Mennonite Studies, 1992), 42-57.

particular, affirms Cheryl Bridges Johns, "has lost sight of the pedagogical role of the Holy Spirit." She says that Pentecostal experience is the "epistemological key" that "radically alters traditional forms of theological education."[60] But, leaving the last word to the Mas, Pentecostal/Charismatic theological education is an integral and necessary part of our "Mission in the Spirit."[61] In this way, we will not lose the dynamic enabling of the Spirit through an overemphasis on rationalistic scholasticism. Both are necessary.

---

[60]Cheryl Bridges Johns, "The Meaning of Pentecost for Theological Education,"*Ministerial Formation* 87 (October 1999): 42.

[61]Julie C. Ma & Wonsuk Ma, *Mission in the Spirit: Towards a Pentecostal/Charismatic Missiology* (Regnum, 2010).

Pentecostal Reflections on Apostolicity

by Harold D. Hunter

Global Pentecostals Are Not "Protestants" and Are Not "Western"

Not unlike Anglican communions, Pentecostals around the world do not accept the generic label of being called Protestants nor as having risen solely from soil of the Global North. Negative perceptions of Pentecostalism can often be traced to the opinions of "independents" who communicate through television, radio, social media, and the web; whereas a more accurate commentary should come from analyzing Pentecostal churches like the Yoido Full Gospel Church in Seoul, South Korea.[1]

The above paragraph attempts to summarize a 2010 course on "Global Pentecostalism," which I taught for Gordon-Conwell Theological Seminary in Africa and Asia. However, even at the inaugural Global Conference for Pentecostal Scholars, known as

---

[1] A good place to start is Allan Anderson's *Introduction to Pentecostalism* (Cambridge: Cambridge University Press, 2004). Margaret Poloma and John C. Green, *The Assemblies of God: Godly Love and the Revitalization of American Pentecostalism* (New York: New York University Press, 2010), 22, 32, document the growing number of European-American congregations in the USA—including Central Assembly in Springfield, Missouri—that can be labeled Evangelical Assemblies of God. This should challenge Grant Wacker and other scholars in the U.S. who consider the Assemblies of God as being the axiomatic typology of global Pentecostalism.

"Brighton '91," I tried to start a conversation between David Barrett and Mel Robeck. Unfortunately, Barrett declined my invitation; so their papers, published under the title "All Together in One Place," give the inaccurate impression that I endorse the concept that the Azusa Street Revival is the epicenter of global Pentecostalism.

The largest organization of Pentecostals is the Pentecostal World Fellowship (PWF), which was formed in 1947. It today consists of approximately fifty Pentecostal denominations or associations spread throughout the world. (Its current chairman is Rev. Dr. Prince Guneratnam, founder and president of Calvary International Ministries in Malaysia.) The PWF does not exercise legislative or jurisdictional oversight but rather, through its triennial conference, encourages the formation of partnerships and cooperation among Pentecostal bodies for the sake of common mission. Although lacking a formal apparatus to engage sister churches, mutual cooperation takes many forms, which expands the reach of the PWF community to represent the majority of Pentecostals around the world.

The PWF network extends deep into the Global South to embrace denominations like the Church of Pentecost in Ghana and the Indian Pentecostal Church in India, which has ties to Syriac Orthodoxy. Not presently included in the network, however, are the African instituted churches, the house churches in China, the autochthonous Pentecostal churches in Latin America, and like groupings.

The 2010 PWF Conference convened in Stockholm and welcomed Dr. Olav Tveit, General Secretary of the World Council of Churches (WCC), to bring greetings. One of the hosts for the 2013 WCC General Assembly in Korea will be Yoido Full Gospel Church, which recently hosted the Global Christian Forum, previously hosted the World Alliance of Reformed

Churches (WARC)-Pentecostal Dialogue and the WCC-Pentecostal Joint Consultative Group (JCG), and has extended an invitation to host future talks between Orthodox and Pentecostals. Yoido's senior pastor Rev. Dr. Young-hoon Lee chairs the National Council of Churches in Korea. Pentecostal fellowships do not have anything comparable to a Pope, Ecumenical Patriarch, or Archbishop of Canterbury. Thus, any attempt to impose foreign ecclesiastical structures on Pentecostals would be seen as betraying our ecclesiology as well as our pneumatology, with an emphasis on gifting and calling. Our pneumatic emphasis insists on accountability to the discernment of the community. At the same time, however, it has been suggested that some of our autocephalous ecclesial structures function in ways not unlike patriarchs.

Apostolicity is frequently depicted by member churches of the PWF as continuity with the life, teachings, and practices of the early church. This consciousness gave birth to names like the Apostolic Faith Movement, the Apostolic Faith, and the Apostolic Faith Church of South Africa. A search for "apostolic" in the digital version of *Bridegroom's Messenger* turns up countless hits in this periodical started by G.B. Cashwell, a minister in the Pentecostal Holiness Church.[2] Apostolicity gained momentum in the 21st century, as can be illustrated by all the Pentecostal churches in Ghana that incorporate "apostolic" in their name.

Pentecostals have two primary sacraments: water baptism and the Eucharist. In addition, most Pentecostals practice Holy

---

[2]See *Bridegroom's Messenger* 2:26 (November 15, 1908), 3, for an article about Beulah Home, referring to it as being an apostolic town with an apostolic Bible and literary school that will teach apostolic music and build an apostolic orphanage. There is an ad in *Bridegroom's Messenger* 1:18 (July 15, 1908), 14, about a meeting in Falcon, North Carolina, that promises "the restoration of Apostolic gifts and power to the Church, Mark 16:17, Acts 2:1, Acts 4:39, and the healing of the sick, according to James."

Unction–the anointing of persons (and of cloths in the absence of the person) with oil as part of the prayer for healing of the sick. Some also practice foot washing (John 13) as a post-baptismal cleansing from sin and thus sacramental in nature.

In January 2011, the International Pentecostal Holiness Church (IPHC) celebrated the centennial of the merger of the Fire-Baptized Holiness Church (FBHC) with the Pentecostal Holiness Church (PHC). That historic achievement of unity, made visible on January 31, 1900, writes plainly the message that much Pentecostal theology has been done in the context of prayer and worship. It is this matrix that caused two churches to realize a common mission and vision. The older, larger church was the FBHC, but a secure anchor was found in the PHC. The group at the merger was small but their vision was big as they sensed a calling to propel the emerging church to far-flung parts of the world.

These saints imbibed a spirituality of the Cross. They continually talked about "being living sacrifices crucified unto Christ" and lived that out through constant prayer, fasting, covenant-keeping, and non-stop church attendance. Their discipline and spirituality, although remarkable, were not particularly unusual in the early 20th century and not exclusively owned by any particular group of Christians in the Global North.

With the fresh winds of the Spirit came the Pentecostal message with its empowering and liberating proclamation of the resurrection. Some of these theological themes coalesce in J.H. King's *Passover to Pentecost*. King wrote this influential thesis in 1914, after returning to the U.S. from Asia, the Middle East, and Europe. At the time of the merger, he was in India making connections important to global Pentecostalism through persons like Pandita Ramabai at the Mukti Orphanage, who had direct ties to a future IPHC affiliate–the Pentecostal Methodist Church of Chile.

Early Pentecostals had a passion for their faith that considered little about anything other than singing, praying, preaching, agonizing, confessing, seeking the anointing, testifying, episodes of ecstasy, studying and memorizing the Bible, and taking light to dark places. These Pentecostals faced threats by fire, hangings, poison, whips, brute force, etc.; yet they were quite literal about bringing in the "poor, the crippled, the blind and the lame" (Luke 14:21, NRSV) as well as going "out into the roads and the country lanes and compel people to come in, so that my house may be filled" (Luke 14:23, NRSV). Their version of social justice usually started with the individual, which was in no small measure explained by them often being the victims of discrimination or persecution. It is likely that the first Pentecostal martyr in the U.S. was killed by police in 1918 due to his commitment to pacifism.[3]

In the context of this discussion, those who surrender to the post-modern paradigm of post-denominationalism and care little about pre-denominational churches should read the commentary on John 17:21 by J.H. King and G.F. Taylor. North Carolina Pentecostal Holiness Church Conference Superintendent A.H. Butler would call on this text during the November 1911 PHC North Carolina Convention as he looked back at recent events. The January 1911 merger of the FBHC and PHC was the first instance of organic unity achieved by Classical Pentecostals in the U.S.[4]

---

[3] See Paul Alexander, *Peace to War: Shifting Allegiances in the Assemblies of God* (Telford, PA: Cascadia Publishing House, 2009), 136-137. Also, email (6/04/2010) from Jay Beaman.
[4] Harold D. Hunter, "Full Communion: A Pentecostal Prayer," in *Ecumenical Trends* 37:1 (January 2008): 1-7, 15. Also see *Proceedings of the Twelfth Annual Convention of the Pentecostal Holiness Church of North Carolina,* November 21-23, 1911 (Goldsboro: Nash Brothers, 1911), 4; G.F.

Miroslav Volf's Participatory Ecclesiology

In light of the fact that there is no agreement on global Pentecostal identity, it would be ludicrous to expect a presentation on ecclesiology that could speak authoritatively even for those Pentecostals that make up the Pentecostal World Fellowship. The wide diversity of ecclesiology found among Pentecostals around the world is easily measured by the number of official documents available now on CDs, DVDs, and websites. In terms of scholarly analysis, we need look no farther than the works on ecclesiology by Shane Clifton (Australia), Simon Chan (Singapore), Wolfgang Vondey (Germany), and Veli-Matti Kärkkäinen (Finland).[5] I would add that while our lack of homogeneity is roundly criticized, no tradition known to me is monolithic.

There is, in fact, no uniform ecclesiastical polity embraced by Pentecostals around the world, as was clearly illustrated in the founding of the PWF itself. Pentecostals bring to life the admission in the Lima, Peru document, *Baptism, Eucharist, and Ministry* that the "New Testament does not describe a single pattern of ministry which might serve as a blueprint or continuing norm for all future ministry in the Church." This

---

Taylor: "Other Organizations," in *Pentecostal Holiness Advocate* 1:24 (October 11, 1917): 9; "Perilous Times," in *Pentecostal Holiness Advocate* 1:49 (April 4, 1918): 4; "Editorial Thoughts" (p. 1) then "Bear With Me" (p. 8), in *Pentecostal Holiness Advocate* 1:50 (April 11, 1918); J.H. King, "A Word to the Ministry and Membership of the Pentecostal Holiness Church," in *Pentecostal Holiness Advocate* 5:4 (May 26, 1921): 2f.

[5] Simon Chan, *Pentecostal Ecclesiology: An Essay on the Development of Doctrine* (Amsterdam: Deo Publishing, 2011); Veli-Matti Kärkkäinen, *An Introduction to Ecclesiology: Ecumenical, Historical & Global Perspectives* (Downer's Grove, IL: InterVarsity Press, 2002); Shane Clifton, *Pentecostal Churches in Transition: Analysing the Developing Ecclesiology of the Assemblies of God in Australia* (Leiden; Boston: Brill, 2009); Wolfgang Vondey, *People of Bread: Rediscovering Ecclesiology* (New York: Paulist Press, 2008).

view of the essence of the church differs from that of those who insist that we really cannot talk about the nature of the church without making certain fundamental assumptions about how it is to be constituted. Is it an episcopate, a council of presbyters, or simply a congregation? The Assemblies of God in the U.S. has in the past officially used the word "fellowship" as its corporate self-designation to indicate its intention to resist the notion that the sociological term "denomination" is fitting.

In contrast to ecclesiological voids emphasized by Frank Macchia, Veli-Matti Kärkkäinen, and other like-minded scholars, Dale Coulter and I have pointed out separately in *Pneuma: The Journal for the Society for Pentecostal Studies* that the Church of God (Cleveland, Tennessee) paid a lot of attention to ecclesiology, particularly in its formative years at the opening of the 20th century.[6] I would go on to say that Pentecostals classed as "Free Churches" speak from a pre-determined ecclesiology, although previously lacking sufficient theological reflection to be published as official documents.

With the aid of Monsignor Peter Hocken, I put together in 1991 the first Global Conference for Pentecostal Scholars, known as the Theological Track of Brighton '91. Our presenters were Roman Catholic, Eastern and Oriental Orthodox, Protestant, and Pentecostal. Everything possible was done to strike a balance between the Global North and Global South. The irony is that I initially tried to link this global event with the World Council of Churches General Assembly, known as Canberra '91. In speaking with WCC General Secretary Emilio Castro in his Geneva office, he was positive about the concept but wanted input from W.H.

---

[6]Dale Coulter, "The Development of Ecclesiology in the Church of God (Cleveland, TN): A Forgotten Contribution?" in *Pneuma: The Journal of the Society for Pentecostal Studies* 29:1 (2007): 59-85; Harold D. Hunter, "A.J. Tomlinson's Emerging Ecclesiology," in *Pneuma* 32:3 (2010): 369-389.

Hollenweger. When Hollenweger was slow to engage the process, I had to move everything quickly to Brighton '91.

Our keynote speaker for Brighton '91 was Professor Jürgen Moltmann, who reserved a chapter of his book *The Spirit of Life* (Minneapolis: Fortress Press, 1992) until after his presentation. Following the conference, he invited me to contribute "We Are the Church: New Congregationalism" in the work he and Karl-Josef Kuschel were publishing titled *Concilium: Revista Internazionale di Teologia*. This volume was devoted to the topic "Pentecostal Movements as an Ecumenical Challenge." Moltmann (or at least Miroslav Volf as seen in his response to my article) wanted me to argue that the democratic presence of the Holy Spirit among Pentecostals accounted for more congregational autonomy than in magisterial traditions; but I cited evidence to the contrary as part of the story in addition to what they expected.

I argued that that, despite our several differences, there is this one common feature that distinguishes Pentecostal churches— Even with the most rigid control from the "top down," the local churches are constantly exhorted to be alive and on fire, with each member expected to be active and "carry the flame." To bend a familiar image, Pentecostals believe in the transformation, not of elements or buildings but of believers. It is in the context of determining the nature of worship (though in a forum sometimes labeled the "sacred theatre of the spirit possessed"[7]) that Pentecostals approach the question of the church dispersed in the world–that is, the witnessing and serving people of the triune God.

---

[7]Daniel Albrecht, *Rites in the Spirit: A Ritual Approach to Pentecostal-Charismatic Spirituality* (Sheffield: Sheffield Academic Press, 1999), 159, acknowledges there is a wide variety of ritual expressions, but "At the center of the variety exists the belief among the congregants that they are actually experiencing the presence of God in an intimate, immediate, mystical way."

For me, there is a striking parallel between how traditional sacramentalists describe what happens at the altar or in water baptism and when someone confesses salvation at a Pentecostal "altar." Pentecostals believe in a real presence when it comes to the people of God gathered together for worship. For some Pentecostals, this is most evident during the Eucharist. Another dimension is apparent when glossolalia is manifest during water baptism or washing the saints' feet or even at a wedding. We also prophesy, report miracles, and seek to manifest divine love. I am saying we affirm the metaphysical reality of the presence of the Holy Spirit regardless of the liturgy that is adopted. Since our critics are quick to dismiss the Charismatic manifestations as irrational, I have long said that the official teachings of our churches rather support the notion that this should be seen as trans-rational or supra-rational (or mystical, if you like). On the other hand, I do not mean to imply anything bordering on the gnostic kind of self-serving revelation.

In terms of being participatory, not only can we use my phrase that "every member should carry the flame," but also group prayer aloud, gifts of the Spirit manifested during worship services, spontaneous spiritual dance, vigorous singing, constant earnest prayer, observing strict discipline, engaging in diligent study and memorizing of the scripture, and evangelism are constant multi-member affirmations of the faith. In short, there was no room for those who were complacent. I was raised on a slogan reportedly printed on a poster carried around by A.J. Tomlinson that said "A work for every member and every member a worker."

This concept of "participatory ecclesiology" gained a wider hearing in Volf's *After Our Likeness: The Church as the Image of the Trinity*. Here Volf's dialogue partners are Pope Benedict (at that time Cardinal Joseph Ratzinger) and the Eastern Orthodox authority John Zizioulas. Volf utilizes the category of "Free

Church ecclesiology" to engage Baptist theologian John Smyth as well as feminist theologians.

Volf soundly rejected what he labels the "episcopocentric ecclesiology" of Ratzinger and Zizioulas in favor of a "polycentric community," saying "Paul seems to envision such a model of ecclesial life with a polycentric participative structure when he tries to re-establish peace within the enthusiastic and chaotic congregation in Corinth" (see 1 Cor. 14:33).[8]

Volf also makes clear that he disowns what he terms the Roman Catholic and Eastern Orthodox notion of the soteriological significance of the church. It is here where he suggests that the "mediation of salvation occurs not only through office-holders, but also through all other members of the church."[9] This is linked to his notion of a polycentric community that leads to talk of a polycentric participative model. So at the end of the day, the church does have soteriological significance but not of the sort associated with magisterial Christianity.

Volf further states that "Ratzinger and Zizioulas understand the Trinity hierarchically and ground the hierarchical relations within the church in part of this basis. In following Jürgen Moltmann, I, by contrast, take as my premise the symmetrical relations within the Trinity. Relations between charismata, modeled after the Trinity, are reciprocal and symmetrical; all members of the church have charismata, and all are to engage their charismata for the good of all others."[10]

There is certainly more to be said about how Volf fleshed out this ecclesiology; but at this point, I want to comment on the paradigm that allows Volf and Kärkkäinen to speak of "Free

---

[8]Miroslav Volf, *After Our Likeness: The Church as the Image of the Trinity* (Grand Rapids, MI: Eerdmans, 1998), 224.
[9]Ibid., 223.
[10]Ibid., 226.

Church ecclesiology." This kind of language works well when drawing a contrast to what can be called a "descending ecclesiology" over against an "ascending ecclesiology." This concept is used in the unique 2009 book co-authored by a Roman Catholic and a Pentecostal scholar, both from Australia, who were consulted in the original paper.[11] Advocating a participatory ecclesiology does not require an exclusive affirmation of the Free Church idea that limits the church merely to a local assembly. Volf's idea of "interecclesial minimum"[12] falls short on many accounts, as this study attempts to make evident.

In *After Our Likeness*, Volf contends that "Diachronic plurality is even more important than synchronic" and observes that "The charismata with which these members serve in the congregation can change; certain charismata come to the fore at certain times, while others become unimportant. Members who are "passive" are not truly "Charismatic," even though there are no members without charisma."[13]

I can sympathize with Volf's point that the *Baptist, Eucharist, and Ministry* document gives too much away to ordained ministers,[14] but then again I do not want to dismiss the concept of leadership that goes beyond the local church. To do otherwise would betray well-known Pentecostal ecclesiologies like the Pentecostal version of "ascending ecclesiology" of my youth as well as that embraced by Roman Catholics and the Eastern Orthodox. Take note of the following relevant commentary by Simon Chan:

---

[11]Neil J. Ormerod and Shane Clifton, *Globalization and the Mission of the Church: Ecclesiological Investigations*, (London: T&T Clark, 2009).

[12]Volf, *After Our Likeness*, 157.

[13]Ibid., 233.

[14]Volf, "A Protestant Response", 40; Volf, *After Our Likeness*, 228 and note 28.

The claim that Pentecostals are predominantly Free Church in their ecclesiology is not borne out by the facts. Historically, there is a wide diversity of ecclesiastical structures in classical Pentecostal denominations ranging from the Free Church-type to Episcopalian-type. The Assemblies of God is usually categorized as a Free Church denomination, but in point of fact, it is partly congregational and partly Presbyterian. Each local church is autonomous, but there is also a central governing body, the general presbytery or executive council, which issues credentials to AG ministers. Perhaps a more telling sign of episcopal inclination is seen in the widespread practice of distinguishing between ordinary Christians as Spirit-filled and the pastor as having a "special anointing."[15]

In defence of this thesis, Chan refers to New Order of the Latter Rain Movement (1940s), the Shepherding Movement (1970s), and the current Apostolic Reformation Movement.

Nature and Mission of the Church 100 Years After Edinburgh 1910

The centennial of the historic 1910 Edinburgh World Missionary Conference was marked with important celebrations in Edinburgh, Cape Town, Japan, and elsewhere around the world. It is often said that global Pentecostalism is barely a century old, so this means that now is an appropriate time to review ecclesiology with an emphasis on the mission of the church. I have often chosen as a dialogue partner the World Council of Churches' Faith and Order working document known as *Nature and Mission of the Church*.

---

[15]Chan, *Pentecostal Ecclesiology*, 112.

Unlike previous reports (e.g., *Baptism, Eucharist, and Ministry* and *Confessing the One Faith*), WCC's *Nature and Mission of the Church* has lagged in terms of official responses. Additionally, to my knowledge, there has never been an official response to any of these conciliar documents by a member church of the Pentecostal World Fellowship, which in and of itself is a commentary on our myriad ecclesiologies. In fact, even member churches of the WCC have been slow in responding to *Nature and Mission of the Church*.[16]

There is no evidence of Pentecostal influence on the current text despite connections to the likes of Miroslav Volf, Mel Robeck, and Veli-Matti Kärkkäinen. I worry that, at this stage, the only way we will show up is in those "gray boxes of divergences," since we seem to have little constructive input given the nature of the document. This provokes the question of whether these "gray boxes" are more a commentary on Pentecostal scholars or the drafters of the document in question.[17]

I published my own reflections on *Baptism, Eucharist, and Ministry* in the *Journal of Ecumenical Studies*. I also published "Confessing the One Faith: An Ecumenical Explication of the Apostolic Faith as It Is Confessed in the Nicene-Constantinopolitan Creed" (381) in *Pneuma*.[18] I come with this

---

[16]*The Nature and Mission of the Church: A Stage on the Way to a Common Statement*, Faith and Order Paper 198 (Geneva: World Council of Churches, 2005).

[17]For constructive input, see Veli-Mati Kärkkäinen, "The Nature and Purpose of the Church: Theological and Ecumenical Reflections," and Frank D. Macchia, "The Nature and Purpose of the Church: A Pentecostal Reflection," in *Pentecostalism and Christian Unity: Ecumenical Documents and Critical Assessments*, edited by Wolfgang Vondey (Eugene, OR: Pickwick Publications, 2010).

[18]Harold D. Hunter, "Reflections by a Pentecostalist on Aspects of BEM," in *Journal of Ecumenical Studies* 29:3/4 (Summer/Fall 1992): 317-345; Harold D. Hunter, "Musings on *Confessing the One Faith*," in *Pneuma: The Journal of the Society for Pentecostal Studies* 14:2 (Fall 1992): 204-208.

background and the added benefit of being on the study commission working on *Nature and Mission of the Church* in the U.S. National Council of Churches' Faith and Order Commission. Our report was sent to Geneva at the end of our 2011 quadrennium. I tried to bring to bear a Pentecostal perspective on our draft, which would become the first such direct impact on this particular conciliar text.

The International Pentecostal Holiness Church has consistently affirmed bishops and sacraments as part of their identity. In general terms, one could say this version of Pentecostal episcopacy does link directly to the sacraments. It is worthy of note that the succession of IPHC presiding bishops involves the laying on of hands. I would argue that such a model is consistent with my version of participatory ecclesiology, although it rejects Volf's ecclesial minimum. I would also point to similar traits found in the Church of God in Christ, the Church of God (Cleveland, Tennessee), and the Church of God of Prophecy among others. Moreover, the distinguished Assemblies of God scholar in Singapore Simon Chan has been depicted as embracing a "hierarchically structured model" in his book *Liturgical Theology: The Church as Worshipping Community*.[19]

Returning to the WCC dictionary quoting *Baptism, Eucharist, and Ministry,* one can easily hear a Pentecostal reading of the following: "Most important, it is the apostolic tradition of the church as a whole which is now regarded as the primary manifestation of apostolic succession, though the ministerial succession (by laying on of hands) is also treated as an expression

---

[19]See Dale M. Coulter, "Christ, the Spirit, and Vocation: Initial Reflections on a Pentecostal Ecclesiology," in *Pro Ecclesia* 19:3 (Summer 2010): 318, who speaks of the "Episcopal wing" of the Pentecostal Movement in the U.S..

of both the permanence and the continuity of the original apostolic mission."

To illustrate the careful distance most Pentecostals have kept from the idea of apostolic succession, Simon Chan notes that the consecration of the first bishops of the Communion of the Evangelical Episcopal Church was carried out in the presence of both a Roman Catholic bishop and an Eastern Orthodox bishop.[20] Some Pentecostal ministers who converted to Roman Catholicism or Eastern Orthodoxy have named apostolic succession as a "missing link" in their ecclesial identity.

Reacting to apostolic succession known to magisterial Christendom, here is a telling snippet from A.J. Tomlinson's annual address delivered to the November 1914 Church of God (Cleveland, Tennessee) General Assembly: "Although we do not claim a line of succession from the holy apostles, we do believe we are following their example."[21]

An extended quotation from the same address reveals more of what is at stake for Tomlinson and echoes what was heard from the Fire-Baptized Holiness Church in 1900:

> The one at Nicaea was disorderly and resulted in division, shame and disgrace, while the one at Jerusalem was orderly and resulted in a closer fellowship and union of the multitudes and brought consolation and joy to all who were interested. And when the decrees (not creed) were delivered to them the churches were established in the faith and increased in number daily. Bear in the

---

[20]Chan, *Pentecostal Ecclesiology*, 1234.

[21]*Historical Annual Addresses,* compiled by Perry Gillum (Cleveland, TN: White Wing Publishing House & Press, 1970) 1:34. Spurling's 1897 "An Appeal" (p. 8) dismissed those who teach apostolic succession and Baptists who make laws and binding rules; this is contrasted to the law of Christ, which he termed "the lost link."

mind that the council at Jerusalem was conducted under theocratic form of government which honoured God and the Holy Scriptures in the final settlement of the matter in question, while the one at Nicaea was operated under episcopal government and not a word of Scripture was given as authority for the creed and nothing said about it being pleasing to the Holy Ghost... We are certainly following in the footprints of the noble and ever-to-be-revered apostles and elders of the early Church when we declare that in all of our deliberations the final decision and settlement of every question must be in harmony with God's Holy Word, and a 'Thus saith the Lord' or 'It seemed good to the Holy Ghost, and to us,' at the end of the decision.[22]

Tomlinson spoke of a united church in the opening centuries of Christianity, depicting Jerusalem as a center linking far-flung churches. By this, he meant to give James first place over Paul or Peter when it came to councils like the one recorded in Acts 15.[23] Tomlinson is less precise when it comes to understanding how local churches related to one another outside such a structure. He conceded that an episcopacy did eventually emerge, but only as the church lost its way. Tomlinson espoused a vision of restoring the apostolic order known as theocracy.[24]

---

[22]*Historical Annual Addresses* 1:40-41; see also p. 39. See *Constitution and General Rules of the Fire-Baptized Holiness Association of America* (1900), 2, under Article II, Object and Design: "It is our intention that the Fire-Baptized Holiness Association shall embody all the essential characteristics and perform all the functions of an Apostolic church."

[23]See his annual address delivered to the Church of God (Cleveland, TN) General Assembly that met November 1–7, 1915, in *Historical Annual Addresses* 1:52. See also A.J. Tomlinson, "Oneness," in *Bridegroom's Messenger* 2:37 (May 1, 1909): A.J. Tomlinson, "The Lord's Church," in *Bridegroom's Messenger* 2:33 (March 1, 1909), 4.

[24]While Tomlinson's intentions of bringing all into "one fold" are abundantly clear, he was hardly alone in this respect. See Harold D. Hunter,

Roger Robins characterizes this quest of leadership by Tomlinson over not only the Church of God (Cleveland, Tennessee) but the entire Pentecostal Movement as seeking "apostolic authority." The term is used parallel to the term "apostolic order" as applied by the likes of Frank Sandford. More telling about Tomlinson is his use of James as his model. One can see the notes scribbled on his collection of *The Ante-Nicene Fathers* that figured into his 1914 annual address. Building on the exalted language about James used by early bishops, Tomlinson raised the stakes by placing James on "his imperial and mediatorial throne."[25]

Volf's emphasis on the "democratic presence of the Holy Spirit" notwithstanding, one would be hard pressed to say that any of the various ecclesial forms generated by the Pentecostal Movement truly espouse the priesthood of all believers. Perhaps it may be more helpful to speak of the "prophethood of Pentecostal believers" in the sense that they seek the Charismatic empowerment of the Holy Spirit to glorify God.

"A.J. Tomlinson's Emerging Ecclesiology," in *Pneuma: The Journal of the Society for Pentecostal Studies*, 376. In contrast to the notion that early Pentecostalism was inherently ecumenical, I first advanced my reading in my 1984 presidential address "What Is Truth?" to the Society for Pentecostal Studies meeting at Gordon-Conwell Theological Seminary, which was not published in *Pneuma*.

[25]*General Assembly Minutes: 1906-1914: Photographic Reproductions of the First Ten General Assembly Minutes*, 302, citing minutes of the 10th Annual Assembly held November 2-8, 1914 in Cleveland, Tennessee, 12; *Historical Annual Addresses: A.J. Tomlinson*, 1:50. Cf. Robins, *A.J. Tomlinson*, 208, 212, 220ff; Daniel D. Preston, *The Era of A.J. Tomlinson* (Cleveland, TN: White Wing Publishing House and Press, 1984), 59ff. I read A.J. Tomlinson's handwritten notes in his personal copies of the *ANF* years before Robins would report this finding in his book on Tomlinson. What I found was incorporated into various dictionary and encyclopedia articles that I wrote about A.J. Tomlinson.

Final Remarks

David Carter's study of Edinburgh 2010 concludes that "In the end, unity and mission are one." This UK Roman Catholic scholar says unity based on John 17:21 should move to "so they may believe." Would this not be a compelling argument for Pentecostals who claim evangelism is a top priority and perhaps even the fifth mark of the church? Carter is captivated with Christian Churches Together in England, even making flattering parallels with the intent of Edinburgh 2010.[26] Many early Pentecostals knew no limits to God's saving grace. G.F. Taylor would say this with clarity, but even the Pentecostal church of my youth saw evangelism as taking light to dark places rather than proselytism.[27]

---

[26]David Carter, "The Edinburgh Missionary Conference Centenary," in *Ecumenical Trends* 39:3 (March 2010): 4-5.
[27]G.F. Taylor, "Our Policy," in *Pentecostal Holiness Advocate* 1:1 (May 3, 1917): 9.

Mission in the Spirit:
From Edinburgh to Canberra
and Athens

by Kirsteen Kim

When the report of the meeting of the International Missionary Council in Willingen, Germany, in 1952 linked mission with the nature of the Trinity and the sending of the Son and Spirit into the world, it established this link as a theological concept and inaugurated the postwar paradigm of mission known as *missio Dei*.[1] When Willingen further stated that mission belongs to the very nature of the church and of the Christian life,[2] it suggested that mission is a spiritual activity. Nevertheless, for most of the twentieth century, mission continued to be separate from spirituality and mission studies from spiritual theology,[3] with some notable exceptions that reflected on Pentecost. In the late twentieth century, Pentecostal-Charismatic perspectives contributed to the understanding of *missio Dei* in pneumatological terms and to reflection on the mission of the Spirit. In the twenty-first century, Wonsuk and Julie Ma are among those who have brought about a renewed understanding of mission not primarily as task or strategy but as

---

[1] "The Theological Basis of the Missionary Obligation", in Norman Goodall (ed.), *Missions Under the Cross* (London: Edinburgh House Press, 1953), 238–45, 241.
[2] "The Theological Basis", 244.
[3] Robert Davies Hughes, III, *Beloved Dust: Tides of the Spirit in the Christian Life* (New York: Continuum, 2008).

spirituality: "mission in the Spirit."[4] This brief paper explores the contribution of Pentecostal-Charismatic perspectives to mission spirituality and mission pneumatology through reflection on the mission of the Spirit.

Pentecost and Mission Spirituality: Edinburgh 1910

The relationship between *missio Dei* and mission spirituality can be understood in several ways. Here we shall look at three of them, each of which can be traced to reflection on Pentecost. The first concerns the spirituality of the missionary. If we go back to the World Missionary Conference in Edinburgh in 1910, we find that it was "firmly Christocentric;" God was thought of as Jesus Christ but rarely as the Holy Spirit or as Trinity.[5] The word *spirit* was used frequently but usually with respect to the human spirit or the spirits of nations and cultures. However, there was reference to "the superhuman factor" which covered many pneumatological concerns in mission. This "superhuman factor" was necessary to "the success of the Kingdom of Christ."[6] It was virtually identified with the spiritual life of the missionaries and their home churches: the "faithfulness and loyalty of His children in prayer" was the condition for "the extension, the progress and the fruitfulness of His Kingdom."[7] In the conference itself, prayer was given a central place and this was remembered afterwards as a highly significant spiritual event. "Earnest prayer" was also to

---

[4] Julie C. Ma and Wonsuk Ma, *Mission in the Spirit: Towards a Pentecostal/Charismatic Missiology* (Eugene, OR: Wipf & Stock, 2010).

[5] Brian Stanley, *The World Missionary Conference, Edinburgh 1910* (Grand Rapids, MI: Eerdmans, 2009), 88.

[6] World Missionary Conference, 1910, *Report of Commission I: Carrying the Gospel to All the Non-Christian World* (Edinburgh & London: Oliphant, Anderson and Ferrier, 1910), 359.

[7] World Missionary Conference, 1910, *Report of Commission I*, 360. Prayer was given a central place in the conference and it was remembered afterwards as a highly significant spiritual event. Stanley, *The World Missionary Conference*, 88–90.

be the guarantee that its Continuation Committee was directed by the Holy Spirit.[8] To the Holy Spirit, or equivalently, to the divine power which "dominates" the missionaries, were attributed revival movements in different parts of the world, the success of evangelistic endeavor, unity in mission, the inauguration and direction of mission, and sustaining strength.[9] In a rare direct reference, the "Spirit of God" could be described as "the great Missioner," to whom the work and the workers are subject if there is any "hope for success in the undertaking to carry the knowledge of Christ to all people."[10] But this affirmation defines the Spirit in terms of the mission, not the other way round, and contributes to the impression given by the Edinburgh papers that the Holy Spirit is simply the human spirit writ large.[11]

Although the presence of the Spirit with the missionaries is not doubted in the Edinburgh reports, the Spirit's presence among native believers appears as something of an afterthought.[12] At the conference itself, Indian native representative, V. S. Azariah, complained that missionaries failed to devolve power to local Christians and held themselves aloof from them. His famous plea for friendship between missionaries and converts was poorly received by the conference and largely

---

[8]World Missionary Conference, *World Missionary Conference, 1910 Vol. 9: History and Records of the Conference* (Edinburgh: Oliphant, Anderson & Ferrier, 1910): 138.

[9]World Missionary Conference, 1910, *Report of Commission I*. See for example, 35–41, 47–48, 351, 353, 356–57.

[10]World Missionary Conference, 1910, *Report of Commission I*, 351.

[11]See Kirsteen Kim, "Edinburgh 1910 to 2010: From Kingdom to Spirit," *Journal of the European Pentecostal Theological Association* 30/2 (2010): 3–20.

[12]Cf. World Missionary Conference, 1910, *Report of Commission I*, 353; Teresa Okure, "The Church in the Mission Field: A Nigerian/African response", in David A. Kerr and Kenneth R. Ross, *Edinburgh 2010: Mission Then and Now* (Oxford: Regnum Books, 2009), 59–73, at 62–63.

rejected in missionary practice until at least the 1940s.[13] In 1912, Anglo-Catholic British missionary Roland Allen, who was also a proto-Charismatic, published a devastating critique of colonial missionary methods in which he argued that this failure to trust converts was the result of a lack of "faith in the Holy Ghost."[14] "We believe that it is the Holy Spirit of Christ which inspires and guides us," he wrote, but "we cannot believe that the same Spirit will guide and inspire them."[15] He found missionary paternalism to be completely contrary to the mission principles practiced by the apostle Paul, who believed in a spiritual reality which was prior to and greater than his mission, and therefore trusted converts to manage their own affairs and himself soon moved on to another city.[16]

A second connection between *missio Dei* and mission spirituality concerns the shift in missionary motivation from obedience to the Great Commission to a response to God's love in Christ, which also emerges from reflection on Pentecost. In 1918, Allen contributed the first article to the *International Review of Missions*[17] to draw ecumenical attention to the significance for mission in the coming of the Holy Spirit at Pentecost.[18] Allen challenged the dominant paradigm that the foundation for mission was obedience to God's command, chiefly as stated in Mt 28:18–20. This understanding of mission

---

[13] V. S. Azariah, "The Problem of Co-operation Between Foreign and Native Workers", in World Missionary Conference, 1910, *The History and Records of the Conference*, 306–15; Stanley, *The World Missionary Conference*, 121–30.

[14] Roland Allen, *Missionary Methods: St. Paul's or Ours?* (London: World Dominion Press, 1956; first published in 1912): 152.

[15] Allen, *Missionary Methods*, 143–44.

[16] Ibid, 126–38.

[17] The *International Review of Missions (IRM)* was journal of the International Missionary Council, the Continuation Committee of Edinburgh 1910.

[18] Roland Allen, "The Revelation of the Holy Spirit in the Acts of the Apostles," *IRM* 7/2 (Apr 1918): 160–67.

as duty was dominant at least until Willingen, which itself addressed "the missionary obligation of the Church." Believing that "The Spirit is prior to the letter," Allen put the work of the "Spirit of Love which eternally desires and strives for the welfare of all" before the Great Commission in missionary motivation.[19] In suggesting that mission is participation in God's Spirit of love, Allen was a prophet far ahead of his time. His work was revisited and taken up by Pentecostal theologians in the mid-twentieth century. In 1961, U.S. evangelical Harry R. Boer's New Testament studies corroborated Allen's view that the Great Commission is descriptive of the natural consequences of Pentecost rather than prescriptive as a command to action.[20] Both Boer and Allen understood the Holy Spirit to be the motivator of Christian mission, which now appeared to be an instinctive response to the internal prompting of the Spirit rather than obedience to an external command. They believed that mission according to the Spirit would be much closer to the New Testament ideal than mission under the Law. As Allen explained, mission is the work of the Spirit and "the Spirit is a missionary Spirit." Mission is a spiritual activity, written on the heart.[21] Or, to put it another way, mission is the outworking of a missionary spirituality.

In light of Allen and Boer's work and other reflection on the biblical texts, mission theologian David J. Bosch argued that even in the case of Mt 28:16–20, response to the Spirit of Christ should be understood as prior to the command. The clause "I am with you always" indicates that it is "because Jesus continues to be present with his disciples [that] they go out in mission."[22]

---

[19]Roland Allen, *Missionary Principles* (Grand Rapids: Eerdmans, 1964 [c. 1910]).
[20]Harry R. Boer, *Pentecost and Missions* (Grand Rapids: Eerdmans, 1961).
[21]Allen, *Missionary Principles*, 16–17, 33–36.
[22]David J. Bosch, *Transforming Mission: Paradigm Shifts in Theology of Mission* (Maryknoll, NY: Orbis Books, 1991), 74–83.

Turning to Luke-Acts, Bosch draws the same conclusions as Allen and Boer when he summarizes Luke's missiology of the Spirit in three terms: the Spirit "initiates," "guides," and "empowers" the disciples' mission.[23] Showing thus that mission takes place by the impulse of the Spirit is another way of saying that mission is a spirituality.[24]

A third way of relating *missio Dei* to mission spirituality is to combine both as "mission in the Spirit." Spirituality is often used to refer to a kind of religion that it not expressed in worldly activity, but in worship, meditation, and often introspection. "Mission," on the other hand, is associated with activism, with goals and strategy, so "mission spirituality" sounds like an oxymoron.[25] At Edinburgh 1910 and in the colonial missionary movement, such was the emphasis on the goals and mobilizing all the resources necessary to meet them that there was a danger of an "end justifies the means" approach. In this context Allen rediscovered the pneumatological perspective of the Gospel of John in which mission is simply breathed into the disciples. John does not emphasize what the church is sent to do so much as the manner of our sending: "As the Father has sent me so I send you." John presents a model or pattern for mission–Jesus Christ–not a mandate. He puts forward a spirituality for mission, not a program of missionary activity. The interest lies not in the missionary task but in the spirit in which it is done.[26] The use of John 20:21 here–the verse used in the Willingen statement–confirms that mission spirituality is a corollary of the *missio Dei*

---

[23] Bosch, *Transforming Mission*, 113–14.
[24] Bosch went on to develop a mission spirituality—a "spirituality of the road"—that it is an engaged spirituality lived out in mission. David J. Bosch, *A Spirituality of the Road* (Scottdale, PA: Herald Press, 1979).
[25] Robert J. Schreiter, "The Spirituality of Reconciliation and Peacemaking in Mission Today," in Howard Mellor and Timothy Yates, *Mission, Violence and Reconciliation* (Sheffield: Cliff College Press, 2004), 29–43.
[26] Allen, *Missionary Principles*, 33–36.

paradigm. Mission is a spiritual endeavor and spiritual life is missional since both are human responses to impulses produced by the mission of the Spirit of God in the whole creation.[27]

Pentecostals and Mission Pneumatology: Canberra 1991

The potential of the *missio Dei* paradigm for the development of mission spirituality was revealed at the Seventh Assembly of World Council of Churches at Canberra, Australia, in 1991 through the dialogue with indigenous spiritualities and reflection on women's spirituality. For the first time in the history of World Council of Churches assemblies, the one at Canberra took a pneumatological theme: "Come, Holy Spirit, Renew the Whole Creation!" This topic was intended to reflect Orthodox emphasis on the distinctive work of the Holy Spirit in the world since creation, the liberation and ecological emphasis on the work of the Spirit represented by the Council's movement for "Justice, Peace and the Integrity of Creation" (JPIC) and the growing interest in theology of the Holy Spirit generated by the Pentecostal-Charismatic movement.

The Canberra Assembly did indeed bring pneumatology to the fore, although not in the way the Orthodox or the Pentecostals expected or hoped. As the theme suggested, Canberra developed *missio Dei* as mission pneumatology by reflecting on the mission of the Spirit of God. What is more, circumstances forced the connection of mission pneumatology with mission spirituality by demonstrating the importance of considering the meaning of the term *spirit* in the word *spirituality*.

---

[27]For further reflection on mission spirituality, see Wonsuk Ma and Kenneth R. Ross, *Mission Spirituality and Authentic Discipleship*. Regnum Edinburgh Centenary Series, Vol. 14 (Oxford: Regnum Books, 2013).

One of the main questions raised in the preparatory papers for the Assembly was whether the Holy Spirit is present and active outside the Christian confession and, if so, where and how.[28] JPIC answered this question by emphasizing the Spirit's work in creation as "Giver of Life" and the importance of joining in the Spirit's work of caring for the earth. This approach often referred to Romans 8:18-27, in which creation is said to be groaning under its bondage to decay, together with "we, who have the first-fruits of the Spirit" and with the Spirit who intercedes for all. In the JPIC report, this passage was interpreted to imply that it is the Spirit who is bringing about the redemption of the whole creation.[29]

As indigenous and women's spiritualities were mined for theological resources for the Assembly, *spirituality* became a prevalent term. The category of "indigenous spiritualities" combined many different local traditions that were portrayed as "earth-centered," "life-affirming" and "feminine." These were presented as an alternative model to the "destructive," "masculine," "missionary" theologies of colonial Christianity, symbolized in this context especially by the issues of aboriginal land rights and by the military action in the first Gulf War, which was being waged at the time. Women's reflections on mission emphasized the relational nature of mission and the spirituality of mission over against a goal-oriented approach, which they saw tended to be accompanied by oppression.[30] In their search for a

---

[28]Kirsteen Kim, "Spirit and "spirits" at the Canberra Assembly of the World Council of Churches, 1991," *Missiology: An International Review* 32/3 (2004): 349–65.

[29]Report of Section I; Report of Section II, in Michael Kinnamon (ed.), *Signs of the Spirit*. Official Report of the Seventh Assembly of the World Council of Churches, Canberra, 1991 (Geneva: WCC, 1991).

[30]See articles in *IRM* 81/322 (Apr 1992). For example, as Mercy Amba Oduyoye explains, "Women have transformed the traditional church, hospital, school into mission as relationships." Mercy Amba Oduyoye, Guest Editorial, *IRM* 81/322 (April 1992): 174.

more feminine image of God that would affirm women as made in that image, feminist theologians argued that the Holy Spirit is primarily feminine in Scripture.[31] They also stressed the scriptural connection between the Spirit and life, especially in the Johannine tradition.[32]

Indigenous and women's concerns were brought together at Canberra in the opening presentation of Chung Hyun Kyung from Korea, who led an exorcist's dance invoking the Holy Spirit and the spirits of suffering, oppressed individuals and peoples, using the imagery of Korean shamanism to inspire women's solidarity and action to bring about the renewal of creation.[33] This was greeted with rapturous applause from those who admired the courage of a young woman in daring to express her faith in such an unconventional and, as they saw it, indigenous way.[34] At the same time, her presentation was immediately condemned by others who thought she had stepped outside the bounds of Christianity and was engaging in syncretism.[35] The presentation provoked great controversy about what was a legitimate theology of the Holy Spirit.

The ensuing debate at Canberra "concentrated on the issue of the action of the Spirit within and outside the church, and on the criteria necessary to recognize the presence of the Spirit."[36] Two groups–Orthodox and Evangelical–voiced their opinions

---

[31] See, for example, Elizabeth Johnson, *She Who Is: The Mystery of God in Feminist Theological Discourse* (New York: Crossroad, 1992).

[32] John, chapters 3 and 4, for instance.

[33] Her theological approach is spelt out in Chung Hyun Kyung, "Ecology, Feminism and African and Asian Spirituality: Towards a Spirituality of Eco-Feminism", in David G. Hallman (ed.), *Ecotheology: Voices from South and North* (Geneva: WCC, 1994), 175–78.

[34] For example, Van Butselaar, "The Gospel and Culture Study: A Survey", *Exchange* (Koninklijke Brill NV, Leiden) 27/3 (1998): 236-47.

[35] For example, Lesslie Newbigin, "Reply to Konrad Raiser," *International Bulletin of Missionary Research* 18/3 (1994): 51.

[36] Emilio Castro, Editorial, *ER* 43/2 (April 1991): 163.

about Chung's presentation and other aspects of Canberra's treatment of the theme, especially its theology of dialogue, in separate responses to the Assembly. The Orthodox participants expressed "alarm" at a lack of discernment in affirming the presence of the Spirit in human movements, without regard for sin and error and they stressed the need to "guard against a tendency *to substitute a 'private' spirit, the spirit of the world, or other spirits for the Holy Spirit*" (italics original). Although stressing their respect for local and national cultures, they also emphasized that pneumatology is inseparable from Christology and theology of the Trinity.[37] Evangelicals at Canberra also found it necessary to make a statement and, while more positive in tone, this echoed the Orthodox concerns. Evangelicals called for a "high Christology to serve as the only authentic Christian base for dialogue with persons of other living faiths" and for clarity about the relationship between the Christological confession of the World Council of Churches, the person and work of the Holy Spirit, and the agenda of the Council.[38]

As the discussion shows, there were many at Canberra, from varied traditions, who were worried about a pneumatological understanding of mission when it was not clear what spirit was intended. They could affirm that the Spirit gives fullness of life, but the nature of that life, and in particular its links to the church, was in question. Though they might be open to the possibility that the Holy Spirit is at work in changing society and amongst people of all faiths, and though they believed that all good things are the work of God, they were not prepared to separate this interpretation of *missio Dei* from the particular expression of the Spirit of God in Jesus of Nazareth and they

---

[37]"Reflections of Orthodox Participants", in Kinnamon, *Signs of the Spirit*, 279–82.
[38]"Evangelical Perspectives from Canberra", in Kinnamon, *Signs of the Spirit*, 282–86.

wished to keep a close connection of the *missio Spiritus* with Christ and his Church.

The divisiveness of Chung's presentation made pneumatological discourse too sensitive for Council discussions.³⁹ Nevertheless, the potential of pneumatology for mission theology was clear for several reasons: First, because of the fact, evident at Canberra, that the discourse of "Spirit", "spirits" and "spirituality" is shared between Christians of very different theological persuasions, which makes it a vehicle of ecumenical discussion. Second, because at Canberra the representatives of almost all strands of Christian tradition applied pneumatology to the full range of ecumenical concerns: to social, economic, and political movements and forces, to matters of the human heart, giftedness, morality, and evangelism, to the forces or spirits of creation, to unity, dialogue, and reconciliation. Third, because a pneumatological approach can affirm cultures, religions, and diversity. It therefore has potential for a theology of mission in plural contexts, in a globalized world and in post modernity in a way that a narrowly Christological approach does not, nor does discourse of the kingdom of God. Fourth, because the words *spirit* and *spirituality* are not the possession of the Christian community alone. Pneumatology facilitates engagement with secular society as well as dialogue with people of other faiths and indigenous spiritualities from a new perspective with more of a level playing field and possibly circumventing the Christological impasse.⁴⁰ Fifth, because pneumatology facilitates the extent of missionary concern beyond anthropocentrism toward solidarity with the rest of

---

³⁹Christopher Duraisingh, Editorial, *IRM* 84/334 (1995): 203.

⁴⁰Amos Yong, *Beyond the Impasse: Toward a Pneumatological Theology of Religions* (Grand Rapids: Baker Academic, 2003); Jacques Dupuis, *Toward a Christian Theology of Religious Pluralism* (Maryknoll, NY: Orbis Books, 1997).

creation and prophetic action against life-destroying agents.[41] Finally, sixth, because pneumatological discourse connected mission with spirituality in a new way, which we will explore in the final section of this paper. The right formulation was not found at Canberra, but what was needed was clear: a mission pneumatology that is sensitive to the action of the Spirit in the wider creation and rejoices in the work of the Spirit wherever it is found, a pneumatology that gives space for other spiritualities and is open to them while not losing sight of the facts of the Spirit's holiness, that the Spirit was shown perfectly in the life and work of Jesus of Nazareth, and that the Spirit was poured out in a special way on the church at Pentecost.

The Mission of the Spirit and the Mission of Christ: Athens 2005

In the late 1990s, the World Council of Churches' Commission for World Mission and Evangelism (CWME), led by Jacques Matthey, dared to take up the theme of pneumatology again in the context of theology of mission. The development of mission pneumatology in CWME was stimulated by further interaction with Pentecostal-Charismatic theology. A statement on mission developed and adopted by CWME in the year 2000, "Mission and Evangelism in Unity Today" took some important steps toward a mission pneumatology that would be more acceptable across the churches. In this document, *missio Dei*, "the source of and basis for the mission of the church" is interpreted in a fully Trinitarian way in that mention is made of two distinct sendings, but they are treated together. The CWME statement recognized the Pentecostal-Charismatic understanding that mission is a spirituality, a heartfelt but spontaneous

---

[41]See, for example, Celia Deane-Drummond, *Creation through Wisdom* (Edinburgh: T&T Clark, 2000).

outworking of the inspiring, transforming, life-giving work of the Holy Spirit. In the concluding "convictions," mission was explained as an outpouring of love from the heart of the Trinity. The theological section goes on to interpret *missio Dei* both in terms of the Word/Christ and of the Spirit while the statement also emphatically rejects any "temptation to separate the presence of God or the Spirit from the Son of God, Jesus Christ." The comprehensive nature of *missio Dei*, which "has no limits or barriers" and "has been at work within the entire human race and the whole of creation throughout history" is affirmed as promoting "a more inclusive understanding of God's presence and work in the whole world and among all people . . . even in the most unexpected places." Furthermore, the document lays a pneumatological basis for mission spirituality, mission and unity, and also for healing and reconciliation. The contribution of Pentecostal-Charismatic theology to the CWME statement of 2000 is seen especially in the recognition that mission is a "natural response" to the transforming power of the Holy Spirit in individuals and churches.[42]

Pneumatology was even more in evidence at the Conference on World Mission and Evangelism arranged by the CWME and held in Athens at the invitation of the Orthodox Church of Greece. Its theme "Come, Holy Spirit, heal and reconcile" was reminiscent of that of Canberra and allowed for application to ecological concern and the healing of creation, but it was also intended to encourage other dialogues. The first was with

---

[42]World Council of Churches, Commission for World Mission and Evangelism, "Mission and Evangelism in Unity Today" (2000), in Jacques Matthey (ed.), *"You Are the Light of the World": Statements on Mission by the World Council of Churches 1980–2005* (Geneva: WCC Publications, 2005), 62–89; also available at www.mission2005.org. The CWME continued its reflections on mission in pneumatological perspective and in 2012 its document "Together Towards Life" was accepted by the Central Committee of the World Council of Churches as its statement on mission and evangelism.

Pentecostal churches particularly. The Korean Pentecostal missiologist Wonsuk Ma was invited to outline the role of pneumatology in Pentecostal-Charismatic mission. He emphasized that Pentecostal-Charismatics represent the "poor," "for whom poverty and sickness are a part of their lives," and that the core of Pentecostal-Charismatic pneumatology is "empowerment" for witness. He pointed out that in Pentecostal-Charismatic churches the Holy Spirit did not only motivate a concern for the poor "other" but that the poor themselves were lifted up and the marginalized were empowered in their "daily human existence." He then showed historically how they were enabled in service, witness and reconciliation. In other words, how "the Lord has brought this movement with its unique set of gifts to the larger body of Christ, particularly in fulfilling God's missions mandate."[43]

The second dialogue was with peacemaking ministries of various sorts since the Athens conference was held in the context of the World Council of Churches' Decade to Overcome Violence (DOV). The impulse to broaden ecumenism to include peace-making was the witness of the "peace churches," such as the Mennonites and Quakers, which have historically taken a pacifist stance. It was also informed by soul-searching about the violence and abuse that had often been associated with the mission enterprise in the name of world evangelization, particularly around the five hundredth anniversary of the conquest of the Americas (1992), which began the colonial era.[44]

---

[43] Wonsuk Ma, "'When the Poor Are Fired Up': The Role of Pneumatology in Pentecostal-Charismatic Mission," in Jacques Matthey (ed.), *"Come, Holy Spirit, Heal and Reconcile!" Report of the WCC Conference on World Mission and Evangelism, Athens, Greece, May 2005* (Geneva: WCC Publications, 2008), 159.

[44] See Gustavo Gutiérrez, *Las Casas: In Search of the Poor of Jesus Christ* trans. Robert R. Barr (Maryknoll, NY: Orbis Books, 1993 [1992]); Leonardo Boff & Virgil Elizondo (eds.), *1492-1992: The Voice of the Victims* (London: SCM Press, 1990), 78-89.

In this context, Latin American and other liberation theologians saw the need to develop a "spirituality of liberation"[45] in order to make the means of mission consistent with its end and to ensure that the medium or messenger embodies the gospel message so that mission is not a mechanism by which one group advances its power over the other but a way of living in the Spirit.[46] Such a spirituality would wage the struggle in a way that does not breed future resentment and bears witness to the rightness of the cause by following the way of Christ and extending Christian love even to enemies (Mt 5:43-48). This way not only protects the integrity of the campaigners but also lays the ground for future reconciliation.[47] Considering mission as being done "in the Spirit" shifted the focus from the missionary task to the ethos and ethics of mission, to the way in which mission is carried out, to the praxis, path, or process of mission. In keeping with this vision, the Athens conference was intended "to empower participants to continue in their call to be in mission together and to work towards reconciliation and healing in Christ in God's world today" and was itself planned as an exercise in healing and reconciliation.

The theme of Athens, "Come, Holy Spirit, heal and reconcile" recognized the foundation of reconciliation in pneumatology and established it as a new paradigm in mission. Preparatory work was done on the themes of healing and reconciliation as ministries of the Spirit, the most important product of which was *Mission as Ministry of Reconciliation* (2005), a document received by CWME and commended as

---

[45]Gustavo Gutiérrez, *We Drink from Our Own Wells: The Spiritual Journey of a People* (Maryknoll, NY: Orbis Books, 1984).
[46]Kirsteen Kim, *Mission in the Spirit: The Holy Spirit in Indian Christian Theologies* (Delhi: ISPCK, 2003)
[47]Dorr, *Mission in Today's World*, 128; cf. Miroslav Volf, *Exclusion and Embrace —A Theological Exploration of Identity, Otherness and Reconciliation* (Nashville, TN: Abingdon Press, 1996), 105.

preparation for the conference. This text focused on the mission of the Spirit, which it described in terms of reconciliation, following the exposition of this ministry in 2 Cor 3-5. It represented a new step in mission pneumatology because it interpreted *missio Dei* consistently as participation in the energy and life of the Holy Spirit; consequently, it deliberately took a pneumatological rather than a Christological perspective, while recognizing that pneumatomonism was as much a danger as Christomonism. The themes of creation and Pentecost are both prominent throughout the document, and the Holy Spirit is seen as the author of both creation and new creation, biological life and spiritual life. The universal Spirit is also the Holy Spirit who empowers the church to participate in Christian ministry of reconciliation. In this document, there are no limits set to the reconciling power of the Holy Spirit, but it is clear that this ministry is only made possible because of the work of Christ. Creation and Pentecost are connected by the cosmic act of reconciliation—Jesus Christ's death and resurrection. It is the Holy Spirit who is sent into the world and creates Christ and the church—the reconciled community, and it is Christ who sends the church in the power of the Spirit to heal and reconcile.[48]

In order to avoid the Athens conference repeating the problems of Canberra, it was necessary to affirm that, although the Holy Spirit is immanent in the creation, the Holy Spirit is also sent from above (Jn 3:5–7; Acts 2:2). Christian doctrine distinguishes the *Holy* Spirit from any other spirit. The Spirit is the Spirit of God, the Lord, Yahweh in the Hebrew Bible. Furthermore, in the New Testament, the Spirit is the Spirit of Jesus Christ. For Christians, the Holy Spirit is not only understood as the source of life but as the principle of life, or life-force. The Holy Spirit is expressed in the person of Jesus Christ,

---

[48]CWME, "Mission as Ministry of Reconciliation" (2005), in Matthey, *"You Are the Light of the World,"* 90-129.

who is born of the Spirit from above (Lk 1). In his life, Jesus Christ is led and empowered by the Holy Spirit (Lk 4:18–19; and other references throughout Luke's gospel) in full knowledge of his heavenly origins (Jn 13:3). Jesus Christ epitomizes the holy and spiritual life, the life of the Holy Spirit. In death, he was raised by the Holy Spirit to a resurrection life that is imparted by and in the Spirit to all who identify with him. In this perspective, Jesus Christ is the focus or concentration of the Holy Spirit, the one on whom the Spirit descends and remains (Jn 1:32, 33). Another way of stating this is that the *ruach*, the Spirit of creation, God's transforming Spirit, the power of the universe, the fullness of God is fully present in him (Col 1:15–17, 19). Christians believe that the Universal Spirit, the Spirit of Life, shines through the life and work of Jesus Christ (cf. the Transfiguration). Since the Universal Spirit, the Spirit of Life, is accessible to all, this confession does not separate but does distinguish Christians and Christian spirituality from others.

The themes of both Canberra and Athens took the form of the *epiklesis*, calling on the Spirit to act. But both also understood that the Spirit is already at work and tried to identify where that might be–renewing the whole creation or healing and reconciling–in order to join in. The Spirit of God is present and active everywhere, but not every development is the work of the Holy Spirit. Although on one occasion the Psalmist declared that he could not escape from God's Spirit in heaven or on earth or under the earth (Ps 139:7–10), on another he is contemplating the absence, or the withdrawal, of the Holy Spirit (Ps 51:11). Furthermore, the biblical writers are aware that there are other spirits abroad: evil spirits (Matt 10:1), cosmic powers and spiritual forces (Eph 6:12). If mission is understood as "joining in with the Spirit," then finding out where and what the Spirit is doing is a crucial first step.⁴⁹ Discerning the Spirit is a complex process about which much more could be written,⁵⁰ but it was necessary to state at Athens that the criterion for Christian discernment is clear: the Holy Spirit is the Spirit that descended and remained on Jesus Christ.

At Athens, four biblical criteria for discernment were suggested,⁵¹ though none alone is proof of the Spirit's presence and all of them need to be qualified. The first is ecclesial: the confession of Jesus as Lord, which is made possible by the Holy Spirit (1 Cor 12:3; 1 Jn 4:2). We hope and expect to find the Spirit in the Christian community, where Jesus Christ is proclaimed and worshipped. However, it is the Spirit that defines the church, not the other way around. Calling "Lord, Lord" is not necessarily a guarantee of a spirit of obedience (Mt 7:21–22). The second criterion is ethical: the evidence of the fruit of the Spirit: love, joy, peace, and so on (Gal 5:22). The Spirit changes our lives, producing Christlikeness. But good works alone are not a sign of the life of the Spirit–they may be the result of unregenerate legalism (Rom 7:6)–the whole character is important.⁵² The third criterion is Charismatic: the practice of the gifts of the Spirit (1

---

⁴⁹Cf. James D. G. Dunn, *The Christ and the Spirit: Collected Essays* Vol. 2: Pneumatology (Edinburgh: T & T Clark, 1998), 72.

⁵⁰For example, Timothy J. Gorringe. *Discerning Spirit: A Theology of Revelation* (London: SCM Press, 1990); *Furthering Humanity: A Theology of Culture* (Aldershot: Ashgate, 2004); Amos Yong, *Discerning the Spirit(s): A Pentecostal-Charismatic Contribution to Christian Theology of Religions* (Sheffield: Sheffield Academic Press, 2000); Kirsteen Kim, *The Holy Spirit in the World: A Global Conversation* (Maryknoll, NY: Orbis Books, 2007).

⁵¹Kirsteen Kim, "Come, Holy Spirit: Who? Why? How? So What?," in Jacques Matthey (ed.), *"Come, Holy Spirit, Heal and Reconcile!" Report of the WCC Conference on World Mission and Evangelism, Athens, Greece, May 2005* (Geneva: WCC Publications, 2008), 150–58.

⁵²These first two criteria were recognized in the reports of the Canberra Assembly. See "Report of the Seventh Assembly," in Kinnamon, *Signs of the Spirit*, 256.

Cor 12:4-11).⁵³ Where there is empowerment to prophecy, ministry, teaching, exhortation, giving, leading, compassion (Rom 12:6-8), we have good reason to believe God is at work (by the Spirit). However, exercise of a spiritual gift is not a sign of the Spirit's presence if it lacks love (1 Cor 13:1-3). The final criterion is liberational: being on the side of the poor.⁵⁴ The effect of the Spirit's anointing on Jesus Christ was that he announced good news to the poor (Lk 4:18), and this must be a touchstone for all spiritual claims. When discerning the Spirit in any activity, we need to ask whose interests are being served, who is benefiting from this. But the criterion of liberation also needs to be qualified. The liberation struggle must be waged in a way that is loving to our enemies (Mt 5:43-48), and does not aim to crush them, but to live in peace with them (Rom 12:18).⁵⁵ These cautions should not be read as trying to restrict the work of the Spirit. It would be foolish indeed if the church were trying to stop the "violent wind" and fire of the Spirit (Acts 2:2-3). It is possible for churches not to receive Christ or do what the Spirit is saying (Rev 2 and 3). But in so far as the church joins herself to the Spirit of Jesus Christ, she has the gift of discerning the spirits (1 Cor 12:10) and a duty to test them (1 Jn 4:1) to identify where the Holy Spirit is, or is not, at work.⁵⁶ Christ gave his Spirit in order to guide the church into all the truth (cf. Jn 16:13).

The presence of God in the world is mediated through both *logos* and *pneuma*. The *missio Dei* is the work of both (Lk 4:18-

---

⁵³This suggestion from the Pentecostal-Charismatic movement has been made by Amos Yong, *Discerning the Spirit(s): A Pentecostal-Charismatic Contribution to Christian Theology of Religions* (Sheffield: Sheffield Academic Press, 2000).

⁵⁴This is suggested by the work of liberation theologian Samuel Rayan, *Come, Holy Spirit* (Delhi: Media House, 1998), 132.

⁵⁵Donal Dorr, *Mission in Today's World* (Blackrock, Co. Dublin: Columba Press 2000), 128.

⁵⁶Cf. John Paul II, *Redemptoris Missio*, para. 29. Available at www.vatican.va.

19).⁵⁷ The two missions of Son and Spirit are simultaneous—neither is prior to the other, and therefore "all Christology is pneumatologically determined and all pneumatology is Christologically determined."⁵⁸ Taking a pneumatological approach is not to detract from Christology but for the sake of a properly Christological understanding. Pneumatology is needed in order for Christology to be truly *Christo*logy, the doctrine of Jesus as the Christ, meaning the one anointed with the Spirit.⁵⁹

Conclusion

In theological terms, "mission in the Spirit" connects the human spirit in mission with the Spirit of God sent into the world. It sets mission spirituality—the church's witness since Pentecost—within the work of the Spirit of God since creation, shifting interest from the Spirit of mission or missionary Spirit to the mission of the Spirit. This broadens the scope of mission to include the whole creation and encourages the cooperation of Christian mission with other movements for justice and peace. "Mission in the Spirit" suggests that Christian mission begins with the spiritual activity of discerning the spirits (according to the revelation of Jesus Christ) in order to discover the "lordship and resources" of the Holy Spirit at work in the world. And it also expresses "human partnership in the plan of God," the invitation to join in with the Spirit's mission.⁶⁰

---

⁵⁷Paulo Suess, "Missio Dei and the Project of Jesus: The Poor and the 'Other' as Mediators of the Kingdom of God and Protagonists of the Churches", *IRM* 92/367: 552–53.

⁵⁸Kilian McDonnell, *The Other Hand of God: The Holy Spirit as the Universal Touch and Goal* (Collegeville, MN: Liturgical Press, 2003), 88.

⁵⁹Alasdair I. C. Heron, *The Holy Spirit: The Holy Spirit in the Bible, in the History of Christian Thought, and in Recent Theology* (London: Marshall Morgan & Scott, 1983), 126–27.

⁶⁰Wonsuk Ma and Julie Ma, *Mission in the Spirit*, xvi; Jürgen Moltmann, *The Church in the Power of the Spirit* (London: SCM Press, 1977); Kirsteen Kim, *Joining in with the Spirit: Connecting World Church and Local Mission* (London: SCM, 2012).

The Blessing of Abraham: Pentecostalism and Ecumenism in African Perspectives

by J. Kwabena Asamoah-Gyadu
Trinity Theological Seminary, Legon, Ghana

There has been growing discussions on the relationship between Pentecostals and the ecumenical movement in recent years.[1] Wonsuk Ma and his wife Julie are Pentecostals with a wonderful ecumenical spirit and this essay is written to celebrate the fact that their work has impacted Africa. There are at least three ways in which this has happened. First, Wonsuk invited me as an African scholar to serve on the board of the Oxford Center for Mission Studies. Second, he has insisted that given the prominence of Africa in world Christianity today, African voices must be heard in the Regnum publications on mission studies. Third, he has courted the friendship of several African leaders encouraging us to bring students to study at OCMS. This spirit of inclusion is exactly why the Spirit of God was poured out at Pentecost and those who participate in that blessing—Jews and Gentiles—can then share in the blessing of Abraham as the "father of nations." In the words of Paul on this matter, "He redeemed us in order that the blessing given to Abraham might come to the Gentiles through Christ Jesus, so

---

[1] See for instance: Wolfgang Vondey ed., *Pentecostalism and Christian Unity: Ecumenical Documents and Critical Assessments* (Eugene, Oregon: Pickwick Publications, 2010).

that by faith we might receive the promise of the Spirit" (Galatians 3:14).

God redeems us in Jesus Christ and by his Spirit dissolves the ethnic and denominational differences that often separate Christians from each other, preventing us from working together as "brothers and sisters in Christ." In spite of recent tensions in sections of Pentecostalism such as the debate relating to "Oneness" or "Trinitarian" baptismal formulas, Walter Hollenweger has noted that all the Pentecostal churches began as ecumenical revival movements. This movement did not want to found new churches, but to bring life to existing ones.[2]

Pentecostalism is inherently ecumenical and this in spite of its reservations with the theological orientation and *modus operandi* of existing historic mission ecumenical communions such as the World Council of Churches. There are difficulties in relationships between Pentecostals and their non-Pentecostal compatriots but the difficulties come from both sides. Pentecostalism, as an experiential movement, is not given to creedal confessions. Pentecostal theology therefore tends to be oral in nature but this often has been seen by historically older denominations to mean a lack of theology. On the other hand, Pentecostal and Charismatic Christians often have pointed to the lack of the power of the Spirit in the lives of Catholic and Protestant denominations, accusing them of being liberal with the Gospel.

---

[2] Walter J. Hollenweger, 'From Azusa Street to the Toronto Phenomenon', in Jürgen Moltman and Karl-Josef Kushel ed., *Pentecostal Movements as an Ecumenical Challenge: Concilium* (London: SCM; Maryknoll, NY: Orbis, 1996/3), 9.

Pentecost and Experience

Whatever one thinks of the Pentecostal emphasis on experience, it is clear that in Africa, it has permanently altered the face of Christianity. Pentecostalism does not only account for the shift in the center of gravity of Christianity in Africa, but in the future, African Christianity would have a stronger pneumatic orientation. Harvey Cox notes that Pentecostalism first arose as a protest movement against "man-made creeds" and the "coldness" of traditional worship. While the beliefs of other religious groups are enshrined in formal theological systems, those of the Pentecostals, Cox further observes, are imbedded in testimonies, ecstatic speech, and bodily movement.[3] However, Pentecostal Christianity is at the same time not oblivious to the ecumenical imports of such confessions as, "I believe in the Holy Spirit; the Holy Catholic Church; and the Communion of Saints" that are outlined in the Apostle's Creed.

Cheryl Bridges Johns speaks of Pentecost as an "ongoing festival that continually calls us to participate in the work of the Holy Spirit." Contrary to historic Christian views of Pentecost as a static historical event, she notes, "the primary mission of Pentecostalism is to renew the meaning of Pentecost for the whole church."[4] The reference to the "whole church" raises the issue of the ecumenical import of Pentecost as an "ongoing festival." There is an inseparable relationship between Pentecostal spirituality and the ecumenical orientation of Pentecostalism as a distinct stream of Christian expression. That

---

[3] Harvey Cox, *Fire from Heaven: The Rise of Pentecostal Spirituality and the Reshaping of Religion in the Twenty-first century* (Reading, MA: Addison-Wesley, 1995), 14, 15.
[4] Cheryl Bridges Johns, "What Can the Mainline Churches Learn from Pentecostals about Pentecost?" in André Droogers, Cornelis van der Laan, and Wout van Laar (eds.), *Fruitful in the Land: Pluralism, Dialogue and Healing in Migrant Pentecostalism* (Zoetermeer, The Netherlands: Uitgeverij Boekencentrum, 2006), 93.

is so because, as Paul pointed out to the Galatians, the Spirit of God is a Spirit of inclusion and not of division and alienation.

This essay is about the relationship between the Spirit and ecumenism and its implications for world Christianity. In world Christian history, the desire to worship and work together is an important evidence of Pentecostal and Charismatic spirituality. Spirituality in the context of this discussion refers to the practical outworking of faith in God or "expressed religion."[5] This explains why Pentecostalism is usually defined by its emphasis on experiential worship. The late Christian G. Baëta of Ghana described some of the manifestations of such experiences as rhythmic swaying of the body to repetitious music, handclapping, poignant cries and prayers, dancing, leaping and various motor reactions expressive of intense religious emotion; prophesying, speaking in tongues, relating dreams and visions and witnessing by recounting publicly one's own experience of miraculous redemption were also noted.[6] The reference to public witness to faith and miracles here is important. For, as André Droogers points out elsewhere, expansion is essential to the Pentecostal movement and "the goals of evangelistic campaigns illustrate that ultimately the message is meant for the whole of humanity."[7] If the Gospel is meant for the whole of humanity, then the implication is that Pentecostal spirituality—encapsulating speaking in tongues, interpretation of tongues,

---

[5] Russell P. Spittler, "Corinthian Spirituality: How a flawed Anthropology Imperils Authentic Christian Experience" in Edith Blumhofer, Russell P. Spittler and Grant Wacker ed., *Pentecostal Currents in American Protestantism* (Urbana and Chicago: University of Illinois Press, 1999), 3-19.

[6] C.G. Baëta, *Prophetism in Ghana: A Study of Some Spiritual Churches* (London: SCM, 1962), 1.

[7] André Droogers, "The Normalization of Religious Experience: Healing, Prophecy, Dreams, and Visions," in Karla Poewe ed., *Charismatic Christianity as a Global Culture* (Columbia, South Carolina: University of South Carolina Press, 1994), 35.

singing in the Spirit, seeing visions and revelations, prophesying and giving words of knowledge—is not denomination-specific.

Diffusion of Pentecostal Spirituality

These pneumatic phenomena have been recurring in the history of the church. In our age, it is the Pentecostal movement that draws the attention of the church to the central place of the Holy Spirit and spiritual gifts in Christian life and ministry. Pentecostalism is innovative. Its spirituality appeals to those who are discontented with over-formalized, staid and institutionalized Christianity. The understanding of spirituality as "expressed religion" is present in Pauline thought. In his writings, the expression "spiritual" is primarily an adjective for the Holy Spirit, referring to that which belongs to, or pertains to the Spirit of God. He expected the church to be Charismatic by functioning in the gifts of grace bestowed by the Holy Spirit. This, on the basis of his letter to the Galatians, he expected would be inspired by a common experience of the Spirit. It was through the experience of the common Spirit of Christ that all believers are grafted into Christ and come to share in the Abrahamic heritage.

Thus, in passages where St. Paul refers to believers as spiritual, he clearly understands they are "people of the Spirit."[8] There may be churches that call themselves Pentecostal on account of their disproportionate attention to Spirit-inspired experiences such as "Spirit baptism," but Pentecostal spirituality as a form of Christian expression is from the biblical viewpoint not denomination-specific. Any stream of Christianity that values, affirms, and consciously promotes the experiential dimension of life in the Spirit as part of normal Christian life

---

[8]Gordon D. Fee, "Some Reflections on Pauline Spirituality" in *Listening to the Spirit in the Text* (Grand Rapids: William B. Eerdmans, 2000), 38, 39.

could be said to be sharing the ecumenical spirit of Pentecostalism.[9] Pentecostalism is, therefore, a particular form of Christian expression that can be found anywhere including within certain non-Pentecostal denominations. The development within contemporary Christianity of renewal groups that form within historic mission denominations usually designated "Charismatic" is testimony to the pervasive and versatile nature of Pentecostal spirituality.

In contemporary experiences of the Spirit of God and the development of Pentecostal and Charismatic spirituality, there is diffusion of a new spirituality that spreads quickly. This often affects and impacts people of different religious, social, and racial persuasions. This ability to spread quickly, widely and fast has been part of the history of the workings of the Spirit of God from the Acts of the Apostles. On the day of the biblical Pentecost, we are told that event quickly developed international significance. Pentecost brought together a diversity of groups from far and near: Parthians, Medes and Elamites, those dwelling in Mesopotamia, Judea and Cappadocia, Pontus and Asia, Phrygia and Pamphylia, Egypt and the parts of Libya adjoining Cyrene, visitors from Rome, both Jews and Proselytes, Cretans and Arabs (Acts 2:9-11).

It is precisely because of its ability to dissolve differences as amply demonstrated by this list of nations that contemporary Pentecostalism has been described as "a religion made to travel."[10] Its informal, exhilarating, expressive and eclectic spirituality ensures a certain versatility, easy adaptability and translatability to different and diverse cultural situations in ways

---

[9] J. Kwabena Asamoah-Gyadu, *African Charismatics: A Study of Independent Indigenous Pentecostalism in Ghana* (Leiden: E.J. Brill, 2005), 12.

[10] Murray W. Dempster, Byron D. Klaus and Douglas Peterson, *The Globalization of Pentecostalism: A Religion Made to Travel* (Carlisle, Cumbria: Paternoster Publishing, 1999).

that one does not find with denominational Christianity. The result of this has been the globalization of Pentecostalism with a simultaneous "pentecostalization" of Christianity. What has happened in urban Africa in particular is that denominational loyalties are gradually eroding among young people, attracted by the non-liturgical worship forms of Pentecostal churches with their contemporary musical worship forms. These churches recognize the gifts and graces of young people who are often excluded by denominational rules and bureaucracies of older churches but are embraced in contemporary Pentecostal churches even as pastors without requiring of them theological degrees and seminary training, which they need elsewhere to become pastors.

One practical way in which to discern the workings of the Spirit of Pentecost in ecumenical forms is to look at the changing nature of participation in holy communion or the Lord's Table in contemporary Charismatic Christianity in Africa. I have pointed out in my work *Contemporary Pentecostal Christianity* that the word "communicant," often used in the historic mission denominations to exclude non-registered members from the Lord's Table, has lost its significance for many people. Denominationalism is fast losing ground because young people no longer have to go through Confirmation rites to be welcomed to take communion. In the average Charismatic church in Africa today, all one needs is to confess Christ as Lord and the privilege of participation is granted.[11]

---

[11] J. Kwabena Asamoah-Gyadu, *Contemporary Pentecostal Christianity: Interpretations from an African Context* (Oxford: Regnum, 2013).

Pentecost, Ecumenism and the African Spiritual Imagination

There is also much in Pentecostal ecumenical spirituality that resonates with the African imagination. The belief in the ancestors as omnipresent in the African understanding underscores the existence of a spiritual world beyond the physical one. The ancestral world is the source of power, strength, protection, vitality, meaning and fulfillment for living. There is in the African traditional religious imagination a profound emphasis on the transcendent source of true life and existential salvation. Related to this worldview is the conviction that the human being is not alone in the universe. A 'cloud of witnesses' that include the Supreme Being and the ancestors who are more powerful and ultimate than human beings surround us. The other significant aspect of traditional African religion that relates to our purposes here is the deep sense that the human being is finite, weak, limited, and imperfect. Thus, in the human world, we stand in need of powers not our own. This 'cloud of witnesses' supplies our needs but more importantly, they protect us against the malevolent powers in the world.[12]

In this vein, one of the most important traditional symbols of the Akan of Ghana depicts the saying, "God, there is something in the skies, let me have it." This traditional African universe, as explained by Ghanaian philosopher Kwame Gyekye, is a spiritual universe, one in which supernatural beings play significant roles in the thoughts and actions of people. In African philosophical thought therefore, "what is primarily real is spiritual."[13] This is evident in the structure of a typical Akan (African) libation prayer in which officiating priests invoke the forces of

---

[12]Kwame Bediako, *Christianity in Africa: The Renewal of a Non-Western Religion* (Edinburgh: Edinburgh University Press, 1995), 94.

[13]Kwame Gyekye, *African Philosophical Thought: The Akan Conceptual Scheme* (Philadelphia: Temple University Press, 1995), 69.

beneficence, observing the Akan religious hierarchy of the Supreme Being, Mother Earth, the pantheon of lesser gods, and the ancestors. The message segment of libation often highlights the occasion and purpose of the prayer. This is followed by solicitation, in which the officiating priest solicits support for the spiritual, moral, and material well being of the lineage or society. The concluding segment of libation prayers is often reserved for cursing evil.[14]

Similarly, the Pentecostal universe is one that is also enchanted. Here in the Pentecostal worldview, that which is 'spiritual' is also real and active, and the spiritual encroaches daily upon human affairs. The story of Pentecost, to cite Cox again, 'is about the experience of God, not about abstract religious ideas, and it depicts a God who does not remain aloof but reaches down through the power of the Spirit to touch human hearts in life's turmoil.'[15] Pentecostal prayers ask for the same things that African libation prayers ask for, that is, beneficence from heaven and curses upon enemies. Additionally, according to the Pentecostal message, the Holy Spirit is in action in these 'last days' to empower people for service wherever they may be and irrespective of their denominational inclinations. He anoints the church also to deal decisively with principalities and powers that hinder holistic Christian living. In the process, certain denominational barriers and inhibitions are broken as even non-Pentecostal communions begin to discover and operate in the power of the Spirit.

---

[14]Kwesi Yankah, *Speaking for the Chief: Ókyeame and the Politics of Akan Royal Otratory* (Bloomington & Indiana: Indiana University Press, 1995), 174.
[15]Cox, *Fire from Heaven*, 5.

Pentecost and the Breaking Down of Barriers

The evidence for the ability of Pentecostalism to attract people from across denominations into its fold is not difficult to find. Physically, Pentecostals have the numbers; they dominate the media through televangelism, book and magazine publications and Internet websites. Pentecostal leaders also play significant socio-political roles across the world. In matters of direct mission and evangelism, there are witnesses who testify to transformed lives, healings, miracles and signs and wonders experienced at Pentecostal evangelistic meetings and through the ministries of Pentecostal churches and movements. Pentecostalism has now found space in secular universities as an area of critical academic study with scholars in religion and theology paying attention to Pentecostalism. At least this is so in Africa, where many research projects are dedicated to the study of the movement. There are academic conferences and associations such as the USA-based Society for Pentecostal Studies whose proceedings are now articulated through such Pentecostal journals as the *Journal of Pentecostal Theology, Pneuma: Journal of the Society of Pentecostal Studies,* the *Asian Journal of Pentecostal Theology* and other related publications. Pentecostalism, through these developments, has become the most ecumenical stream of Christianity in terms of its effects on world Christianity.

Pentecostalism's translatability, the uncanny ease with which the movement settles comfortably into cultures has been one of its major ecumenical strengths. Cox, speaking about the worldwide effects of early 20th century North American Pentecostal revivals, comments on how the movement "became Russian in Russia, Chilean in Chile [and] African in Africa. It was a religion made to travel, he notes, and it seemed to lose nothing in the translation."[16] In the last two decades or so, a number of African-initiated churches have burgeoned in western European cities, underscoring the shift in the center of gravity of Christianity from the northern to the southern continents. What is often lost on those who comment on these developments is the fact that most of these churches in the Diaspora belong to the Pentecostal/Charismatic stream of Christianity. According to a *New York Times* article of April 18, 2004:

> These new African [Pentecostal] churches are bringing new vitality and new ways of [being Christian]. People walk in and find community—friendly African hospitality. As [these] African churches attract increasing numbers of white worshippers, they can serve as a bridge between the races.

The African churches in question are leading the way in what it means to be truly ecumenical in the former heartlands of Christianity by bridging Christian racial gaps. These attempts at reversing Christian mission go back to the focus of the modern Pentecostal movement as a religion dedicated to preaching Christ in all nations. And indeed a strong call has gone out to European churches to abandon their attitudes and feelings of hostility towards their new immigrant compatriots and in grateful joy perceive the work of the Holy Spirit outside the confines of their own organized pastoral activities, and recognize the genesis of new African churches and congregations in European soil as "the grace of God".[17]

---

[16]Cox, *Fire from Heaven*, 102.
[17]Claudia Währisch-Oblau, "'We shall be Fruitful in this Land': Pentecostal and Charismatic New Mission Churches in Europe," in André Droogers, Cornelis van der Laan and Wout van Laar eds., *Fruitful in this Land: Pluralism, Dialogue and Healing in Migrant Pentecostalism* (Zoetermeer, The Netherlands: Uitgeverij Boekencentrum, 2006), 46.

The view that the globalization of contemporary Pentecostalism should be credited to Charles F. Parham's 1901 revival or William J. Seymour's 1906 Azusa Street revival in North America is contentious. However, particularly in the case of Seymour, we could say that a revival movement led by a black man in early 20th century North America, which succeeded in bringing races together, constituted a phenomenal re-enactment of the original Pentecost and a reversal of the curse of Babel. The doyen of the academic study of Pentecostalism, Walter J. Hollenweger, quoting pioneer British Pentecostal Alexander A. Boddy, captures for us part of the ecumenical spirit of the Azusa Street revival:

> It was something very extraordinary, that white pastors from the South were eagerly prepared to go to Los Angeles to the Negroes, to have fellowship with them and to receive through their prayers and intercessions the blessings of the Spirit. And it was still more wonderful that these white pastors went back to the South and reported to the members of their congregations that they had been together with Negroes, that they had prayed in the Spirit and received the same blessings as they.[18]

The Assemblies of God, which is the leading North American classical Pentecostal denomination in the world, affirmed the ecumenical importance of the Azusa Street revival under Seymour in a "Spiritual Committee Report." This report was cited by Hollenweger: "The Azusa Street revival witnessed the breakdown of barriers which normally divided people from one another through race, class, gender, wealth, language,

---

[18]Walter J. Hollenweger, *The Pentecostals: The Charismatic Movement in the Churches* (London: SCM, 1972), 24.

education, church affiliation and culture.[19] Frank Bartleman also described the Azusa Street revival as an event that "washed away the color line in the blood [of Christ]." Commenting on this statement, Allan Anderson notes as follows:

> Not only did blacks and whites mix freely at Azusa Street; but so did Hispanics and other ethnic minorities . . . Not only did [Seymour] encourage people to remain in their churches after they had received Spirit baptism, but he saw the Pentecostal experience as that which dissolved distinctions of race, class and gender created one common family.[20]

Elsewhere, Cox describes the Azusa Street revival as "the principal point in western history at which the pulsating energy of African American spirituality, wedded by years of suffering to the Christian promise of the Kingdom of God, leaped across the racial barrier and became fused with similar motifs in the spirituality of poor white people."[21] When this dissolution of racial barriers occurred in North America, it did so as a contemporary fulfillment of God's promise, "I will pour out my Spirit upon all flesh" (Joel 2:28). In other words, Pentecost brought together people from across ethnic and racial and perhaps even religious divides to hear in each group's own mother tongue the mighty works of God. As one scholar argues, the miracle of Pentecost lay as much in the speaking of tongues as it was in the *hearing* of the word of God.[22]

---

[19] Walter J. Hollenweger, *Pentecostalism: Origins and Developments Worldwide* (Peabody, MA: Hendrickson Publishers, 1997), 23.
[20] Allan Anderson, *An Introduction to Pentecostalism* (Cambridge: Cambridge University Press, 2004), 61.
[21] Cox, *Fire from Heaven*, 99.
[22] Luke Timothy Johnson, "Glossolia and the Embarrassments of Experience," *The Princeton Seminary Bulletin*, vol. 18, 2 (1997): 117.

Pentecostals, Ecumenism and the World Missions Conference

Typically, many Pentecostals consider the World Council of Churches (WCC) as synonymous with the Ecumenical movement. They often report negative news about the WCC and describe their own alliances and constituencies in positive terms. Early Pentecostal literature spoke of the visible unity of the church but this was to occur only on Pentecostal terms. In a useful essay titled, "Pentecostals and Ecumenism in a Pluralistic World," Cecil M Robeck, Jr., notes how Pentecostals generally assume that all ecumenism is,

I. An attempt to compromise doctrinal standards to the lowest common denominator in such a way as to affirm not only questionable forms of Christian expression, but also the classic religions of the world in a human scheme to embrace all of humankind in a

II. Relativistic international organization that will usurp the rights and freedoms of existing denominations in such a way as to promote 'unity' at the expense of truth, or at least of genuine Christian faith and life, an organization which will

III. Ultimately and inevitably be united with the Roman Catholic Church in such a way as to form the infamous Babylon of Revelation 17 and 18 [See 18:4][23]

In the early 1960s, Klaus Kendrick suggested two reasons why Pentecostals and the older denominations had been unable to work together. Firstly, the older denominations regarded Pentecostals as not yet qualified for recognition. Secondly, the

---

[23]Cecil M. Robeck, Jr., "Pentecostals and Ecumenism in a Pluralistic World," in Murray W. Dempster, Byron D. Klaus and Douglas Peterson ed., *The Globalization of Pentecostalism: A Religion Made to Travel* (Oxford: Regnum, 1999), 343.

Pentecostals also entertained serious objections to the various ecumenical councils as then constituted.[24] The dissociation of classical Pentecostals from bridge-building efforts of Pentecostal ecumenists like David Du Plessis in the 1960s is a classic example of this suspicion.

The 2005 Conference on World Missions and Evangelization (CWME) in Athens, held under the auspices of the World Council of Churches, heightened some of these concerns as it sought to create space for ecumenical dialogue with Pentecostal and Charismatic Christians (PCCs). PCCs at the CWME gathering in Athens sent a letter to the organizers protesting aspects of the program that did not adequately take care of their concerns. This letter, to which I was a signatory, started with a word of appreciation to the WCC for at least giving PCCs some significant space in the event. That portion of the letter read: "We have sensed the genuine openness in the leadership of the conference to the potential of Pentecostal contributions to the future of global Christianity." The letter went on to note that "Pentecostals are often misunderstood, misrepresented, and even unfairly caricaturized." It is significant for our purposes here that the protest letter also admitted Pentecostals are equally responsible for the mutual suspicions and misunderstandings between them and other Christian communions.

Thus, in his listener's report for the CWME, Birmingham University professor of Pentecostal theology Allan Anderson, also a signatory to the letter mentioned, noted as follows: there is some resistance among some WCC members to enter into dialogue with and welcome involvement by Pentecostals, who are still regarded as schismatic and not really Christian. These mutual suspicions, he noted, "are formidable barriers to

---

[24]Klaus Kendrick, *The Promise Fulfilled: A History of the Modern Pentecostal Movement* (Springfield, MO: Gospel Publishing House, 1961), 203-4.

overcome."[25] There is reason to be hopeful, though, because as the years have gone by, the experiential nature of Pentecostal spirituality, which constitutes the basis of its understanding of ecumenism, is gradually being understood and appreciated. To quote Anderson again:

> When PCCs think of the Holy Spirit, they usually think of an experience with the Spirit, often ecstatic and personal, in which believers receive the power promised by Christ and received by the disciples on the day of Pentecost. This experience is often seen as subsequent to their conversion and accompanied by "signs" or "gifts of the Spirit", especially speaking in tongues. The difference between PCCs and most other Christians used to be that PCCs believed that the gifts of the Spirit, . . . continue in the time between the Ascension and the Parousia of Christ. Most other churches, particularly Protestant ones influenced by modernism and rationalism, believe that the time of miracles has ceased.[26]

This dichotomy, Anderson is quick to add, no longer exists as sharply as it did before. The ecumenical movement acknowledges the active presence of the Spirit in the church through spiritual gifts and the PCCs admit that other forms of healing (such as medical science) are also part of the economy of God.[27] At the forum where these observations were captured, we were delighted, as people of Pentecostal and Charismatic persuasions, not only to be represented at such an august international ecumenical gathering but also with the amount of

---

[25] Allan Anderson, "The Holy Spirit, Healing and Reconciliation: Pentecostal/Charismatic Issues at Athens 2005," *International Review of Mission*, vol. 94, 374 (July 2005): 335.
[26] Ibid., 336.
[27] Ibid.

space given for the symbolic representation of the ecumenical spirit. The opening plenary featured speeches from the Primate of the Church of Greece, the WCC General Secretary, Kirsteen Kim, a British Reformed theologian, and Wonsuk Ma, a Korean Pentecostal. As Anderson observed, "the symbolism of an Ecumenical, an Orthodox, an Evangelical and a Pentecostal leader sharing the same platform was not lost on anybody."[28]

Pentecost and Gentile Inclusion

I started this essay with reference to Paul's epistle to the Galatians in which he addresses the theme of the Spirit as a Spirit of inclusion defining it as the real meaning of inheriting the blessing of Abraham. God's exercise in ecumenism did not only take off from the day of Pentecost but was demonstrated in many ways, including the events that took place in the house of Cornelius. One implication of these developments is that Pentecost is about experiencing the Spirit of God and that experience is not the prerogative of any Christian denomination. It is noteworthy that St. Peter confesses in the house of Cornelius after being struck by the reality of the ecumenical nature of Pentecost: "in truth I perceive that God shows no partiality but in every nation whoever fears Him and works righteousness is accepted by him" (Acts 10:34-5).

In the house of the Gentile Centurion Cornelius, the outpouring of the Spirit, which the disciples of Jesus had experienced previously, also occurred outside Pentecostalism. The Holy Spirit defied religious protocol of the time and literally invaded Gentile territory in order to affirm his own ecumenical mission. Peter narrated the sequence of events concerning how this happened to his colleagues who did not understand how he

---

[28]Ibid.

found himself in a situation in which the Gentiles also experienced Pentecost: "you went in to uncircumcised men and ate with them!" Peter explained to them how the vision God had instructed him not to refer to anything he has created as "unclean." Subsequently, he found himself in the house of Cornelius "and as I began to speak, the Holy Spirit fell upon them, as upon us at the beginning." When the other Apostles heard these things, they became silent; and they glorified God saying, "Then God has also granted to the Gentiles repentance to life." (Acts 11:1-18). The events surrounding Peter's encounter with Cornelius underscores a simple fact that in God's scheme of things, Pentecost could occur outside Pentecostalism.[29]

Pentecost can occur outside Pentecostalism because, according to Hollenweger, what unites the Pentecostal churches is not found in a doctrine but in a religious experience.[30] The phenomenal success of Pentecostalism in Africa is due largely to the emphasis on the experience of the Spirit. Pentecostalism has done well in Africa because it provides ritual contexts within which people may experience God's presence and power in forceful and demonstrable ways. Mine is not a novel attempt at pointing to the importance of the non-rational in religion. In his classic work, *The Idea of the Holy,* Rudolf Otto lamented how the marginalization of the non-rational aspect of religion by 'orthodoxy' had resulted in the 'idea of the holy' being given a one-sidedly intellectualistic approach. Otto states, "So far from keeping the non-rational element in religion alive in the heart of the religious experience, orthodox Christianity manifestly failed

---

[29] Cephas N. Omenyo, *Pentecost Outside Pentecostalism: A Study of the Development of Charismatic Renewal in the Mainline Churches in Ghana* (Utrecht: Boekencentrum, 2002).
[30] Hollenweger, "Azusa Street," 7.

to recognize its value, and by this failure gave to the idea of God a one-sidedly intellectualistic and rationalistic interpretation."[31]

Whatever else can be said about them, Russell Spittler writes, the Pentecostal and Charismatic movements have democratized individual religious experience.[32] In *Reinventing American Protestantism,* Donald E. Miller picks up the same theme of the centrality of religious experience in Pentecostalism when he notes that the new paradigm churches, as he calls them, are changing the way Christianity looks and is experienced. Miller describes the new paradigm churches as groups that have discarded many of the attributes of establishment religion. Appropriating contemporary cultural forms, these churches "are creating a new genre of worship music" and "are restructuring the organizational character of institutional religion; they are democratizing access to the sacred by radicalizing the Protestant principle of the priesthood of all believers."[33] In short, they offer people hope and meaning that is grounded in a transcendent experience of the people.[34]

Pentecost, New Tongues and Ecumenism

Another way to appreciate the influence of Pentecostalism is to look at its cardinal theological emphasis of speaking in tongues or *glossolalia.* Glossolalia is the Spirit-inspired utterance that Pentecostals believe must accompany baptism in the Holy Spirit following conversion. Speaking in tongues plays a democratizing role in worship. The gift of tongues allows people to pray in non-rational meditative language that is not mediated.

---

[31] Rudolf Otto, *The Idea of the Holy* (Oxford: Oxford University Press, 1923), 3.
[32] Spittler, "Corinthian Spirituality," 5-6.
[33] Donald E. Miller, *Reinventing American Protestantism: Christianity in the New Millennium* (Los Angeles: University of California Press, 1997), 1-2.
[34] Ibid., 3.

There are certain things that are clear about the experience of glossolalia, which have a direct bearing on the ecumenical nature of Pentecostal spirituality. Tongues is unintelligible speech that is basically directed toward God (I Corinthians 14:2, 14-15, 28). St. Paul held tongues speaking in the highest esteem as a means of communicating with God. To that end, Paul's reference to "inarticulate groaning too deep for words" in Romans 8:26-27 must be understood as referring primarily to glossolalia.[35]

Tom Smail describes speaking in tongues as an experience,

> "that escapes from a complicated conceptuality and a second dependence on such liturgical resources as prayer-books and hymn-books, and responds in immediacy and freedom to the contact with the living Lord that the Spirit makes possible and, in joyous serenity, rejoices and mediates upon his poured-out grace and his revealed glory."[36]

This observation in fact reiterates Paul in I Corinthians 14:14, "For if I pray in a tongue, my spirit prays, but my understanding is unfruitful." The expression "unfruitful" is a word, which, as Ralph Martin explains,

> implies that the human intellect in this kind of ecstatic praying lies dormant, contributing nothing to the process of articulating thoughts into words. . . . It suggests an enraptured fellowship with God when the human spirit is in such deep, hidden communion with the

---

[35]This point has been forcefully argued by Frank D. Macchia, "Sighs too Deep for Words: Toward a Theology of Glossolalia," *Journal of Pentecostal Theology*, Issue 1 (1992): 47-73.

[36]Tom Smail, "In Spirit and in Truth: Reflections on Charismatic Worship," in Tom Smail, Andrew Walker, and Nigel Wright, *Charismatic Renewal* (London: SPCK, 1995): 109-110.

divine Spirit that "words"–at best broken utterances of our secret selves–are formed by a spiritual upsurge requiring no mental effort.[37]

The fact that glossolalia "by-passes the rational faculties" and makes possible free access to the living God, means it cannot be colonized within any particular Christian tradition and precisely for that reason, glossolalia can have a strong and profound ecumenical significance for Christians worldwide.

The Spirit as God's Empowering Presence

The Holy Spirit, as Gordon D. Fee describes him, is "God's Empowering Presence." The empowering effect of God the Holy Spirit is evident for example in the speaking of tongues. "We do not know how to pray" says St. Paul, so the Spirit helps us in our weakness in order that, against the backdrop of limited human speech and comprehension, we are enabled to speak mysteries unto God in prayer. It is the same enabling influence that fired up the apostles to boldly proclaim the word of God following the experience of Pentecost. There is a non-negotiable connection between the reception of power through the presence of the Holy Spirit and the ability to witness. In the words of Latin American Pentecostal theologian Juan Sepúlveda:

> [The] constitutive act of the Pentecostal movement is the offer of a direct and particularly intense encounter with God which makes possible a profound change in the life of the person who experiences it. The reference to the Holy Spirit—which from the doctrinal point of view is

---

[37]Ralph P. Martin, "Aspects of Worship in I Corinthians 14:1-25," in Cecil M. Robeck, Jr., ed. *Charismatic Experiences in Christian History* (Peabody, MA: Hendrickson Publishers, 1985), 74.

the characteristic accent of Pentecostalism–has to do, fundamentally, with the direct character of the encounter. Through the Holy Spirit, God makes himself directly accessible to the believer who seeks him, thus destroying the necessity of every kind of external priestly mediation.[38]

In the contemporary Western church, this supernatural dimension in the mission of the church has been seriously downplayed in Christian ministry and the results have been the anemic Christianity and empty chapel buildings that we are now seeing. Wherever Christianity is doing well, it is doing well because God's Holy Spirit, his Empowering Presence is active. Therefore, in putting the emphasis on the experience of the Holy Spirit as essential to Christian identity and mission, the different streams of Pentecostal movements identify the critical element in the mission of the church.

Pentecost: 'God Inhabits the Praise of His People'

We have spoken about the "pentecostalization" going on in contemporary African Christianity; music has played a critical role in this. One of the greatest lessons that non-Pentecostal Christianity in Africa has picked up from the Pentecostal and Charismatic compatriots is that there is a close relationship between "music" and "religious experience." The informal, affective, emotional and expressive nature of Pentecostal meetings facilitated by its music makes the point that "worship requires more than a cognitive assent."[39] Praise and worship of

---

[38] Juan Sepúlveda, "Reflections on the Pentecostal Contribution to the Mission of the Church in Latin America," *Journal of Pentecostal Theology*, Issue 1 (1992): 100.

[39] Margaret Poloma, *Mainstream Mystics: The Toronto Blessing and Reviving Pentecostalism* (New York: Altamira, 2003), 41.

God, Margaret Poloma avers, is believed to be the medium through which the presence of God is made manifest, as reflected in the oft-cited scripture verse, "God inhabits the praise of his people."[40] "Praise and Worship" is now an integral part of the liturgical practices of non-Pentecostal services. "Praise" consists of singing an electrically charged locally and internationally composed repertoire of choruses that celebrates God's power, goodness and majesty. This high amperage music is gradually brought down, and meetings then enter into a "worship" segment that "allow the worshipper to enter into a time of contemplative intimacy with God."[41]

In a personal quest for the reasons accounting for the quick diffusion of Pentecostal Christianity across the world, Cox cites music as one of them. Music, he writes, is not used by Pentecostals just as an embellishment, but "as the wavelength on which the message is carried."[42] There is no question about Cox's submission that music is integral rather than peripheral to Pentecostal worship.[43] In my view, music is the heartbeat of Pentecostal religiosity, and it is through that medium that it has most affected non-Pentecostal liturgies. Music plays a critical role in this therapeutic and edifying process of Pentecostal/Charismatic worship. Pentecostals worship in expectation that in the midst of the singing and prayer, the Holy Spirit will visit and that people will encounter his presence as he does so. It is a mode of religious expression that appeals very much to African religious sensibilities because of its experiential and therapeutic nature.

---

[40]Ibid.
[41]Ibid., 42.
[42]Cox, *Fire from Heaven*, 121.
[43]Ibid., 122.

Conclusion

In Pentecostalism, I believe, with Miller, "we are witnessing a second reformation that is transforming the way Christianity will be experienced in the new millennium."[44] The Pentecostal reformation challenges the medium through which the message of Christianity is articulated.[45] In Africa, where Pentecostalism has become the representative face of Christianity, Anderson also speaks of the situation as an *African Reformation*. This reformation is thoroughly experiential in character and ecumenical in orientation because it is unbounded by denominational bureaucracy and the restraint of tradition.

Pentecostalism is not only a Christianity of the present, it is also the Christianity of the future. Its greatest strength is its emphases on Christianity as an *experience* or *encounter* and the ecumenical nature of its spirituality. Right from its biblical origins in the prophecy of Joel through the promise of the Spirit after the resurrection of Christ and its fulfillment on the day of Pentecost, Pentecostalism has been thoroughly ecumenical. The expression 'ecumenical' must not been interpreted in the restrictive sense of denominations working together but in a broader sense of the possession of a form of religion that is not defined by denominational boundaries. In other words, Pentecostal spirituality is not a denomination; it is an experience that can be encountered within and without denominational, ethnic, social, geographical, economic, political, and ecclesiastical boundaries.

Pentecost, unlike Babel, was a divine action in which God reached out to 'all flesh' by the outpouring of his Spirit. Whereas the tower of Babel created confusion and dispersion of nations,

---

[44]Miller, *American Protestantism*, 11.
[45]Ibid.

Pentecost announces the possibility of a new unity among people, in effect a new ecumenism. This unity, which transcends linguistic differences and gives communal value to the individual emotional experience, transforms Pentecostalism into the greatest expression of religious communication. Wherever it is found today, Pentecostalism breaks down rigid traditional ecclesiastic structures and joins the secular, modern world, reaching out in all languages to all peoples and nations.[46] "To celebrate Pentecost is not to recall an event that is locked in time and space. Rather, it is to participate in a continuing festival that is ever more mysterious, frightening and wonderful than we can ever imagine."[47] That is what ecumenism is about. Rather than allow denominational inclinations to divide us, each one of us should be open to the Spirit, sincerely desiring the gifts of the Spirit so that when God reaches out to us, his presence can be recognized wherever we meet. For in Christ, St. Paul tells the church at Ephesus, we "also are being built together for a dwelling place of God in the Spirit" (Ephesians 2:22).

---

[46]Waldo César, *From Babel to Pentecost: A Social-Historical-Theological Study of the Growth of Pentecostalism* (Bloomington and Indianapolis: Indiana University Press, 2001), 31, 32.

[47]Wout van Laar, "Introduction: It's Time to Get to know Each Other," in André Droogers, Cornelis van der Laan and Wout van Laar eds., *Fruitful in this Land: Pluralism, Dialogue and Healing in Migrant Pentecostalism* (Zoetermeer, The Netherlands: Uitgeverij Boekencentrum, 2006), 14.

Pentecostal Feeling in Conversation with William James and Rudolf Otto: A Preliminary Exploration

by Ekaputra Tupamahu

Introduction

I met Dr. Wonsuk Ma for the first time during the orientation of incoming students at Asia Pacific Theological Seminary in the Philippines in 2003. I have come to know him since then as a leading Asian Pentecostal thinker who has a deep conviction that the task of constructing theology has to be undertaken from within a real human context.[1] This essay is rooted in a similar conviction. I will attempt to approach Pentecostal spirituality from a standpoint of human religious experience.

Pentecostalism[2] has grown remarkably around the world in the last one hundred years. Mark Noll notes:

> One of the most momentous developments in the twentieth century history of Christianity must certainly

---

[1] See Wonsuk Ma, "Toward an Asian Pentecostal Theology," *Asian Journal of Pentecostal Studies* 1, no. 1 (January 1998): 1–19.

[2] I use the term "Pentecostal" in a broad sense that includes the classical Pentecostal movement, Charismatic movement and the third wave movement. For further discussions on the definition of Pentecostalism, see Allan Anderson, "Varieties, Taxonomies, and Definitions," in *Studying Global Pentecostalism: Theories and Methods*, ed. Allan Anderson et al. (Berkeley, CA: University of California Press, 2010), 13–29.

be the emergence of Pentecostalism as a dynamic force around the world. In 1900 there were, at most, a bare handful of Christians who were experiencing special gifts of the Holy Spirit similar to those recorded in the New Testament. By the end of the century, as many as 500 million (or more than a quarter of the population of affiliated Christian adherents) could be identified as Pentecostal or Charismatic.[3]

Pentecostals have reached people from many different nationalities, races, languages, and social status.[4] This inevitably leads to a great diversity within the movement and Allan Anderson has rightly pointed out that, "it is very difficult to find some common unifying features or distinctiveness by which they might be defined."[5] However, it is certainly true that Pentecostalism is greatly diverse, yet it can also be argued that one of the most important characteristics of this movement is the display of emotion or feeling in both public and personal worship. Pentecostal worship is filled with emotional expressions such as crying, laughing, and shaking. Harvey Cox observes that this emotional expression is what attracts modern people who have been deeply trapped in 'the ecstasy deficits' to the Pentecostal movement.[6]

---

[3] Mark A. Noll, *Turning Points: Decisive Moments in the History of Christianity* (Grand Rapids, MI: Baker Books, 1997), 299.
[4] According to a 2008 research by Pew Forum, Pentecostalism in North America consists of White (70%), Black (11%), Asian (3%), Latino (12%), others (3%). Even though Pentecostalism in the US was started as mainly a black movement in the early twentieth century, it is now dominated by white people. See Pew Forum, "Palin V.P. Nomination Puts Pentecostalism in the Spotlight" http://pewforum.org/docs/?DocID=345 (Accessed November 22, 2009)
[5] Allan Anderson, *An Introduction to Pentecostalism: Global Charismatic Christianity* (Cambridge, U.K.: Cambridge University Press, 2004), 10.
[6] Harvey G. Cox, *Fire from Heaven: The Rise of Pentecostal Spirituality and the Reshaping of Religion in the Twenty-First Century* (Reading, MA: Addison-Wesley, 1995), 24.

In this essay, I will explore this special characteristic of the Pentecostal movement through the lens of the phenomenological analysis of religion. I am going to discuss two leading thinkers of the phenomenology of religion, namely William James and Rudolf Otto. In doing so, I attempt to show that when Pentecostals go beyond theological and biblical explorations, they can take many things from the scholars of the phenomenology of religion to help explain their emotional religious expression.

James and Otto on Religious Feeling

William James and Rudolf Otto are two noted thinkers in the field of religious studies. This section is intended to explore their discussion on mysticism, especially the idea of feeling (Otto: non-rationality) as a way of religious knowing, and how feeling has become an expression of human religiosity. After discussing them, I will move further to use their theoretical proposal as a framework to explain Pentecostal religious feeling.

William James, professor of psychology at Harvard University, gave his Gifford Lectures in 1901 and 1902 on the topic of religious experience. The lecture, *The Varieties of Religious Experience: A Study of Human Nature*, subsequently became one of the most significant works in the field of religious studies in the twentieth century. James's discussion on mysticism and religious feeling has made him sort of "the father of modern study of mysticism."[7]

James points out in the lecture, pertaining to the reality of the "unseen" God (lecture III), that every experience of feeling is always directed toward some object. One cannot have feeling in

---

[7]Louise Nelstrop, Kevin J. Magill, and Bradley B. Onishi, *Christian Mysticism: An Introduction to Contemporary Theoretical Approaches* (Farnham, UK: Ashgate, 2009), 3.

itself. Feeling should be oriented and in relation to an object(s). By using Immanuel Kant's concept that in the religious context the objects of religious experience are God, creation, soul, freedom, and life after death, James contends that these abstract belief objects are in close relation to our religious feeling. Many religious people operate within the mechanism of religious feeling. According to James, "it is as if there were in the human consciousness *a sense of reality, a feeling of objective presence, a perception* of what we may call *'something there,'* more deep and more general than any of the special and particular 'scenes' by which the current psychology supposes existent realities to be originally revealed."[8] People still hold firmly to this "reality-feeling" in spite of its unclearness or vagueness. It is similar to the phenomenon of hallucination, James argues, in which "a person affected will feel a 'presence' in the room, definitely located, facing in a more particular way, real in the most emphatic sense of the word, often coming suddenly, and as suddenly gone; and yet neither seen, heard, touched, or cognized in any of the usual 'sensible' ways."[9] James discusses this feeling of the divine presence as an 'ontological imagination' within which "unpicturable beings are realized, and realized with an intensity almost like that of an hallucination."[10]

The religious feeling is the primary element in the religious expression and experience of the mystics, and the opposing position to the mysticism is *rationalism*. Interestingly, for James, religious experience goes far beyond a rational state of being. James explains, "Your whole subconscious life, your impulses, your faiths, your needs, your divinations, have prepared the premises, of which your consciousness now feels the weight of

---

[8] William James, *The Varieties of Religious Experience: A Study in Human Nature*, A Centenary Edition (London: Routledge, 2004), 50.
[9] Ibid.
[10] Ibid., 61.

the result; and something in you absolutely knows that that result must be truer than any logic-chopping rationalistic talk, however clever, that may contradict it."[11] In addition, James is convinced that every logical argument in the metaphysical and religious discourse would confirm the prior conclusion that has been taken through non-logical feelings. James states: "The truth is that in the metaphysical and religious sphere, articulate reasons are cogent for us only when our inarticulate feelings of reality have already been impressed in favor of the same conclusion."[12] It means that the rational articulation is a product of the feelings that have occurred in the first place. This, moreover, seems to be the reason that James dedicates two long lectures (XVI and XVII) just to explain the religious phenomenon of mysticism.

Mysticism, according to James, is a 'state of consciousness' that is very ambiguous in its outward expression. So in order to identify it, James proposes four signs of mystical experience. The first one is *ineffability*.[13] The mystical experience cannot be expressed. It is, in other words, a "negative" state of mind. James explains, "in this peculiarity mystical states are more likely states of feeling than like states of intellect. No one can make clear to another who has never had a certain feeling, in what the quality or worth of it consists. One must have musical ears to know the value of a symphony; one must have been in love oneself to understand a lover's state of mind."[14] Second, mystical experience has a *noetic quality*. James argues that mystical states are not only experienced in the level of feeling, but they also have an intellectual quality. "They are illuminations, revelations, full of significance and importance, all inarticulate though they remain; and as a rule they carry with them a curious sense of

---

[11] Ibid., 62.
[12] Ibid.
[13] Ibid., 295.
[14] Ibid.

authority for after time."[15] The third mark of mysticism is *transiency*. What this means is that mystical states take place only temporarily. James observes that they can last only about an hour or two, and then they will fade away.[16] The fourth mark is *passivity*. The person who experiences the mystical states will feel "as if his own will were in abeyance, and indeed sometimes as if he were grasped and held by a superior power."[17] These four marks, for James, are enough to indicate the mystical states. He calls the people who are experiencing this, "the mystical group."[18] Also, James observes that the goal of religious mystical experience is to be in union with the Divine. The methods of this mystical union can vary from tradition to tradition. It can take the form of music, poetry, meditation, etc.

Otto, who published his book in 1923, also picks up the same theme of religious feeling as the main center point of his work. Otto begins his discussion by making a distinction between rational and non-rational natures of religion. God can be explained through concepts and ideas, and then the concepts and ideas are structured in a certain system of theology. For Otto, one can call this "rational religion."[19] Rationalism is the dominant expression throughout the history of Christianity. Otto nonetheless observes that the rationalistic system of concepts or attributes of God is far from "exhausting the idea of deity."[20] The ideas or concepts of God only "imply a non-rational or supra-rational Subject of which they are predicates."[21] The non-rational

---

[15]Ibid.
[16]Ibid.
[17]Ibid., 495.
[18]Ibid., 496.
[19]Rudolf Otto (1869-1937), *The Idea of the Holy: An Inquiry into the Non-Rational Factor in the Idea of the Divine and Its Relation to the Rational*, trans. John W. Harvey, 2nd ed., Oxford Paperbacks (London: Oxford University Press, 1958), 1.
[20]Ibid., 2.
[21]Ibid.

dimension of God goes deeper than just a series of concepts about God. The difference between rational and non-rational is not about the debate concerning miracles. It is the "quality in the mental attitude and emotional content of religious life itself."[22] The depth of the non-rational reality of God is what the mystics throughout history try to maintain.

In relation to this, Otto says that the idea of "holy" has been partially understood in a moral sense as completely good. Holy does not only mean that, it goes beyond the ethical or moral meaning. For Otto, in its original sense, the word "holy" actually refers to the idea of feeling. Since God is completely separate (i.e., wholly other) from human beings, the only way people can experience this wholly other is through feeling. So, the event or the moment of feeling is holy. Otto believes that this is the core of religion. "There is no religion in which it does not live as the real innermost core, and without it no religion would be worthy of the name."[23] Therefore, it is crucial to distinguish two different Latin terminologies, namely *numen* and *numinous*, that Otto uses throughout the book. Numen is the divine in itself, whereas numinous is the undefined "state of mind" that reaches out to the divinity. *Numinous*, therefore, is a process. Otto takes a further step from Schleiermacher's conception of "feeling of dependence" because for him it is not enough to explain the complexity of mystical experience. So he proposes a new term *creature-consciousness* or *creature-feeling*. Otto explains that "it is the emotion of creature, submerged and overwhelmed by its own nothingness in contrast to what is supreme above all creatures."[24] Just like the first criterion of mystical experience in James's work [ineffability], Otto also proposes that this feeling "cannot be expressed verbally, and can only be suggested indirectly through

---

[22]Ibid., 3.
[23]Ibid., 6.
[24]Ibid., 10.

the tone and content of a man's feeling-response to it. And this response must be directly experienced in oneself to be understood."[25]

Furthermore, Otto contends that the *creature-feeling* is experienced in two ways: "*mysterium tremendum et fascinans*" (overwhelming and fascinating mystery). The emotion or feeling of fear toward God does not only carry the meaning of awefulness (reference), but also overpoweringness and energy or urgency. Since God is the 'wholly other', it is inherent in this moment of feeling an experience of mystery. For Otto, the Latin term *stupor* fits this feeling of aweful mystery before the presence of the wholly other. "It [*stupor*] signifies blank wonder, an astonishment that strikes us dumb, amazement absolute."[26] Furthermore, the other way people experience the creature-feeling is through the element of fascination. It is the feeling of fascination or amazement. The mystery of the wholly other is not "merely something to be wondered but something that entrances him [human being]; and beside that in it which bewilders and confounds, he feels a something that captivates and transports him with a strange ravishment, rising often enough to the pitch of dizzy intoxication; it is the Dionysiac element in the numen."[27]

Pentecostal Scholarship Encountering James and Otto

Let us now examine how Pentecostal scholarship has encountered William James and Rudolf Otto. Ken Smith's presentation at the 2005 Society for Pentecostal Studies annual meeting is worth mentioning first because he closely examined James's pragmatism. In discussing how Pentecostals can learn from James, Smith argues that Pentecostals can gain a lot from

---

[25]Ibid.
[26]Ibid., 26.
[27]Ibid., 31.

James's critique of rationalism. Smith writes, "The Jamesian critique of rationalism–and of systems generally–seems to mesh well with Pentecostal temperament. The practice of speaking in tongues (leaving aside for the moment the doctrinal formulations regarding tongues) may be the most tangible element of Pentecostalism's rejection of rationalism."[28] But, Smith also offers a critical assessment of James's underlying philosophical assumptions. Smith argues that Pentecostal mystical experience is rooted in the Pentecostal's belief in God who leads and directs the universe to a certain purpose or goal (teleology). He contends,

> The Jamesian abandonment of teleology in history and his rejection of rational logic as a revealer of essential reality–both of which are set forth in A Pluralistic Universe–therefore are acutely problematic. Even more significantly, James's radical sublimation of divine transcendence to human immanence makes a full embrace of Jamesianism untenable for believing Christians, whether of Pentecostals or other traditions.[29]

Smith seems to disagree with James from a theological point of view. He rightly points out that James sees God in "the context of effects" because James does place a very strong emphasis on experience.[30] However, it needs to be clarified also that James himself acknowledges that he is not a theologian, and his work is not a theological work.[31] Therefore, criticizing him from a

---

[28]Kenneth L. Smith, "Spirit, Word, and Stream of Consciousness: Some Implications of Jamesian Pragmatist Theory for Pentecostal Thought and Practice" (presented at the 34th Annual Meeting of the Society for Pentecostal Studies, Regent University, 2005), 14.

[29]Ibid., 15.

[30]Ibid., 11.

[31]James explains in the opening remarks of his lectures that: "As regards the manner in which I shall have to administer this lectureship, I am neither a

theological standpoint, as though James is constructing a theological system, has missed the point of James' work.

Beside Smith, Pentecostal scholarship in general has been reluctant to deal with James and Otto. There are only a handful of Pentecostal thinkers who mention in passing either James or Otto in their works. Frank Macchia, for example, in his article on speaking in tongues, writes: "I recall being struck as a graduate student by Rudolf Otto's depiction, in his *Idea of the Holy*, of one's encounter with the *mysterium, tremendum et fascinosum*. Otto wrote of the awesome, overwhelming and alien mystery without which one misses the heart of religious experience."[32] Macchia, unfortunately, does not engage Otto further because it is not the focus of his article. But, one can see that his discussion on tongues is deeply inspired by Otto's concept of the *mysterium*. Russell Spittler also quickly mentions William James in his discussion on the question of the possibility of studying religious experience.[33] Just like Macchia, Spittler does not spend more than one sentence to engage James.

In spite of the lack of interest among Pentecostal scholars [scholars who come from a Pentecostal background], sociologists who study the Pentecostal movement as a social movement interestingly tend to rely on the work of James or/and Otto. Two

---

theologian, nor a scholar learned in the history of religions, nor an anthropologist. Psychology is the only branch of learning in which I am particularly versed. To the psychologist the religious propensities of man must be at least as interesting as any other of the facts pertaining to his mental constitution. It would seem, therefore, that, as a psychologist, the natural thing for me would be to invite you to a descriptive survey of those religious propensities." See James, *The Varieties of Religious Experience: A Study in Human Nature*, 8.

[32]Frank D. Macchia, "Sighs Too Deep for Words: Toward a Theology of Glossolalia," *Journal of Pentecostal Theology* 1, no. 1 (1992): 57–8.

[33]Russell P. Spittler, "Corinthian Spirituality: How a Flawed Anthropology Imperils Authentic Christian Existence," in *Pentecostal Currents in American Protestantism*, ed. Edith Waldvogel Blumhofer, Russell P. Spittler, and Grant Wacker (Urbana, IL: University of Illinois Press, 1999), 5.

examples can be listed here. First, Donald E. Miller and Tetsunao Yamamori, both professors of religion and sociology at the University of Southern California, utilize William James's discussion on religious experience to articulate their underlying conceptual framework in their recent collaborative work on global 'progressive'[34] Pentecostalism. While acknowledging that Pentecostals believe that they are led and guided by the Holy Spirit, Miller and Yamamori argue that their work is mainly concentrated on social engagement of Pentecostals, and not their theology. So, instead of using theological categories to explain Pentecostal religious experience, they write, "we are philosophical pragmatists, with William James being a guiding light in much that we do."[35] Moreover, in the discussion of the "research assumptions" of the book, Miller and Yamamori argue that they embrace both the views of Rudolf Otto and William James.[36] Second, in her work on the Assemblies of God, sociologist Margaret M. Poloma contends that her work is dependent on William James's concept of religious experience. Regarding spirituality in the Assemblies of God, Poloma explains it in a conversation with James. She writes: "If William James (1902), and others following his lead, is correct in the thesis that the evidence for God lies primarily in inner personal experiences rather than in abstract philosophical systems, the Assemblies of God is successfully promoting such experiences in ways that are conducive to the growth of the denomination."[37] Speaking in

---

[34]Progressive Pentecostals in this book are defined as "Christians who claim to be inspired by the Holy Spirit and the life of Jesus and seek to holistically address the spiritual, physical, and social needs of people in their community." See Donald E. Miller and Tetsunao Yamamori, *Global Pentecostalism: The New Face of Christian Social Engagement* (Berkeley: University of California Press, 2007), 3.

[35]Ibid., 4.

[36]Ibid., 12ff.

[37]Margaret M. Poloma, *The Assemblies of God at the Crossroads: Charisma and Institutional Dilemmas* (Knoxville, TN: University of Tennessee Press, 1989), 91.

tongues, according to Poloma, has become an important element in Pentecostal spirituality.

Why do scholars who come from a Pentecostal background not engage James or Otto in discussing their spiritual experience? One of the reasons I can give is that Pentecostals too often talk about their spiritual experience in theological terms. Theologian Amos Yong argues that it is the "experiences of the Holy Spirit" or "pneumatological imagination" that bind Pentecostals and Charismatics together.[38] God becomes the primary cause of their emotional spiritual experience. Theology, therefore, is the key to understanding the experience. In order to understand what speaking in tongues is, for example, Pentecostals connect to the idea of baptism in the Holy Spirit. Instead of seeing it as a human religious experience, they are more eager to search for its theological articulation. It is not a surprise that most publications in the last two or three decades have been dedicated to either biblical or theological discussions. Pentecostals seem to be nervous when their spiritual experience is explained and analyzed in the context of human religious experience. They do not talk about their spirituality as a human religious experience probably because it can leave an impression of being carnal or fleshy. Feeling therefore is often associated with the "anointing of the Holy Spirit." In this paper, I aim to do an experiment, of course with the help of James and Otto, to explain Pentecostal spirituality in human terms, rather than theological terms.

---

[38] Amos Yong, *Discerning The Spirit(s): A Pentecostal-Charismatic Contribution to Christian Theology of Religions* (Sheffield: Sheffield Academic Press, 2000), 161.

Some Potential Areas of Conversation

First of all, it needs to be pointed out that feeling or emotion is a normal human experience. Some people leave Pentecostalism because they think that the movement has become too feeling-oriented, and it leads to an anti-intellectual attitude. Roger Olson, a Baylor University theology professor, for instance, writes this about Pentecostalism: "Endemic to Pentecostalism is a profoundly anti-intellectual ethos, which is manifested in a deep suspicion of scholars and educators and especially biblical scholars and theologians."[39] It became one of the reasons why he left Pentecostalism. This is only one of many examples, and the list of those who have left Pentecostalism goes longer. My point is that people have seen feelings in Pentecostalism as a problem.

I am fully aware that this essay will not give all the answers to or completely reveal the mystery of religious feeling in the Pentecostal psyche. Nevertheless, I am going to propose several areas in which Pentecostals can gain from James and Otto in order to provide a theoretical framework for understanding feeling as a valid religious experience. First, James and Otto have rightly demonstrated that "feeling" does not necessarily lead to anti-rationalism or anti-intellectualism. For them, reason only is not enough to explain the complexity of religious experience. Otto prefers to use the term "non-rational" instead of "irrational" simply because he does not want to leave an impression that feeling is an irrational state of being. The point is that a mere rationalistic approach to religion is inadequate. Philosopher James K.A. Smith, in his discussion on Pentecostal epistemology, has teased this area. He argues that Pentecostal worship and spirituality "constitutes a kind of performative postmodernism,

---

[39]Roger E. Olson, "Pentecostalism's Dark Side," *The Christian Century* 123, no. 5 (2006): 27.

an enacted refusal of rationalism."[40] This way, Smith thinks that Pentecostalism is actually not "anti*rational*, but antirationa*list*." Drawing his analysis from Pentecostal testimony, Smith writes:

> While Pentecostals (like all sorts of other evangelical Christians) might be prone to fall into anti-intellectualism, I don't think this is endemic to Pentecostal spirituality as such. Rather, it attends the populism that characterizes most expressions of Pentecostalism. But if we filter our analysis more carefully, and try–at least theoretically–to sort out populist anti-intellectualism from the Pentecostal practice of testimony, I think we can discern in Pentecostal spirituality a sort of inchoate epistemic grammar, perhaps best described as a hermeneutic–a tacit understanding of what constitutes 'knowledge' and the means by which we know . . . It is not a critique or rejection of reason as such but rather a commentary on a particularly reductionistic model of reason and rationality, a limited, stunted version of what counts as "knowledge." If the Pentecostal practice of testimony is a kind of critique of our "idolatrous reliance on reason," it's not reason that is the target, but our idolatrous construction of it.[41]

What Smith is trying to highlight is well-taken and it clearly resonates with James and Otto. There is no straightforward path that would lead Pentecostalism with its non-rationalistic approach to spirituality and religious experience to anti-intellectualism.

---

[40]James K. A. Smith, *Thinking in Tongues: Pentecostal Contributions to Christian Philosophy*, Pentecostal Manifestos (Grand Rapids, MI: Eerdmans, 2010), 59.
[41]Ibid., 53.

Second, James and Otto's proposal that feeling can be a way to knowing the 'unseen' God (James) or the wholly Other (Otto) can potentially be a theoretical framework to understand Pentecostal feeling. As we have discussed above, James and Otto both agree that reason is not the only way to the knowledge of God. They bring to the front table the experience of mystical tradition to show that feeling or emotion is also a valid religious experience of the divine. Again, let me put James and Otto in conversation with Smith on this issue. Smith, interestingly, brings attention to Carl Plantinga's film theory to explain Pentecostal affectivity or emotion. Basically, Plantinga argues against the 'cognitivist theory' of film that when people engage with a movie, the initial encounter is not in a cognitive level. In other words, instead of analyzing a movie rationally when people are watching it, the initial reaction usually takes place on an affective or emotional level. For Smith, the same is true also with everyday life, "we *feel* our way around the world more than we *think* about it, *before* we think about it."[42] This is what Smith has to say about Pentecostal emotion:

> I would even grant that there is something *like* a psychoanalytical moment to Pentecostal worship. I suggest this cautiously since many critics and skeptics would like to reduce Pentecostal experience to psychosis, or at least to some kind of mass therapeutic paradigm explainable in naturalistic terms. However, I don't mean to suggest that; rather, it seems to me that affectivity and emotion are central to Pentecostal spirituality because they implicitly recognize that our being-in-the-world is primarily and for the most part 'driven' at an unconscious, affective, predeliberative level. Thus Pentecostal worship digs down past and through the

---

[42]Ibid., 72.

cognitive, conscious, and deliberative register to the affective and emotional core of our identity–a noncognitive core that directs much more of our action and behavior than we'd like to admit.[43]

This statement, I believe, can summarize the core of Smith's argument. The difference between Smith and James or Otto, however, is that neither James nor Otto put feeling or affection prior to thinking. Smith's emphasis on the importance of this *pre*cognitive experience somehow leaves an impression that there is a separated sequential stage of human experience, namely affective and then cognitive experience. For James, however, feeling especially among mystics is a way of knowing. James would not categorize it as a stage before cognitive knowledge. It is a way of knowing that has its own logic that is different from reason. James writes:

> As a matter of psychological fact, mystical states of a well-pronounced and emphatic sort are usually authoritative over those who have them. They have been "there" and know. It is vain for rationalism to grumble about this. If the mystical truth that comes to a man proves to be a force that he can live by, what mandate have we of the majority to order him to live in another way? We can throw him into a prison or a madhouse, but we cannot change his mind–we commonly attach it only the more stubbornly to its beliefs. It mocks our utmost efforts, as a matter of fact, and in point of logic it absolutely escapes our jurisdiction. Our own more

---

[43] Ibid., 77.

'rational' beliefs are based on evidence exactly similar in nature to that which mystics quote theirs.[44]

So for James, the mystical experience is as valid as rational knowledge. On the one side, Smith tries to integrate both ways of knowing by putting affection in a *precognitive* level or stage. James, on the other side, understands it as a 'different' way of knowing, and as I have shown earlier, the emotive knowledge can even go deeper than the rationalistic method of knowing. He even calls theology and philosophy secondary products. James contends:

> I do believe that feeling is the deeper source of religion, and that philosophic and theological formulas are secondary products, like translations of a text into another tongue . . . When I call theological formulas secondary products, I mean that in a world in which no religious feeling had ever existed, I doubt whether any philosophic theology could ever have been framed.[45]

If we could ask James to give advice to Pentecostals, what would it be? He would probably say, "Do not be discouraged by all the negative attacks you receive from the rationalist critics against your religious experience. The way you know and experience the unseen God is as valid as those who are busy building theological systems to explain who God is."

Third, let us examine specifically the possibility of Pentecostals to engage Otto. Otto's concept of *mysterium tremendum et fascinans* (overwhelming and fascinating mystery) can be helpful, just as Macchia has shown, to understand

---

[44]James, *The Varieties of Religious Experience: A Study in Human Nature*, 328.
[45]Ibid., 334.

Pentecostal religious experience. Even though Pentecostals are very free and spontaneous in the worship, God is experienced as a mystery or wholly other. A famous Pentecostal singer today, Chris Tomlin, expresses it well in his poetic song lyrics:

> Indescribable, uncontainable,
> You placed the stars in the sky
> and you know them by name.
> You are amazing God
> All powerful, untameable,
> Awestruck we fall to our knees as we humbly proclaim
> You are amazing God

For Pentecostals, God is a great mystery and the response of human beings to this mystery is through worship in the feeling of amazement. Pentecostals' singing section in their worship gathering is always called "praise and worship." Most of the time, Pentecostal songs are not intended to convey theological arguments or teachings, but emotionally oriented exaltation and praise to God. Songs become an important way of expressing their fascination toward God. In addition, James has shown that one of the ways mystics attain union with the divine is through music. It is obvious that Pentecostal worship is full of music. Music is often loud in Pentecostal gatherings so that everyone can participate in worship. Miller and Yamamori have rightly pointed out that,

> The engine of Pentecostalism is worship. Whether in a storefront building with bare fluorescent tubes hanging from ceiling or in a theater with a sophisticated sound system, the heart of Pentecostalism is the music. It touches emotions. It is populist in tone and

instrumentation. The lyrics give voice to feelings–the pain, the joy, the hope for new life.[46]

In other words, music and Pentecostal religious experience are inseparable. Music functions to enhance Pentecostal experience.

The fourth point I should like to discuss here is the Pentecostal feeling of the presence of God and James's concept of hallucination. Just as we have discussed above, hallucination is a feeling of a presence of something in the room, and it is real for those who experience it. Not only that, James also describes that mystical experience as ineffable in nature. The feeling of the presence of God real, but it is ineffable. The experience itself is beyond explanation. Just like the experience of listening to music or falling in love, James argues that one needs to have "musical ears" or falling in love oneself, in order to understand the value of that music or the meaning of "a lover's state of mind."[47] Pentecostals have a deep desire to feel and experience the presence of God. The expressions such as "God is here" or "His anointing is in this place" or "I can see Him moving in this place" –yes, Pentecostals always employ masculine language for God– are common among Pentecostals. Pentecostal worship is designed to give room for people to feel and experience the presence of God. Daniel Albrecht, one of the few scholars who study Pentecostal rites and rituals, explains:

> Experiencing God is the fundamental goal of Pentecostal service. This experiencing and encountering God is often symbolized as a felt presence of the divine. The sense of the divine presence is a primary component, and aim, of

---

[46] Miller and Yamamori, *Global Pentecostalism*, 23–24.
[47] James, *The Varieties of Religious Experience: A Study in Human Nature*, 295.

Pent/Char spirituality. In the services this is evidenced by the use of 'Pentecostal icons', chiefly used to help the faithful 'come into the [felt] presence of God.' Pentecostal efforts to develop and maintain pathways into the presence point to the centrality of mystical element in Pentecostal spirituality, the strong desire and claim to experience God directly and intimately.[48]

This description is true among many Pentecostal groups across the economic level, geographical location, and age. The felt presence of God has become the central aim of Pentecostal worship. Pentecostals are striving to experience God in a real and personal way. However, the question remains; is Pentecostal experience ineffable, like what James describes about the mystics? Paul Lewis, a Pentecostal theologian, argues against the idea of ineffability of Pentecostal experience. He writes:

> Pentecostal experience is not 'ineffable' as ascribed by mystics, rather Pentecostal perspectives demand the concreteness of the experience. Pentecostal experience is concrete in that it takes the form of the charismata, missiological endeavors, participatory worship, among other things, which are and needs to be testable by the leaders of the community. It is this practicality and concreteness, which also expresses the Pentecostal necessity for practicality while still emphasizing the supernatural.[49]

---

[48]Daniel E. Albrecht, *Rites in the Spirit: A Ritual Approach to Pentecostal/Charismatic Spirituality* (Sheffield, UK: Sheffield Academic Press, 1999), 149.

[49]Paul W. Lewis, "Towards a Pentecostal Epistemology: The Role of Experience in Pentecostal Hermeneutics," *The Spirit & Church* 2, no. 1 (2000): 105–106.

Lewis seems to equate ineffability with inconcreteness. He, moreover, relates concreteness to the practice of testing the experience by the leaders of the community particularly in the context of the exercise of spiritual gifts, mission, worship, and so on. Not only that, Lewis also connects the concreteness to practicality as opposed to supernatural. This is quite different from what James explains about the mystics. The mystical experience is concrete in a sense that it is an experience of–or directed to–an object, namely God. But, the person who has the experience would not be able to fully articulate it. This is why James contends that in order to understand a mystical experience, one will not be able to explain it to another person. The other person needs to experience it himself/herself. As a matter of fact, some of the early Pentecostal testimonies in the Apostolic Faith show the phenomenon of ineffability of their religious experience. For example, Myrtle K. Shideler who wrote her testimony from New York, apparently on her way to Africa, said that in a prayer meeting in New York, she saw a vision of Jesus coming to her while they were singing a song. She recalls:

> By the time the chorus ended, the power of God was so heavy upon me, I could scarcely open my mouth, and every fiber of my being was trembling. Yet my feet felt glued to the floor and my knees stiff, so I could not sit down. I only got out a few broken sentences that I remember. (I never fainted in my life and was never unconscious, but God certainly took me out of myself.) He showed me things which there are not words enough in the English language to express . . . I do not know how long I stood and praises to God just burst from me. They tell me I sang in a tongue. I was not conscious of singing at all. From seeing others under the power, I had thought it must be a terrible nervous tension, but it was

the most perfect surrender and relaxation . . . I was under the power for the remainder [of the] meeting, and for three days was as one drunken, and had no sense of either hunger or thirst. Since then, such waves of power roll over me from time to time. I can scarcely keep my feet, and I am sure if my old friends in California could see me, they would think I was indeed insane.[50]

This is precisely what James was talking about when he discusses the ineffability of mystical experience. Pentecostal experience is ineffable because it cannot be fully articulated. For the past many years, this is why theology, as a rational exercise in articulating human religiosity, does not attract Pentecostals. Only in the last two decades have we seen a growing number of theologians begin to articulate Pentecostal experience in a rational and systematic manner.

Conclusion

Peter Berger's acknowledgement that "Pentecostalism is an exceedingly important movement in the contemporary world" is worth noting.[51] The importance of Pentecostalism in the study of religion today can no longer be overlooked. Their emphasis on feeling, affection, passion, and emotion has fascinated many scholars. Unfortunately, the articulation of Pentecostal feeling has been dominated by theological and biblical exercise. This paper is intended to bring the phenomenology of religion, through the works of James and Otto, to the table of discussion.

---

[50]Myrtle K. Shideler, "Received Her Pentecost," *The Apostolic Faith*, January 1907.

[51]Peter Berger, "Pentecostalism-Protestant Ethic or Cargo Cult?" *The American Interest: Religion and Other Curiosities*, Accessed December 5, 2013, http://blogs.the-american-interest.com/berger/2010/07/29/pentecostalism-%E2%80%93-protestant-ethic-or-cargo-cult/.

My hope is that there will be more Pentecostal scholars in the future who will seriously engage James and Otto.[52]

---

[52] I am grateful to Frank Macchia, Paul W. Lewis, Menghun Goh, Kenneth Smith, Anna Hymes, and Steve Forsberg who have helped me read and have given their critical comments to this essay.

Peter, Women, and the Holy Spirit in the Bezan Text of Acts[1]

by R.G. dela Cruz

Introduction

Codex Bezae Cantabrigiensis is a major New Testament (NT) uncial Greek-Latin bilingual manuscript that has preserved remarkable variant readings in the Acts of the Apostles.[2] These textual variations, fossilized in particular within the Greek text of the manuscript, present a challenge to students of the text of the NT.[3] Its textual form and history, though, are not of concern

---

[1] This essay is a substantially revised version of a paper originally read in February 2006 at the 14th William W. Menzies Lectureship held at Asia Pacific Theological Seminary, Baguio City, Philippines. I am delighted to present this article as my contribution to the collection of writings in honor of Wonsuk and Julie Ma.

[2] See the important study of Stanley E. Porter, "Developments in the Text of Acts before the Major Codices," in *The Book of Acts as Church History: Text, Textual Traditions and Ancient Interpretations / Apostelgeschichte als Kirchengeschichte: Text, Texttraditionen und antike Auslegungen*, ed. Tobias Nicklas and Michael Tilly, Beihefte zur Zeitschrift für die neutestamentliche Wissenschaft 120 (Berlin & New York: Walter de Gruyter, 2003), 31-67. See also in the same volume Marco Frenschkowski, "Der Text der Apostelgeschichte und die Realien antiker Buchproduktion," 87-107.

[3] Cf. J. Keith Elliott, "An Eclectic Textual Study of the Book of Acts," in *The Book of Acts as Church History: Text, Textual Traditions and Ancient Interpretations / Apostelgeschichte als Kirchengeschichte: Text, Texttraditionen und antike Auslegungen*, ed. Tobias Nicklas and Michael Tilly, Beihefte zur Zeitschrift für die neutestamentliche Wissenschaft 120 (Berlin &

here.⁴ It is known, however, that from the St. Irenaeus monastery in Lyon, Codex Bezae (also referred to as the D text)⁵ received contemporary attention when the Council of Trent in 1546 borrowed it.⁶ The origin of the text of codex D has not been settled, albeit it is unquestionably a regularly utilized bilingual manuscript.⁷

New York: Walter de Gruyter, 2003), 9-30. Cf. also in the same volume Christopher Tuckett, "How Early Is 'the' 'Western' Text of Acts?," 69-86.

⁴It is appropriate to mention that the historical development of its enigmatic textual form was evolving rather than a one-time widespread editing. This view is in agreement with D. C. Parker, *An Introduction to the New Testament Manuscripts and Their Texts* (Cambridge: Cambridge University Press, 2008), 289: By a comparison of the Greek and Latin columns, I concluded that the form of text of Acts found in the manuscript was due to evolution rather than to a single comprehensive revision. The evidence lies in differences between the columns, where the Latin often seems to be a witness to a form of Greek text which lies somewhere between the form in [B]03 and that in [D]05.

⁵Codex Bezae is also known as 05. However, for the sake of convenience, it will be consistently referred to in this paper as the D text or D, as it is represented by this letter symbol in the textual apparatus of critical editions of the Greek New Testament.

⁶Frederick H. Scrivener, ed., *Bezae Codex Cantabrigiensis, Being an Exact Copy, in Ordinary Type, of the Celebrated Uncial Graeco-Latin Manuscript of the Four Gospels and Acts of the Apostles, Written Early in the Sixth Century, and Presented to the University of Cambridge by Theodore Bezae, A.D. 1581* (Cambridge: Deighton, Bell and Co., 1864; repr., Pittsburgh: Pickwick Press, 1978; and Eugene: Wipf and Stock Publishers, n.d.), vi. See E. A. Lowe, "The Codex Bezae and Lyons," in *Palaeographical Papers 1907-1965*, 2 vols., ed. Ludwig Bieler (Oxford: Clarendon Press, 1972), 1:182-6; repr. from *Journal of Theological Studies* 25 (1924): 270-4, for a discussion of the manuscript's relation with St. Irenaeus monastery in Lyons.

⁷J. Neville Birdsall, "The Geographical and Cultural Origin of Codex Bezae Cantabrigiensis: A Survey of the *Status Quaestionis*, Mainly from the Palaeographical Standpoint," in *Studien zum Text und zur Ethik des Neuen Testaments: Festschrift zum 80. Geburtstag von Heinrich Greeven*, ed. Wolfgang Schrage, Beihefte zur Zeitschrift für die neutestamentliche Wissenschaft 47 (Berlin: Walter de Gruyter, 1986), 102-14. See also D. C. Parker, *Codex Bezae: An Early Christian Manuscript and Its Text* (Cambridge: Cambridge University Press, 1992), for the many hands that touched the text of the manuscript in its existence as a codex. The many hands that put their imprints on the manuscript show how it was well used in late antiquity.

This manuscript eventually ended up with Theodore Beza.[8] In due course, it came to the Cambridge University Library, as a letter from Beza in 1581 indicates that he sent the codex to England that year.[9] However, it was in 1582 that the Cambridge vice-chancellor and senate recognized the manuscript's arrival.[10] Thus, because it was Beza who had passed it on to Cambridge (where it still resides), it was identified with this renowned scholar and named Codex Bezae Cantabrigiensis.

Codex D has brought an enduring perplexity to textual students of early NT manuscripts ever since it was summoned up and referred to in preparing critical editions of the Greek NT.[11] Accordingly, the textual problem caused by D is one of a methodological challenge. In what way can these "unique readings"[12] of the D text fit in the text of the NT? The peculiar

---

[8]Scrivener, *Bezae*, vi.

[9]See the reprinted letter of Theodore Beza (dated 6 December 1581) that went together with the D manuscript when he donated it to Cambridge University and the response of the vice-chancellor and senate (dated 18 May 1582) in Scrivener, *Bezae*, iv.

[10]The precise time of D's arrival in Cambridge is unidentified. Thomas Kipling, *Codex Theodori Bezae Cantabrigiensis Evangelia et Apostolorum acta complectens quadratis literis Graeco-Latinus* (Cantabrigiae: E prelo Academico impensis Academiae, 1793), xxii, indicates that based on Beza's correspondence with Walter Travers, Codex D only found its way in Cambridge at about the start of spring time in 1582.

[11]See Scrivener, *Bezae*, viii-xi, for the list of the first scholars who studied D. Most recently, Josep Rius-Camps and Jenny Read-Heimerdinger, eds., *Luke's Demonstration to Theophilus: The Gospel and the Acts of the Apostles According to Codex Bezae*, English trans. Helen Dunn and Jenny Read-Heimerdinger (London & New York: Bloomsbury, 2013); and Jenny Read-Heimerdinger and Josep Rius-Camps, *A Gospel Synopsis of the Greek Text of Matthew, Mark and Luke: A Comparison of Codex Bezae and Codex Vaticanus*, New Testament Tools, Studies and Documents 45 (Leiden: E. J. Brill, 2014) continue the scholarly interest on Codex Bezae with their publications of these significant tools.

[12]The phrase "unique readings" also "peculiar," "distinctive," "odd," and "unusual" are used to describe the deviating D text from the accepted superior textual witness, particularly the B text. However, the use is not only limited to singular variant readings of D. Rather, singular readings are only part of the larger unusual variants that may have parallels with other Greek manuscripts or

variants of D against the other important witnesses represented by Codex Vaticanus (or the B text), which immensely influenced the text of the familiar modern critical editions of the Greek NT, have been a matter of interest and investigation among scholars, both then and now.[13] It is also noteworthy that the complete digital images of the codex is now exhibited on the Internet[14] and that there is a website fully devoted to its text.[15] The accessibility of these digital images on the Internet plus the websites devoted to biblical textual criticism make the study of the distinctive readings of D attractive to more students of the NT text.[16]

There are three areas of interest or issues with regard to post-apostolic Christianity that are relevant in studying the variant readings of the D text of Acts.[17] They include: (1) the apostolic

---

early translations that are different from the recognized "better-quality" manuscripts. For the sorting and analysis of the peculiar variant readings of the D text, see James D. Yoder, "The Language of the Greek Variants of Codex Bezae Cantabrigiensis" (Th.D. diss., Princeton Theological Seminary, 1958). Yoder's linguistic approach to D is grammatical in nature.

[13]Parker, *Codex Bezae*, 183-4, is concerned with instituting a "correct" methodology that will seriously consider the bilingual tradition of the D text. He also observes that those who assert that D "approximates to the original" become so absorbed "to discredit other texts."

[14]See http://cudl.lib.cam.ac.uk/view/MS-NN-00002-00041/1 (cited 14 August 2013).

[15] See http://codexbezae.perso.sfr.fr/cb/acc.html (cited 14 August 2013).

[16]A couple of websites devoted to biblical textual criticism are http://rosetta.reltech.org/TC/TC.html (cited 14 August 2013) and http://evangelicaltextualcriticism.blogspot.com (cited 14 August 2013).

[17]Eldon J. Epp, "Toward the Clarification of the Term 'Textual Variant'," in *Studies in New Testament Language and Text: Essays in Honour of George D. Kilpatrick on the Occasion of his Sixty-Fifth Birthday*, ed. J. K. Elliott, Supplements to *Novum Testamentum* 44 (Leiden: E. J. Brill, 1976), 153-73; repr. in Eldon J. Epp and Gordon D. Fee, *Studies in the Theory and Method of New Testament Textual Criticism*, Studies and Documents 45 (Grand Rapids: Wm. B. Eerdmans Publishing Co., 1993), 47-61, clarifies that there is a difference between "variant" and "reading." See also Gordon D. Fee, "On the Types, Classification, and Presentation of Textual Variation," in Eldon J. Epp and Gordon D. Fee, *Studies in the Theory and Method of New Testament Textual* Criticism, Studies and Documents 45 (Grand Rapids: Wm. B. Eerdmans Publishing Co., 1993), 62-79. In this essay, "variant" and "reading" are used interchangeably, for both categories that Epp describes are applicable

hierarchy, which is symbolized by the exaltation of Peter; (2) the public status of early Christian women, who were marginalized; and (3) the divine authority of believers as manifested by the presence of the Holy Spirit. These three issues are profitable subjects to investigate in relationship with the way the D text of Acts was shaped in light of the patristic views, sociological milieu, and political climate under which this significant early Christian majuscule text was produced.[18] This essay attempts to address each one of these issues.

---

to the unusual readings of D in various functions. The main interest of this present investigation is the different effect that the D text produces caused by its odd readings. However, the following slight distinction should be pointed out—When the term "variant" is used, the implied stress is on the variant itself as a word, phrase or clause; but when the expression "reading" is used, the assumed emphasis is on the nuance of the reading of the variant. The goal of this essay is not to reconstruct the original text of Acts or to probe whether the D text is original or not but rather to explain the reason for being of D's deviating textual variant readings.

[18]The shaping of the text according to the circumstances of the community where it belongs are well discussed by Bart D. Ehrman, *The Orthodox Corruption of Scripture: The Effect of Early Christological Controversies on the Text of the New Testament* (New York: Oxford University Press, 1993); Kim Haines-Eitzen, *Guardians of Letters: Literacy, Power, and the Transmitters of Early Christian Literature* (New York: Oxford University Press, 2000); Wayne C. Kannaday, *Apologetic Discourse and the Scribal Tradition: Evidence of the Influence of Apologetic Interests on the Text of the Canonical Gospels*, Society of Biblical Literature Text-Critical Studies 5 (Atlanta: SBL, 2004); and D. C. Parker, *The Living Text of the Gospels* (Cambridge: Cambridge University Press, 1997). See also D. C. Parker, "Scribal Tendencies and the Mechanics of Book Production," *Textual Variation: Theological and Social Tendencies?*, ed. D. C. Parker and H. A. G. Houghton, Papers from the Fifth Birmingham Colloquium on the Textual Criticism of the New Testament, Texts and Studies: Third Series 5 (Piscataway: Gorgias Press, 2008). And in the same volume, cf. Ulrich Schmid, "Scribes and Variants–Sociology and Typology," 1-23.

Apostolic Hierarchy: The Case of Peter

The post-apostolic church needed to deal with who should succeed Peter and the apostles.[19] The hierarchy in the church was beginning to be established.[20] As the most prominent among the apostles, Peter became the paradigm of leadership.[21] Clement of Alexandria calls him "the blessed Peter, the chosen, the preeminent, the first of the disciples, for whom alone and Himself the Saviour paid tribute."[22] Tertullian poses a rhetorical question: "Was anything withheld from the knowledge of Peter, who is called 'the rock on which the church should be built,' who also obtained 'the keys of the kingdom of heaven,' with the power of 'loosing and binding in heaven and on earth?'"[23] Whereas Origen notes that "Peter, on whom the Church of Christ is built, against which the gates of hell shall not prevail, left only one epistle of acknowledged genuineness,"[24] Cyprian reminds that "Peter, upon whom by the same Lord the church had been built, speaking one for all, and answering with the voice of the Church, says, 'Lord to whom shall we go? Thou hast the

---

[19] Cf. Georg Strecker, "On the Problem of Jewish Christianity," Appendix 1 of Walter Bauer, *Orthodox and Heresy in Earliest Christianity*, 2nd ed., trans. and ed. Robert Kraft and Gerhard Krodel (Philadelphia: Fortress Press, 1971; repr. Mifflintown: Sigler Press, 1996), 241-85.

[20] The discussion of Elaine Pagels, *The Gnostic Gospels* (New York: Random House, Inc., 1979; repr., London: Penguin Books, 1990), 55-70, is helpful in understanding the background of the development of church hierarchy in the post-apostolic period.

[21] See Robert M. Grant, *Augustus to Constantine: The Thrust of the Christian Movement into the Roman World* (London: William Collins Sons & Co. Ltd., 1971), 184, 222.

[22] Clement of Alexandria, "Salvation of the Rich Man," XXI, in *Ante-Nicene Fathers*, 10 vols., ed. Alexander Roberts and James Donaldson, rev. A. Cleveland Coxe (repr., Peabody: Hendrickson Publishers, 1994), 2:597. Hereafter, all citations from *Ante-Nicene Fathers* will use the abbreviation *ANF*.

[23] Tertullian, "The Prescription Against Heretics," XXII, *ANF*, 3:253.

[24] Origen, "Origen's Commentary on the Gospel of John," V.3, *ANF*, 9:346.

words of eternal life."'"[25] John Chrysostom, in his homilies in Acts, explicitly claims that Peter "as having been put in trust by Christ with the flock, and as having precedence in honor"[26] is "on all occasions he goes about, foremost."[27] It is apparent from the patristic witness that the apostle Peter was indeed considered in Christian antiquity as 'up there' on the ecclesiastical ladder. He was indeed a reflection of the developing hierarchy of the post-apostolic church.

In looking at the D text of Acts, Peter's role is lifted up. Crehan,[28] Epp,[29] Pervo,[30] and CroweTipton[31] have already observed this tendency of exalting Peter. The unusual readings of D in Acts can easily be noted in the critical apparatus of *Nestle-Aland Novum Testamentum Graece*, 28th edition (symbolically known as NA[28]).[32] The peculiar variants in the D text are claimed to be showing a pattern that Peter is exalted in comparison with

---

[25]Cyprian, "The Epistles of Cyprian," LIV.7, *ANF*, 5:341.

[26]John Chrysostom, "A Commentary on the Acts of the Apostles," III, in *Nicene and Post-Nicene Fathers*, 1st series, 14 vols., ed. Philip Schaff (repr. Peabody: Hendrickson Publishers, 1994), 11:18. Henceforth, all quotes from *Nicene and Post-Nicene Fathers*, 1st series, will use the abbreviation *NPNF1st*.

[27]John Chrysostom, "A Commentary on the Acts of the Apostles," XXI, *NPNF1st*, 11:136.

[28]Joseph Crehan, "Peter According to the D-text of Acts," *Theological Studies* 18 (1957): 596-603.

[29]Eldon J. Epp, *The Theological Tendency of Codex Bezae Cantabrigiensis in Acts*, Society for New Testament Studies Monograph Series 3 (Cambridge: Cambridge University Press, 1966), passim.

[30]Richard I. Pervo, "Social and Religious Aspects of the 'Western' Text," in *The Living Text: Essays in Honor of Ernest W. Saunders*, eds. Dennis E. Groh and Robert Jewett (Lanham: University Press of America, 1985), 229-41.

[31]Vaughn Eric CroweTipton, "*Ad Theophilum*: A Socio-Rhetorical Reading of Peter in Acts in Codex Bezae Cantabrigiensis" (Ph.D. diss., Baylor University, 1999), passim.

[32]I also used James D. Yoder, *Concordance to the Distinctive Greek Text of Codex Bezae*, New Testament Tools and Studies 2 (Leiden: E. J. Brill, 1961); and Reuben J. Swanson, ed., *New Testament Greek Manuscripts: Variant Readings Arranged in Horizontal Lines Against Codex Vaticanus: The Acts of the Apostles* (Sheffield: Sheffield Academic Press, 1998) in verifying the unique readings in D.

a base text (i.e., the B text) of NA²⁸.³³ There are three odd variant readings of D in Acts that may be adequately used as representative examples to show how Peter was placed on a pedestal by this textual tradition.³⁴ The first is a change of spelling, second is the addition of a word, and third the omission of a word. Following is a brief discussion of each.

In Acts 1:23, the reading of the D text elevates Peter's authority as the only one who was in charge of selecting the candidates by putting the verb ἵστημι in the singular form ἔστησεν from the plural ἔστησαν. Probably, the original reading of 1:23 was in the plural form. Pervo contends that if the original was indeed plural, there is an inference "that the community put forward two qualified candidates."³⁵ Hence, Pervo continues, that by making the verb singular in D, "Peter alone [becomes] responsible for screening candidates for office."³⁶ The antecedent of the verb then becomes Peter and no longer the apostles in general. Epp's observation is correct when he points out that by rendering the verb in singular form, the allusion is obviously made to Peter.³⁷ He further argues that: "Thus, it is Peter who presents or nominates the two candidates, showing an anxiety in the D text to accentuate the role of Peter in the church government."³⁸

---

³³I utilized the transcription of Scrivener, *Bezae*, for the D text, which is the text analyzed in this study. I used the transcription of Constantinus Tischendorf, ed., *Novum Testamentum Vaticanum, post Angeli Maii aliorumque imperfectos labores ex ipso codice* (Lipsiae: Giesecke et Devrient, 1867) for Codex Vaticanus, 03 or the B text, which is the collating base text.
³⁴I am indebted to the works of Crehan, "Peter;" Epp, *Theological*; Pervo, "Social;" and CroweTipton, "*Ad Theophilum*" for the quick identification of the passages that I am citing from the D text of Acts that exalt Peter.
³⁵Pervo, "Social," 232.
³⁶Ibid.
³⁷Epp, *Theological*, 158.
³⁸Ibid.

The B text in Acts 1:23 is: καὶ ἔστησαν δύο, Ἰωσὴφ τὸν καλούμενον Βαρσαββᾶν, ὃς ἐπεκλήθη Ἰοῦστος καὶ Μαθθίαν, which reads: "And they (the apostles) presented two, Joseph the one called Barsabbas, who is surnamed Justus, and Matthias."

The D text in Acts 1:23 is: καὶ ἔστησεν δύο, Ἰωσὴφ τὸν καλούμενον Βαρνάβαν, ὃς ἐπεκλήθη Ἰοῦστος, καὶ Μαθθίαν, which reads: "And he (Peter) presented two, Joseph the one called Barnabas, who is surnamed Justus, and Matthias."

There is clear indication here that the textual variation between B and D is not just a matter of wrong spelling,[39] but rather a significant change in D to the effect that makes Peter appear as the most prominent apostle. He gains all the attention from the apostles in endorsing the candidates. As Pervo puts it: "Since lots will decide between the two, the people have lost their power."[40] The D text makes Peter the only apostle with authority in making an important selection of the two qualified candidates, which shows his preference even in the presentation of their names.[41]

---

[39]Another seemingly wrong spelling in this verse is D's Βαρνάβαν, Barnabas, as against B's Βαρσαββᾶν, Barsabbas. Probably D was consequently modified against the familiar reading, which is that of the B text. See Jenny Read-Heimerdinger, "Barnabas in Acts: A Study of His Role in the Text of Codex Bezae," *Journal for the Study of the New Testament* 72 (1998): 23-66, who argues that the D text intentionally refers to Barnabas as one of the choices set forth in Acts 1:23. See also the discussion of Josep Rius-Camps and Jenny Read-Heimerdinger, "The Message of Acts in Codex Bezae: A Comparison with the Alexandrian Tradition," *Journal for the Study of the New Testament Supplement Series/Library of New Testament Studies*, 4 vols. (London & New York: T&T Clark/Continuum, 2004-2009), 1:129-31.
[40]Pervo, "Social," 232.
[41]See Rius-Camps and Read-Heimerdinger, *Message*, 1:129-31, who argue that in the D text Peter prefers Joseph the one called Barnabas, who is surnamed Justus than Matthias. However, Peter's plan did not work out the way he wanted the result of the election for the replacement of Judas to be.

In another case of the preserved variant of D, there is the resulting addition of the word πρῶτος in Acts 2:14. This word places Peter as the first among the apostles to speak, hence making him the principal speaker. The inserted word πρῶτος is seen as supporting Peter's primacy among his fellow apostles. Crehan states his observation of Peter's primacy in the insertion of πρῶτος is a kind of "fussy addition by someone who is anxious to show the reader that, although in 2:6 the glossolalia is quite general on the part of the Twelve, and although Peter then stands up to speak with the rest, he is heard first and then the others have their turn."[42] Furthermore, Epp thinks that, along with the other textual variations in the D text in 2:14, the role of Peter becomes even more prominent.[43] This observation can be noticed immediately when D is compared with B.

> The B text in Acts 2:14 is: σταθεὶς δὲ ὁ Πέτρος σὺν τοῖς ἕνδεκα ἐπῆρεν τὴν φωνὴν αὐτοῦ καὶ ἀπεφθέγξατο αὐτοῖς, which reads: "But Peter having stood with the eleven lifted up his voice and declared to them:"
>
> The D text in Acts 2:14 is: τότε σταθεὶς δὲ ὁ Πέτρος σὺν τοῖς δέκα ἀποστόλοις ἐπῆρεν πρῶτος τὴν φωνὴν αὐτοῦ καὶ εἶπεν, which reads: "But then Peter having stood with the ten apostles lifted up his voice first and said:"

The notable difference in the reading of B against D as seen above is intriguing. It is obvious in D that Peter is the foremost person in this scene, that he is not merely "as the spokesman for the apostles but his speech as the first among the other apostolic discourses not cited in the Acts account (cf. 2:42)."[44] Pervo contends that "Peter spoke as chief."[45] Although it may be argued

---

[42] Crehan, "Peter," 597.
[43] Epp, *Theological*, 158-9.
[44] Rius-Camps and Read-Heimerdinger, *Message*, 1:168.
[45] Pervo, "Social," 232. The underline is original.

that, even without the alterations in the D text of Acts 2:14, the B text has already presented the position of the most prominent apostle. However, what is made obvious in the variant readings of the D text is a strengthened distinction between him as the chief and the other ten apostles as under him.[46]

A final example, found in Acts 2:37, is the consequent omission of the word λοιπούς in D. The absence of this word makes Peter detached from the rest of the apostles, who were subsequently decreased in position.[47] This unique reading of D puts the apostles in another group not connected or co-equal with Peter, who becomes the prominent person addressed by the crowd. Epp asserts that the lack of λοιπούς in the D text implies that "there were two ranks, Peter and then the apostles,"[48] which, Epp claims, takes the removal of λοιπούς in the reading of D among other variants in Acts 2:37 as indicating that Peter is taken away from his fellow apostles.[49] Looking at the textual variants in D against B helps to resolve the point.

The B text in Acts 2:37 is: ἀκούσαντες δὲ κατενύγησαν τὴν καρδίαν εἶπόν τε πρὸς τὸν Πέτρον καὶ τοὺς λοιποὺς ἀποστόλους· τί ποιήσωμεν, ἄνδρες ἀδελφοί;, which reads: "And having heard this they were pierced to the

---

[46] The plausible explanation of why D has mentioned only 10 apostles plus Peter is due to the rejection of Matthias by the textual tradition of D. It is also notable that, in any textual tradition of Acts, Matthias is never mentioned again after his election as the twelfth apostle. In the D text, Barnabas and not Barsabbas of the B text is the other candidate that D prefers. This view is what Read-Heimerdinger argues in her article "Barnabas in Acts." For Read-Heimerdinger, if Barnabas of D is the one commonly known as Barsabbas of B and actually the one who lost the election to Matthias, then the apostles made a mistake in rejecting Barnabas, who became prominent in Acts. See also the commentary of Rius-Camps and Read-Heimerdinger, *Message*, 1:178ff., on the implications of the textual alterations in the D text of Acts 2:14.

[47] CroweTipton, "*Ad Theophilum*," 122.
[48] Epp, *Theological*, 159.
[49] Ibid.

heart, then they said to Peter and the rest of the apostles, What should we do men, brothers?"

The D text in Acts 2:37 is: <u>τότε πάντες οἱ συνελθόντες καὶ ἀκούσαντες κατενύγησαν τῇ καρδίᾳ, καί τινες ἐξ αὐτῶν εἶπαν πρὸς τὸν Πέτρον καὶ τοὺς ἀποστόλους· τί οὖν ποιήσομεν, ἄνδρες ἀδελφοί; ὑποδείξατε ἡμεῖν,</u> which reads: "Then all those who were gathering and hearing were pierced in the heart, and some from them said to Peter and the apostles, What therefore should we do men brothers? Show us."

What this case in point above plus the other examples presented earlier show is the tendency of the D text to place Peter on a higher status.[50] The other variants observable in the rendition of D in Acts 2:37 as contributing data indicate that the changes transpired in the text are more consequential and not a scribal error.[51] There are other similar illustrations discussed in the works of scholars quoted above in their studies of the D text of Acts where Peter is put in a pedestal. The examples that I presented are representative of how, through the change of spelling, addition of word(s), or omission of word(s), the reading of D in Acts could relay a different message about Peter's apostolic level.

---

[50]Cf. Rius-Camps and Read-Heimerdinger, *Message*, 1:165-92, on their critical evaluation of "[Acts] 2:14-40: Peter's Two-Part Response and Its Outcome."

[51]Epp, *Theological*, 73-4, explains the reason for the odd readings of D in 2:37 as an anti-Judaic. Epp, *Theological*, 73, maintains the theological bias of D against the Jews:

> Is τινὲς ἐξ αὐτῶν read by D merely because the whole crowd cannot speak to the apostles, as Haenchen says; or is it not more likely that the D text has this and the opening words, τότε πάντες οἱ συνελθόντες, in order to make distinction between the whole crowd, which was cut to the heart and the τινὲς ἐξ αὐτῶν who were ready to follow conviction with action *(ὑποδείξατε ἡμεῖν)*? In this latter case, the text of D minimizes the response from the Jewish audience and does not expect the repentance of all the Jews then listening.

For a long time, the unique readings in the D text were considered scribal errors, with the copyist of this controversial manuscript being branded as careless.[52] But Parker, who was the first to do a thorough study of the whole manuscript, argues that the one who reproduced the manuscript was, in fact, a careful copyist.[53] For him, the issue is not that the scribe of D was careless and committed many errors in his transmission of the text of Acts, but rather the implications of his cautiousness as a scribe. It may be that the exemplar or the *vorlage* of the manuscript that he used in copying what is now known as the D

---

[52] The basic assumption of those who provide explanations for the distinct text of D is that the manuscript is erratic and the scribe is overzealous. See e.g. Frederic G. Kenyon, *Handbook to the Textual Criticism of the New Testament* (London: Macmillan & Co., Ltd., 1901), 79, who views D as a manuscript that "is very full of scribal errors." Another scholar, Alexander Souter, *The Text and Canon of the New Testament* (London: Duckworth, 1912), 27, maintains that: "The vulgarisms and errors in [the D text] forbid us to suppose that it was intended for formal and public reading. Neither side is simply a rendering of the other. There are many discrepancies between the two, and the two texts are in a sense of separate origin." Also, A. T. Robertson, *An Introduction to the Textual Criticism of the New Testament* (London: Hodder & Stoughton, 1925), 87, gives this opinion about D: "The scribe has also made numerous slips in matters of detail, blunders due perhaps partly to the manuscript and partly to the copyist himself who may have known Latin better than he did Greek....A dozen scribes in later time made corrections." George Milligan, *The New Testament and Its Transmission: The Baird Lectures for 1929-30* (London: Hodder and Stoughton, 1932), 52, further points out that the general character of the D text actually "varies largely from the normal type in the way of additions and omissions." Likewise, Robert C. Stone, *The Language of the Latin Text of Codex Bezae with Index Verborum*, Illinois Studies in Language and Literature 30 (Urbana: University of Illinois Press, 1946), 10, makes his observation that: "The scribe of Codex Bezae was frequently careless in the technical execution of his work". Moreover, G. D. Kilpatrick, "The Transmission of the New Testament and Its Reliability," 3-14, in *The Principles and Practice of New Testament Textual Criticism: Collected Essays of G. D. Kilpatrick*, ed. J. K. Elliott, Bibliotheca Ephemeridum Theologicarum Lovaniensium 96 (Leuven: Leuven University Press, 1990); repr. from *Proceedings of the 945th Ordinary General Meeting of the Victoria Institute on 15 April, 1957* (Croydon: Victoria Institute, 1957), 92-101; also *The Bible Translator* 9 (1958): 127-36; 4, states that D is "the most erratic" among the great uncial witnesses to the text of the New Testament.

[53] Parker, *Codex Bezae*, 285, convincingly concludes that: "Codex Bezae is a free text, but is essentially not a careless one."

text already contained those 'free readings.' It could also be possible that, instead of a more controlled reading, alteration of D was a more loosed text. There is freedom in the process of copying the source text, thus there is a difference between being careless and being free in copying. What this analysis of the D text contributes is that it provides a window for a historical-sociological development of the early church. This kind of study reveals how a text of Acts was shaped by the development of the church hierarchy. Peter in the D text of Acts becomes the later paradigm for a bishop.

Public Status: The Case of Women

The D text in Acts preserves textual variations that imply women were marginalized in Christian antiquity.[54] It appears that the attitude of the Church Fathers toward women is reflected in the D text.[55] For example, the Apostolic Constitutions states: "We do not permit our 'women to teach in the church,' but only to pray and hear those that teach; for our Master and Lord, Jesus Himself, when He sent us the twelve to make disciples of the people and of the nations, did nowhere

---

[54]See for example the critical notes of Ben Witherington, "The Anti-Feminist Tendencies of the 'Western' Text in Acts, *Journal of Biblical Literature* 103/1 (1984): 82-4. See also Michael W. Holmes, "Women and the 'Western' Text of Acts," in *The Book of Acts as Church History: Text, Textual Traditions and Ancient Interpretations / Apostelgeschichte als Kirchengeschichte: Text, Texttraditionen und antike Auslegungen*, ed. Tobias Nicklas and Michael Tilly, Beihefte zur Zeitschrift für die neutestamentliche Wissenschaft 120 (Berlin & New York: Walter de Gruyter, 2003), 183-203. And in the same volume, cf. Ann Graham Brock, "Appeasement, Authority, and the Role of Women in the D text of Acts," 205-24. Cf. also Dominika A. Kurek-Chomycz, "Is There an 'Anti-Priscan' Tendency in the Manuscripts? Some Textual Problems with Prisca and Aquila," *Journal of Biblical Literature* 125/1 (2006): 107-28.

[55]Cf. David E. Malick, "The Contribution of Codex Bezae Cantabrigiensis to an Understanding of Women in the Book of Acts," *Journal of Greco-Roman Christianity and Judaism* 4 (2007): 158-83.

send out women to preach."⁵⁶ Clement of Alexandria observes that apostles' "spouses went with them, not as wives, but as sisters, in order to minister to housewives,"⁵⁷ having limited the women in ministry. Gregory the Great asserts that the "canonical authority has decreed, [bishops] are not to leave wives whom they ought to govern chastely."⁵⁸ In addressing the question as to why only Miriam was punished by God and not Aaron when they went against Moses, Irenaeus states: "First, because the woman was the more culpable, since both nature and the law place the woman in a subordinate condition to the man."⁵⁹ Lactantius sees men's power in terms of relationships: "But I speak of those in particular who are in our own power as slaves, children, wives, and pupils; for when we see these offend, we are incited to restrain them."⁶⁰

It is significant that the way the D text's unusual readings relate to women suggests a patriarchal suppression of their roles. Others have already recognized the degradation of women in the D of Acts; among them are Pervo,⁶¹ Menoud,⁶² Fiorenza⁶³ and Parker.⁶⁴ A few examples with different textual variations may

---

⁵⁶"Constitutions of the Holy Apostles," III.i.6, *ANF*, 7:427.

⁵⁷Clement of Alexandria, "The Stromata, or Miscellanies," III.vi, *ANF*, 2:390-1. The English translation from the Latin is mine.

⁵⁸Gregory the Great, "Selected Epistles," LX, in *Nicene and Post-Nicene Fathers*, 2nd series, 14 vols., ed. Philip Schaff and Henry Wace (repr., Peabody: Hendrickson Publishers, 1994), 13:16. Heretofore all references from *Nicene and Post-Nicene Fathers*, 2nd series, will use the abbreviation *NPNF2nd*.

⁵⁹Irenaeus, "Fragments from the Lost Writings of Irenaeus," XXXII, *ANF*, 1:573.

⁶⁰Lactantius, "A Treatise on the Anger of God," XVII, *ANF*, 7:274.

⁶¹Pervo, "Social," 235-40.

⁶²P. H. Menoud, "The Western Text and the Theology of Acts," *Studiorum Novi Testamenti Societas*, Bulletin 2 (1951): 19-32; repr., in *Bulletin of the Studiorum Novi Testamenti Societas*, nos. 1-3 (Cambridge: Cambridge University Press, 1963), 19-32.

⁶³Elisabeth Schüssler Fiorenza, *In Memory of Her: A Feminist Theological Reconstruction of Christian Origins*, 2d ed. (London: SCM Press, 1995), 52.

⁶⁴Parker, *Codex Bezae*, 191-2, recognizes the argument raised by Fiorenza.

help to illustrate the way women were perceived in the post-apostolic period.

The first example is in Acts 1:14. Here in the D text were added words καὶ τέκνοις. The definite article is also placed before γυναιξίν after the preposition σύν. Thus, the reading of D becomes σὺν ταῖς γυναιξὶν καὶ τέκνοις–i.e., "with the women and children."[65] The construction of the D text with these additional words takes the women and kids as one group that is secondary to the male apostles.[66] The addition of the extra qualifying words in this case makes women followers of Jesus as mothers associated with children.[67] Therefore, the status of these women, who were part of the group of disciples, has been degraded as mere housewives or mothers with their children. Fiorenza's point which says "Codex D adds in Acts 1:14 'and children,' so that the women who were gathered with the apostles and Jesus' brethren become the 'wives and families' of the apostles"[68] should be adjusted. The women here in this case cannot be associated with the wives of the apostles in totality. The neutral term "women" is a better word than "wives." Jesus had many women followers that were not relatives of the

---

[65]Contra Walter Thiele, "Eine Bemerkung zu Acts 1.14," *Zeitschrift für die neutestamentliche Wissenschaft* 53/1-2 (1962): 110-11, who points out that the reading of the D text implies that now the women became family members of the apostles and they are no longer taken as a separate entity alongside the apostles anymore. It should be pointed out against Thiele that not all of those women would be wives of the apostles. Jesus had many female disciples, with their children coming with them. It is most unlikely that these women can simply be equated to the wives of the apostles. Moreover, the following verse in Acts 1:15b indicates the presence of about (ὡς) 120 ($\overline{ρκ}$) people. There would be more women in this group than just the family members of the apostles.

[66]See the thoughts and insights of Rius-Camps and Read-Heimerdinger, *Message*, 1:98-106, about the treatment of women in the D text's account of the ascension of Jesus from Olives and the return to Jerusalem of the disciples. See also Curt Niccum, "A Note on Acts 1:14," *Novum Testamentum* 36/2 (1994): 196-9.

[67]Cf. the discussion of Menoud, "Western," 31, fn. 42.

[68]Fiorenza, *In Memory*, 52.

apostles. These women then became inferior as witnesses for Christ, and thus a less important group of followers of Jesus.[69]

Another instance is the dropping of the definite article αἱ (before θυγατέρες) in the D text of Acts 2:17. Thus, D reads καὶ προφητεύσουσιν οἱ υἱοὶ αὐτῶν καὶ θυγατέρες αὐτῶν, which can be literally translated as "and the sons of them and daughters of them will prophesy." Although this may seem to be a scribal oversight or an honest mistake in the process of copying the text, such a deletion can produce a different effect to the reader.[70] If the theory is that the women are degraded in D, then it would make sense to demean the daughters of women in prophesying.[71] This means that, although all the sons will be prophesying, only *some* of the daughters may do so. Pervo's comment is noteworthy: "It may be intentional that by dropping the article D appears to imply that only some of their daughters will prophecy [sic], as opposed to all their sons."[72] Pervo's insight is not impossible; rather, it is highly possible that the dropping of this article before "daughters" indicates the indefinite reference to their potential to prophesy.

The third telling case is the occasion of the reference to the "leading women converts in Thessalonica." Eventually, these prominent women converts of Paul become wives of leading

---

[69]Pagels, *Gnostic*, 81-8, documents how Christian women were suppressed by men. Her reconstruction of the church environment in the post-apostolic Christianity is helpful in understanding why marginalized women are plausibly reflected in the D text of Acts.

[70]It is disappointing that Rius-Camps and Read-Heimerdinger, *Message*, 1:169-70, have not observed the D text's deletion of the definite article before "daughters" in Acts 2:17.

[71]The theory of Deborah M. Gill, "The Disappearance of the Female Prophet: Twilight of Christian Prophecy," in *The Spirit and Spirituality: Essays in Honour of Russell P. Spittler*, eds. Wonsuk Ma and Robert P. Menzies, Journal of Pentecostal Theology Supplement Series 24 (London & New York: T&T Clark/ Continuum, 2004), 178-93, is helpful in imagining this kind of limitation for females to prophesy.

[72]Pervo, "Social," 237. The underlines are original.

men in the D text of Acts 17:4.[73] The variant of the D text may be a suspect for a scribal error due to the different spelling from the B text, which is γυναικῶν in the genitive plural form. And yet, the D text has γυναῖκες in the nominative plural form. Accordingly, the reading of D is modified into καὶ γυναῖκες τῶν πρώτων οὐκ ὀλίγαι–i.e., "and not a few wives of prominent men."[74] Menoud admits that in D the sense of the text is now alluding to wives of the leading men.[75] Pervo suggests that the change of meaning may imply that: "[S]uch converts are quite acceptable, provided that their status comes from their husbands, who will doubtless keep them in line, rather than from their own pedigree or achievements."[76] What becomes obvious in the alteration of spelling is the indication that women are subject to the men, even if they are prominent in their society. Once again, in this illustrative example in the D text, the women are marginalized and put under the shadow of men.

The above examples are significant in pointing out how women can be degraded even in the readings of NT text. Adding his weight to Fiorenza's claim, Parker maintains that the D text preserves "clear instances of the way in which all changes have a theological significance" and "how the text has been modified as

---

[73]Kim Haines-Eitzen, *The Gendered Palimpsest: Women, Writing, and Representation in Early Christianity* (New York: Oxford University Press, 2012), 90-1, includes Acts 17:12 and 34 with 17:4 in her discussion of the eventual alterations in the D text. Haines-Eitzen, *Gendered*, 91, provides an insightful point to ponder:
> These are subtle changes textually, but they have significant implications for interpretation. I am not suggesting here that an "egalitarian" text has been reformulated into one that promotes subordination; rather, that the different readings may well betray different conceptions about the roles of women and permit the text to function toward different ends.

[74]See Rius-Camps and Read-Heimerdinger, *Message*, 3:311-7, for an investigation of the textual matters of Acts 17:4 as well as the surrounding contextual and textual study of the section in Acts where it belongs.

[75]Menoud, "Western," 30.

[76]Pervo, "Social," 238.

a consequence of an issue within the early church."⁷⁷ The sociological structure of men and women in the early church is reflected in the D text of Acts.⁷⁸ Harris suggests Montanism's influence on D,⁷⁹ but this suggestion cannot be a plausible explanation for the unique readings of the Spirit passages in this controversial text. This is so because, although women were participating freely in prophesying in the Montanist movement, they were degraded in the textual tradition of D. Harris' theory is highly implausible, for the text is not supportive of female prophets.⁸⁰

Divine Authority: The Case of the Spirit

The post-apostolic testimony linking the Holy Spirit and heavenly authority is significant. The manifestations and operations of the Spirit of God in the life and ministry of the early Christians indicate that they had received divine power. Of particular interest is the prophetic or inspired speech experience with the Spirit. Athenagoras affirms that: "The Holy Spirit Himself also, which operates in the prophets, we assert to be an effluence of God, flowing from Him, and returning back again like a beam of the sun."⁸¹ The notion that "the mouth of the Lord the Holy Spirit has spoken these things" in Clement of Alexandria acknowledges the authority that the prophetic

---

⁷⁷Parker, *Codex Bezae*, 192.
⁷⁸Cf. L. Curt Niccum and Jeffrey W. Childers, "'Anti-Feminist' Tendency in the 'Western' Text of Acts?," in *Essays on Women in Earliest Christianity*, 2 vols. ed. Carroll D. Osburn (Joplin, MO: College Press, 1993-1995; repr. Eugene, OR: Wipf & Stock Publishers, 2007), 1:469-92.
⁷⁹See J. Rendel Harris, *Codex Bezae: A Study of the So-called Western Text of the New Testament*, Text and Studies: Contributions to Biblical and Patristic Literature, ed. J. Armitage Robinson, vol. 2/1 (Cambridge: Cambridge University Press, 1891), particularly 148-59, 191-214, 226ff. for his exploration of Montanist evidence.
⁸⁰So is the conclusion of Menoud, "Western," 30.
⁸¹Athenagoras, "A Plea for the Christians," X, *ANF*, 2:133.

experience of the Spirit brings with it, and every word will be fulfilled.[82] Origen also recognizes that the outpouring of the Holy Spirit after Christ's ascension, wherein "before that, [the gift of the Holy Spirit] was upon the prophets alone, and upon a few individuals" and then "the prediction of the prophet Joel was fulfilled," stressing the prophetic role of the Spirit.[83] In addition, the idea of authority due to the retention of the Holy Spirit in the apostles' lives is explained this way by Novatian: "He is therefore one and the same Spirit who was in the prophets and in the apostles, except that in the former, He was occasional, in the latter always."[84] Thus, as Basil the Great puts it: "For there is not even one single gift which reaches creation without the Holy Ghost; when not even a single word can be spoken in defence of Christ except by them that are aided by the Spirit."[85]

Among the other books of the NT that are included in the D manuscript, the Spirit passages were modified the most in Acts. It is obvious that His role in the apostolic church was important. However, in the D text, the changes made in those passages concerning the Holy Spirit are related to issues of spiritual authority and prophetic speech[86] which attracted much attention from scholars. Observations about the variant readings in these passages have been noted in the works of Epp,[87] Black,[88] Read-

---

[82]Clement of Alexandria, "Exhortation to the Heathen," IX, *ANF*, 2:195.

[83]Origen, "De Principiis," II.vii.2, *ANF*, 4:285.

[84]Novatian, "A Treatise of Novatian Concerning the Trinity," XXIX, *ANF*, 5:640.

[85]Basil the Great, "De Spiritu Sancto," XXIV.lv, *NPNF2nd*, 8:35.

[86]On the subject of Spirit, authority, and prophecy, see Laura Nasrallah, *"An Ecstasy of Folly": Prophecy and Authority in Early Christianity*, Harvard Theological Studies 52 (Cambridge: Harvard University Press, 2003).

[87]Epp, *Theological*, passim.

[88]Matthew Black, "The Holy Spirit in the Western Text of Acts," in *New Testament Textual Criticism, Its Significance for Exegesis: Essays in Honour of Bruce M. Metzger*, ed. Eldon J. Epp and Gordon D. Fee (Oxford: Clarendon Press, 1981), 159-70.

Heimerdinger,[89] and Pervo.[90] Three particular example verses will be treated here relative to the concept of authority in relationship to the presence of the Spirit manifested through inspired utterance.

The first one is the addition of τῷ ἁγίῳ in D to clarify the reference of the Spirit as the 'Holy' Spirit in Acts 6:10. This is important, as in D, it underscores the spiritual authority of Stephen. The notable thing about this interpolation or expansion in the D text is that it formulates an unambiguously clear reference to the Holy Spirit.[91] Epp puts the purpose of the addition of τῷ ἁγίῳ in proper perspective for Stephen as follows:

> In the D-text here, at one and the same time, Stephen is enhanced and the Jewscome off in a poorer light. Notice, first of all, that in the D-text there is no doubt that Stephen is inspired in speech: τῷ ἁγίῳ post πνεύματι. The additional material in D gives the reason for the Jews' inability to withstand his wisdom and inspired speech: 'Because they were refuted by him with all forthrightness.'[92]

In other words, the presence of the Spirit in Stephen's confrontation with the Jews reflects the spiritual authority that he had–so much so that this authority seen in Stephen is coupled with wisdom. The following suggestion of Ruis-Camps and Read-Heimerdinger in the Acts 6:10 reading of D is noteworthy:

---

[89] Jenny Read-Heimerdinger, *The Bezan Text of Acts: A Contribution of Discourse Analysis to Textual Criticism*, Journal for the Study of the New Testament Supplement Series 236 (London: Sheffield Academic Press, 2002), especially 145-72.
[90] Pervo, "Social," 232-5.
[91] Black, "Holy Spirit," 161.
[92] Epp, *Theological*, 132-3.

The explicit mention of the adjective 'holy' by the Bezan text is due to no mere scribal fondness for the adjective nor is it simply the reflection of a theological tendency. Its purpose is to underline the prophetic nature of Stephen's speech which transmitted not his own thoughts but those of God. Within the scheme of the narrative, it demonstrates how faithfully Stephen puts into practice the teaching of Jesus to his disciples that they were to rely on the Holy Spirit to answer their accusers.[93]

Read-Heimerdinger notes that the case of the D text adding the adjective "Holy" to the Spirit only happened in Acts 6:10 and in 8:18.[94] In both cases is the remark about the Holy Spirit "in relation to a specific event where ἅγιον is an expression either of the prophetic context or of the insistence on the identity of the Spirit."[95] Here, the usage of the Holy Spirit is in a prophetic context and His identity is specified. These notions of the Spirit fit well with the theory of Nasrallah that the discourse on the prophetic in the early church and post-apostolic Christianity is primarily to establish spiritual authority.[96] It is possible then to point out that the insertion of τῷ ἁγίῳ in the D text of Acts 6:10 is to place an unambiguous paradigm of spiritual authority on Stephen.

The next instance is the insertion of ἐν πνεύματι in the D text of Acts 15:7, which gives the divine authority to Peter. The Spirit is associated with ecclesiastical authority in this particular case.[97]

---

[93]Rius-Camps and Read-Heimerdinger, *Message*, 2:41.
[94]Read-Heimerdinger, *Bezan*, 167.
[95]Ibid.
[96]Nasrallah, *Ecstasy*.
[97]Cf. Bruce M. Metzger, *A Textual Commentary on the Greek New Testament*, 2d ed. (New York: American Bible Society, 1994), 378.

The distinctive reading of D here is rendered as ἀνέστησεν ἐν πνεύματι Πέτρος–i.e., "Peter rose up in the Spirit." It is noteworthy that Black even thinks that the reading of D here is original.[98] However, it is more probable that the ἐν πνεύματι is actually an addition that enhances Peter's spiritual authority.[99] The analysis of Pervo sheds light as follows: "'Western' variants have James 'rise and speak' in v 13, thus completing the parallel with Peter, v 7. This similarity...heightens the contrasting imputation of inspiration to Peter (by adding [ἐν] πνεύματι in v 7). In v 12, the πρεσβύτεροι formally endorse Peter's statement. With such compliant presbyters Ignatius would have been well pleased."[100]

In this kind of explanation, the principle that Peter stands for becomes "pneumatic" utterance because of the authority of the Holy Spirit.[101] The position of Peter is placed above the status of James because in the D text of Acts 15:7 he has stood up by the influence of the Spirit while James spoke to find a middle ground.[102] Consequently, in the way D presents Peter in its peculiar reading in Acts 15:7 he becomes preeminent among others.[103]

A concluding example is Paul being guided by the Holy Spirit in the D text of Acts 20:3, instead of making a decision himself in his travel plans. This is clearly the case as the reading of D in Acts 20:3 is εἶπεν δὲ τὸ πνεῦμα αὐτῷ ὑποστρέφειν διὰ τῆς Μακεδονίας,–i.e., "but the Spirit said to him to return through

---

[98]Black, "Holy Spirit," 162.
[99]Cf. Read-Heimerdinger, *Bezan*, 160. Cf. also Epp, *Theological*, 104.
[100]Pervo, "Social," 232-3.
[101]Epp, *Theological*, 104.
[102]Ibid.
[103]What is apparent in Peter's general representation in D is that he is chief among other apostles. In this particular case in Acts 15:7 Peter has a good grasp of the dispute because of the guidance of the Holy Spirit. See the investigation of the issue from the perspective of the D text in Rius-Camps and Read-Heimerdinger, *Message*, 3:194ff.

Macedonia."[104] Such a variant reading makes the Holy Spirit the one who dictates to Paul.[105] This is similar to prophetic encounter of the Spirit of God. The reading of D is unlike the B text, which makes Paul the one who is determined to return through Macedonia. Black picks up this important difference but maintains that the variant preserved in D is Luke's style.[106] In any case, whether the reading of D is Lukan or not, it is distinct from B. The D text in Acts 20:3 brings a clear divine prophetic authority in Paul, who is guided by the Spirit in his decision-making.[107]

---

[104] Cf. the analysis of Rius-Camps and Read-Heimerdinger, *Message*, 4:85ff., on Paul's intentions and the D text's emphasis on the influence of the Holy Spirit in Paul's travel plans.

[105] Metzger, *Textual*, 420-1.

[106] Black, "Holy Spirit," 165.

[107] Cf. Epp, *Theological*, 143-4; and Read-Heimerdinger, *Bezan*, 233. Earlier, in the beginning part of the previous chapter, Paul's divine authority in praying for the disciples to receive the gift of the Spirit supports the view that is advanced here. It is notable in Acts 19:1-2 the way the coming of the Holy Spirit to the followers of John the Baptist is introduced. There is clear indication in verse 1 how the D text expands on the Spirit's direction to Paul: Θέλοντος δὲ τοῦ Παύλου κατὰ τὴν ἰδίαν βουλὴν πορεύεσθαι εἰς Ἰεροσόλυμα εἶπεν αὐτῷ τὸ πνεῦμα ὑποστρέφειν εἰς τὴν Ἀσίαν, διελθὼν δὲ τὰ ἀνωτερικὰ μέρη ἔρχεται εἰς Ἔφεσον. And thus, the authority of Paul in laying hands to the followers of John the Baptist in 19:6 brings out an interesting reading in D. The omission of the article τὰς in D (and in this case it is similar to B and other important witnesses) from the plural noun χεῖρας emphasizes the quality of the process of laying of hands rather than the definiteness of Paul's act. This understanding of a resulting rendition of the apostle's hand as anarthrous from the point of view of the authority of Paul to pray for the disciples is further strengthened by the replacement of the well supported reading of ἦλθε in terms of the coming of the Spirit after the laying on of Paul's hand with εὐθέως ἐπέπεσεν. This reading of D is notably stressing the immediacy of the reception of the Spirit. It is a straight falling of the Spirit onto the Baptist's followers in Ephesus. But the immediate reception of the Spirit by the Ephesian disciples is not really the emphasis. Rather, it is actually in the compound verb ἐπιπίπτω that is used by the D text. It is the same word that is used in Acts 8:16, 10:44, and 11:15. All of these instances are connected to Peter's authority to bring down the Spirit to the believers. It indicates here in the D text of Acts 19:6 that Paul has the clear authority to let the Spirit fall on the people that he lays his hand upon (in the same manner as that of Peter).

The way D narrates the stories of Stephen, Peter, and Paul as experiencing the prophetic occurrence of the Holy Spirit makes them a carrier of a special kind of spiritual authority. It has been posited that the text of Acts could be posthumously published into two versions, as argued earlier by Blass[108] and revived by Strange.[109] There is also that tension between those who contend that a theological tendency exists in the D text of Acts, including Crehan,[110] Epp,[111] and Pervo,[112] versus Ropes[113] and Barrett,[114] who believe that the emphasis the others see as a theological tendency is already there, thus nothing new is added. Rather than a theological tendency, Ropes and Barrett claim that the unique readings in D are simply for clarification, emphasis, or expansion. Nonetheless, the obvious difference that exists should not be overlooked when the story of Acts is read in the textual tradition of D against that of the popular reading represented by the B text. This means that the distinctive Holy Spirit passages in the D text of Acts make the stories different from the usually preferred textual tradition reflected in NA[28].

---

[108]Friedrich Blass, ed., *Acta apostolorum sive Lucae ad Theophilum liber alter. Editio philologica. apparatu critico, commentario perpetuo, indice verborum illustrata* (Göttingen: Vandenhoeck & Ruprecht, 1895).

[109]W. A. Strange, *The Problem of the Text of Acts*, Society for New Testament Studies Monograph Series 71 (Cambridge: Cambridge University Press, 1992), passim.

[110]Crehan, "Peter."

[111]Epp, *Theological*.

[112]Pervo, "Social."

[113]Ropes, *Text of Acts*, ccxxxiii.

[114]C. K. Barrett, "Is There a Theological Tendency in Codex Bezae?," in *Text and Interpretation: Studies in the New Testament Presented to Matthew Black*, ed. Ernest Best and R. McL. Wilson (Cambridge: Cambridge University Press, 1979), 15-27.

Conclusion

Issues in Christian antiquity, especially during the time of the Church Fathers, can be observed as reflected in the D text of Acts. Studies of textual variants can be a 'window' into looking at the socio-political world of post-apostolic Christianity. It has been suggested that there is a theological tendency in Acts. Harris is perhaps the first to suggest such a tendency when he claimed that D was a Montanist and Marcionite document.[115] However, it is Epp who popularized the anti-Judaic tendency in the D text in his study of Acts.[116] Rice in Luke verified Epp's view.[117] I also did my own studies of the D text, focusing on the Lukan parables that resulted in basic agreement with the central thesis of Epp and Rice.[118]

The outcome of the studies in D that leads to the assumption of a theological tendency in its textual tradition has been both affirmed due to its textual digression[119] and challenged because of

---

[115]Harris, *Codex Bezae*, especially 148-59, 191-214, 226-8, for his investigation of the Montanist evidence; and 226-34, 235-40, for his exploration of the Marcionite readings in the D text of Acts.

[116]Epp, *Theological*. See also the more recent reflection of Eldon J. Epp, "Anti-Judaic Tendencies in the D-text of Acts: Forty Years of Conversation," in *The Book of Acts as Church History: Text, Textual Traditions and Ancient Interpretations / Apostelgeschichte als Kirchengeschichte: Text, Texttraditionen und antike Auslegungen*, ed. Tobias Nicklas and Michael Tilly, Beihefte zur Zeitschrift für die neutestamentliche Wissenschaft 120 (Berlin & New York: Walter de Gruyter, 2003), 111-46. Cf. Philip Maertens, "Vos pères' ou 'nos pères': la question de l'appartenance ethnique dans le texte grec du livre des Actes du Codex Bezae (D 05)," *New Testament Studies* 58/3 (2012): 401-15.

[117]George E. Rice, "The Alteration of Luke's Tradition by the Textual Variants in Codex Bezae" (Ph.D. diss., Case Western Reserve University, 1974).

[118]Roli Garcia dela Cruz, "Allegory, Mimesis and the Text: Theological Moulding of Lukan Parables in Codex Bezae Cantabrigiensis" (Ph.D. thesis, University of Birmingham, 2004).

[119]Kurt Aland and Barbara Aland, *The Text of the New Testament: An Introduction to the Critical Editions and to the Theory and Practice of Modern Textual Criticism*, 2d ed. trans., Erroll F. Rhodes (Grand Rapids: Wm. B.

its anachronistic approach.[120] However, few would question that, in the process of textual transmission, the copyists, readers, bishops, or any tradent of the text will effectually leave their stamps on it because they need to interpret the text that they transmit.[121] Thus, the approach used in this essay seems both appropriate and safe. The methodology of comparing B as the base text due to its controlled textual transmission against the D text, which is known for a free textual tradition, is valid.

The result of studying the peculiar readings of D in light of the situation in the patristic period is fruitful, supplying insights into the socio-political tension within the ancient Christian communities. Although the D manuscript copy could be safely dated at about 400 CE, the textual tradition of the D text should be much earlier.[122] Accordingly, it is proper to assume that there

---

Eerdmans Publishing Co., 1989), 69, states: "The text found in Codex Bezae Cantabrigiensis (D) of the fifth century, however, represents (in its exemplar) the achievement of an outstanding early theologian of the third/fourth century."

[120] Parker, *Codex Bezae*, 189-93.

[121] See Harry Y. Gamble, *Books and Readers in the Early Church: A History of Early Christian Texts* (New Haven: Yale University Press, 1995). See also Anthony Grafton and Megan Williams, *Christianity and the Transformation of the Book: Origen, Eusebius and the Library of Caesarea* (Cambridge: Harvard University Press, 2006).

[122] See Parker, *Codex Bezae*, 30, 35, 281, who based his dating of 400 CE on palaeographical ground. Cf. the palaeographical discussion of the date of the Latin text by Bernhard Bischoff, *Latin Palaeography: Antiquity and the Middle Ages*, trans. Dáibhí Ó Cróinín and David Ganz (Cambridge: Cambridge University Press, 1990), 72-5. Cf. also Stone, *Language*, 67-8, who put the date of D in the fifth-century based on his analysis of the Latin text of d. For further discussion on the fifth-century dating of Codex D, see F. C. Burkitt, "The Date of Codex Bezae," *Journal of Theological Studies* 3 (1901-1902): 501-13; J. Chapman, "The Order of the Gospels in the Parent of Codex Bezae," *Zeitschrift für die neutestamentliche Wissenschaft* 6 (1905): 339-46; Ropes, *Text of Acts*, lvii-lviii; E. A. Lowe, "A Note on the Codex Bezae," in *Palaeographical Papers 1907-1965*, 2 vols., ed. Ludwig Bieler (Oxford: Clarendon Press, 1972), 1:224-8; repr. from *Bulletin of the Bezan Club* 4 (1927): 9-14; Scrivener, *Bezae*, xiv-vi. Cf. Kurt Aland, "The Significance of the Papyri for Progress in New Testament Research," in *The Bible in Modern Scholarship: Papers Read at the 100th Meeting of the Society of Biblical Literature, December 28-30, 1964*, ed. James Philip Hyatt (London: Carey

are several scribes, editors, or tradents who placed their imprints on the evolving textual tradition of D.[123] Furthermore, there are already layers of traditions behind the distinctive readings of the D text as we have it now in its textual form. As a result, the odd readings that are currently observed in the D of Acts were already fossilized within the textual tradition of the manuscript.

An understanding of the issues that the Church Fathers faced in the early centuries of the church will facilitate an appreciation of the developing nature of the unusual variants in the D text of Acts.[124] Hence, the issues facing the church of its time shaped the D text of Acts exegetically and theologically. Some of those issues that influenced D are the subjects dealt with in this paper– namely, the development of the ecclesiastical hierarchy with Peter as the model paradigm, the marginalization of women, and the spiritual authority associated with the presence of the Holy Spirit.

Kingsgate Press, 1966), 334, who insinuates a sixth-century date. Cf. also K. Sneyders de Vogel, "Le codex Bezae est-il d'origine sicilienne?," *Bulletin of the Bezan Club* 4 (1927): 10-3, who views D from a seventh-century dating. See also Hermann Josef Frede, *Altlateinische Paulus-Handschriften*, Aus der Geschichte der lateinischen Bibel 4 (Freiburg: Verlag Herder, 1964), 18-9, especially footnote 4, that D "im 4. Jahrhundert entstanden ist." Cf. Bonifatius Fischer, "Das Neue Testament in lateinischer Sprache," in *Alten Übersetzungen*, 41 footnote 133, who thinks that D has a fourth-century date when he insinuates: "Wenn der gelegentliche Einfluß der Vulgata-Evangelien sicher nachgewiesen wäre, dann hätte man damit einen *terminus post quem* gewonnen, nämlich das Jahr 383."

[123] Parker, *Codex Bezae*, passim.

[124] Cf. Bart D. Ehrman, "The Use and Significance of Patristic Evidence for NT Textual Criticism," in *New Testament Textual Criticism, Exegesis and Church History: A Discussion of Methods*, ed. Barbara Aland and Joël Delobel, Contributions to Biblical Exegesis and Theology 7 (Kampen: Kok Pharos Publishing House, 1994), 118-35.

Baptism in the Holy Spirit vs Spirit Possession in the Lowland Philippines: Some Considerations for Discipleship

by Dave Johnson

Introduction

"**If** I ask the Lord to baptize me in the Holy Spirit, is it possible that a demon might possess me instead?" This is the question I have heard asked on more than one occasion by Filipinos seeking the Spirit's infilling, highlighting the need for a careful analysis of the Philippine animism as it relates to biblical teaching on the baptism in the Holy Spirit. What is the Philippine worldview that drives this and other related questions and what are the implications of this worldview for discipleship and teaching regarding Spirit baptism?

Numerous writers have indicated that the Pentecostal/Charismatic sector is the fast growing, with researchers like Peter Wagner attributing at least some of the growth to the fact that Pentecostalism, with its emphasis on power encounter, is the part of Christianity that best deals with the animistic worldviews that are prevalent throughout the Majority World.[1] This fact further underscores the need for clear biblical teaching that

---

[1] C. Peter Wagner, "A Church Growth Perspective on Pentecostal Missions," in *Called and Empowered: Global Mission in Pentecostal Perspective* ed. Murray A. Dempster, Byron D. Klaus and Douglas Petersen, 265-284 (Peabody, MA: Hendrickson Publishers, 1991), 271-272.

addresses these world view issues within the cultural framework of animists.

This article will focus on how Filipinos understand the baptism in the Holy Spirit within their cultural framework. It will also include an attempt to contextualize biblical teaching regarding Holy Spirit baptism. To do this, I will attempt to fulfill two components so necessary for contextualization: faithfulness to the biblical text and an accurate exegesis for Filipino culture. Dean Gilliland writes that "contextualization declares that truth, however absolute, cannot be abstracted from the particularity of the context."[2] The understanding here is that the message of the gospel, including Spirit baptism, must be relevant and understandable within the cultural framework of the receptor because, regardless of how the message is communicated, the receptors will interpret it according to their worldview. If the Gospel message is not conceptualized within that framework, the distortion of the message and the resultant syncretism and heresy are virtually guaranteed.

Research Questions

This study will attempt to answer two simple questions. First, when Filipinos from an animistic background hear about the Spirit baptism, how do they understand it within their worldview? Second, what does the Bible say about the baptism of the Holy Spirit that answers the concerns of Filipinos?

Scope and Limitations

Virtually all writers in the field agree that the similarities between the lowland cultures of the Philippines greatly outweigh

---

[2]Dean Gilliland, ed., *The Word Among Us: Contextualizing Theology for Mission Today*. (Dallas: Word Publishing, 1988), 59.

the dissimilarities, mainly due to nearly 450 years of Roman Catholicism that has deeply impacted the lowlands. Also, the author's nearly twenty years of missionary experience in the lowlands confirms that although this field research is limited to the Waray people of Leyte and Samar, this essay is relevant throughout the lowlands.

Much research is available on the Filipino's view of the spirit world and the activities of the spirit beings that occupy it. Likewise, the literature available on a Pentecostal understanding of the Holy Spirit is numerous. This essay will focus primarily on issues related to Holy Spirit Baptism, which is defined here as subsequent to salvation and is evidenced by speaking in unknown tongues and with the purpose of empowering the believer to live a sanctified life and be an effective witness for Christ.

The Filipino Religious Worldview in Relation to Spirit Baptism[3]

A brief survey of the Filipino religious worldview brings into focus how Filipinos may view Holy Spirit baptism. While most Filipinos are Roman Catholic, the Filipino worldview is heavily animistic, leading one scholar to describe it as "split-level Christianity."[4] For Melba Maggay, a Filipino social anthropologist, this syncretized Catholicism is mainly a "transaction of powers, between the various spirit beings and humans."[5] Like animism the world over, Filipinos view gaining,

---

[3]Because of the similarities of the lowland cultures' worldview, they will be referred to as a singular whole as a simple writing convention.

[4]Jaime Bulatao, S.J., *Split-Level Christianity* (Manila: Ateneo de Manila Press, 1956), n.p.

[5]Melba Maggay, 1999, "Towards Sensitive Engagement with Filipino Indigenous Conciousness." *International Review of Missions* 87 (346): 362.

using, channeling and maintaining supernatural power as the primary reason for participation in animistic practices.

The Three-Tier Occupants of the Spirit World

A brief worldview sketch is in order here to give some backdrop to the problems Filipinos may face when they try to understand Spirit baptism biblically. Using Paul Hiebert's organic, three-tier analogy,[6] Filipinos perceive God alone as at the top, but he is often seen as unapproachable, at least in a direct way. The middle tier is comprised of the Virgin Mary and the Catholic saints who are perceived as much closer to people, attentive to their needs and prayers and interceding before God on their behalf. Virtually every town in the lowlands has an annual fiesta with special masses said in honor of the saints. These fiestas are often accompanied by a religious procession where images of saints are carried in the backs of open vehicles such as pickup trucks and carts. In January, 2014, for example, the annual fiesta and procession of the image of the Black Nazarene in Quiapo drew an estimated crowd of twelve million according to at least one newscaster. Many surged around the image trying to touch it in belief that it would bring healing or other kinds of blessings. By comparison, the estimated crowd at the World Youth Day in the same area of Manila featuring Pope John Paul II in 1995 drew an estimated international crowd of only four million. This example serves to confirm that the appeal of animism remains strong even after 450 years of Catholicism and must be reckoned with in matters of discipleship of believers regarding the Holy Spirit and the spirits.

---

[6]Paul Hiebert, "The Flaw of the Excluded Middle," in *Perspectives on the World Christian Movement,"* *4th* ed.407-414, (William Carey Library: Pasadena, CA, 2009), 410.

Besides Mary and the saints, this second tier is also occupied by an army of spirits, including ancestors, whose names and classifications vary from region to region. Some are regarded as always good and others are always perceived to be evil. The vast majority, however, are perceived as amoral and capricious and can be manipulated through sacrifices, incantations and rituals to do either good or evil, depending on the mood of the spirit or the desire of human trying to engage the spirit's attention. *For our study, the most significant issue regarding this second tier is that the Waray people among whom I conducted field research placed the Holy Spirit in this category.*[7] Hiebert's bottom or third tier is occupied by humans, animals and plants.

While these categories can be neatly drawn for descriptive purposes for outsiders, the lines are almost purely academic and are often blurred or non-existent in the minds of the local people. Therefore, one must be careful in drawing the lines too sharply. However, the fact that the Holy Spirit may not be considered to be in the same category as God may be significant to many Filipinos.

Spiritual Practitioners and their Spiritual Power

Some understanding of Filipino spiritual practitioners may shed light on how Filipinos might view ministry in the power of the Holy Spirit. There are a multitude of classifications and sub-classifications of spirit world practitioners that range from fortunetellers to faith healers and everything in between, most of whom fall outside of the parameters of this study. Yet the primary purpose of all of them is to maintain contact with the

---

[7]Dave Johnson, *A Study of the Animistic Practices of the Waray People of the Leyte-Samar Region of the Philippines.* (M.A. thesis, Asia Pacific Theological Seminary, 2000), 27.

spirit world and try to manipulate the spirits through sacrifices, incantations and other rituals to benefit mankind.

One of the ways spiritual practitioners channel spiritual power is through spirit possession, suggesting that when someone speaks of the baptism of the Holy Spirit as an enduement of power, Filipinos easily associate power with spirit possession. In Philippine animistic practice, the first purpose of spirit possession is to bring healing; the second is for the purpose of trans channeling messages from the spirit world and is often associated with divination. A third instance of spirit possession is also common—when people become spirit possessed without intending to do so.

Intentional Spirit Possession

In doing the field work for my master's thesis, several spiritists spoke of going into an altered state of consciousness (ASC) where they would become spirit possessed in order to heal their patients.[8] My assistants and I were able to observe this phenomenon on two separate occasions. One of the spiritists was a medium, who was using a Bible to trans channel messages from the spirit world in a healing meeting and the other was known as a psychic healer. Psychic healers are a sub classification of spiritists that are able to place their hands inside the body of the patient and perform "surgery" without the aid of any medical instrument, but that can only be done in an ASC. Jaime Bulatao reflects the non-dualistic Filipino worldview when he suggests that the ability to go into a trance is a divine gift, allowing the person to step into the spirit world, which really isn't separated from the natural one.[9] Leonardo Mercado adds that after the

---

[8] Johnson, 2000, 88.
[9] Jaime Bulatao, *Phenomena and Their Interpretation: Land Mark Essays, 1597-1989*, (Manila: Ateneo de Manila University Press, 1992), 67.

medium returns to a normal state of consciousness, he or she cannot remember what they said while they were in the ASC, and my research bore this out.[10]

Several spiritists to whom I spoke during my research claimed that a spirit takes possession of them in order to heal people. When the healing session is done, the spirit leaves. All of this raises critical issues related to a theology of the Holy Spirit in the Philippine context. Where these spirits come from and who they work for are questions seldom asked by the Waray, but are critical in light of Scripture.

Unintentional Spirit Possession

As mentioned earlier, spirit possession is not only pursued with purpose, but it also may be unintentional. When asked if people could be controlled by an evil spirit, 81.1 percent (369 out of 462 respondents) of the ordinary Waray people responded affirmatively and 85.4 percent (420 out of 492 respondents) of the AG sample population agreed with them.[11] The difference between the two groups here was not significant, (χ^2=3.09 < $F_{crit.}$ 3.84). What is clear in the responses here is that the belief that demons can possess people is widespread among ordinary people and believers alike. However, when interviewed about the Waray's opinion of evil spirits, 88.1 percent of the general population and 98.6 percent of the AG said it was bad.[12] When asked why this was so, over 98 percent of the respondents said it was because it gave control of one's body and mind to demons

---

[10]Leonardo Mercado, *Inculturation and* Theology. Manila: Divine Word Publications, 1992, 110.

[11]Dave Johnson, *An Analysis of the Worldview and Religious Beliefs of the Waray People of the Philippine and the Factors Leading to the Growth of the Assemblies of God in the Region With Implications For the Development of a Contextual Theology for the Waray,* D.Miss Dissertation, Asian Graduate School of Theology, 2004, 180.

[12]Ibid., 181.

and because it would involve losing one's consciousness and not knowing what was going on while the spirit was in control.[13] Many respondents said that the demon possessed walk and talk differently, describing such things as removing their clothes, talking incoherently with bad words, becoming stronger than normal, mental derangement, loss of consciousness, and going crazy. I personally witnessed this kind of behavior once when a lady at an evangelistic rally we were conducting came up to me, started tugging on my shirt and continually repeating John 14:6 in flawless English. I sensed that there was demonic activity going on, but felt I should wait until later in the evening to deal with it. Later a pastor and I went to her house, but were not allowed inside because she was ranting and raving—which we could clearly hear from outside. We were told that she owed someone a considerable about of money and when she was unable to pay, the person went to a sorcerer and had a curse put on her. We prayed for her deliverance, but could do nothing more. The next morning the pastor went back to visit and was told that she was delivered from the demon, but had left town.

Fear then, of evil spirits, is widespread and, given the Philippine worldview, understandable. Many Filipinos respond to this fear by wearing an amulet which, in many cases, is seen as more effective if blessed by the local Catholic priest. Others go to the priest or pastor for special prayer, believing that the one who claims to represent God has greater spiritual power than ordinary laymen.[14]

---

[13] Ibid., 182.
[14] Ibid., 177.

How Filipinos View the Holy Spirit and Spirit Baptism

In my master's thesis research, I discovered that the Waray spiritual practitioners regarded the Holy Spirit as one of a number of spirits (in the second tier) that could be used for healing and did not regard him as the Spirit of God who is *sui generis*, wholly other.[15] In my doctoral research I asked members or adherents (known as sympathizers in the Philippines) what they knew about the Holy Spirit before they came to Christ and what they know now.

TABLE 1[16]
BELIEFS ABOUT THE HOLY SPIRIT

	Before Christ (477 Resp.)		After Christ (478 Resp.)	
	Yes	No	Yes	No
1. I knew little or nothing about the Holy Spirit.	397 (83.2%)	80 (16.8%)	124 (25.9%)	354 (74.1%)
2. That the Holy Spirit is just like the other spirits in that he can heal people through the spiritist.	203 (42.9%)	270 (52.1%)	57 (11.9%)	421 (88.1%)
3. That the Holy Spirit is God.	359 (75.7%)	115 (24.3%)	463 (97.5%)	12 (2.5%)
4. That the Holy Spirit possesses all who trust in God and abides with them forever.	290 (60.8%)	187 (39.2%)	461 (96.6%)	16 (3.4%)
5. That every believer can be baptized in the Holy Spirit and speak in unknown tongues.	133 (27.9%)	344 (72.1%)	438 (91.6%)	40 (8.4%)

---

[15] Johnson, 2000, 27.
[16] Johnson, 2004, 207.

Chi-square analysis reveals differences are significant here on questions one through five (χ^2=336.16, p <.001), (χ^2=115.04, p <.001), (χ^2=96.8, p <.001), (χ^2=182.98, p <.001), and (χ^2=403.57, p <.001), respectively. The results are hardly surprising and, again, give evidence of a real paradigm shift in the thinking of the AG people since they became followers of Jesus Christ. How and why this happened will be noted later. It can be noted here that 24.3 percent of non-Christians do not believe that the Holy Spirit is God, but only 2.5 percent of Christians believe the same.

Most of the respondents indicated that they knew little or nothing about the Holy Spirit before coming to Christ and what they did know does not appear to follow any pattern of consistency. The one statistic that is a bit surprising is that so many said that they knew that people could be filled with the Holy Spirit and speak in tongues *before* the respondents themselves became believers. This percentage is higher than in the first question where they indicated that they were not familiar with the person and work of the Holy Spirit before they became believers. How can this be? One explanation may be that witchdoctors and other spiritual practitioners use *orasyons*, prayers that are believed to be in Latin. Maggay holds that this practice may have stemmed from the time when the mass was said in that language and, therefore, unintelligible to the hearer.[17] Perhaps some may confuse this with speaking in other tongues. A second explanation is that these respondents may have had friends and relatives who preceded them into the Assemblies of God who may have related their experience with the Holy Spirit to them.

---

[17]Melba Maggay, *A Clash of Cultures: Early American Protestant Missions and Filipino*, n.p.

Biblical Teaching on the Holy Spirit, Spirit Baptism and Spirit Possession

Having looked at several key elements of the Filipino Religious Worldview, one of the critical questions to consider is what enters the mind of the Filipinos when they are taught that the Holy Spirit will come upon them (Ac. 1:8)? When the Holy Spirit comes, does He leave again just like the other spirits? If not, in what ways is he different? A true contextual theology of Spirit baptism will answer these questions and challenge the gospel messengers themselves to live lives "full of the Holy Ghost and of power." With a basic understanding of cultural issues in mind, these issues can now be looked at in biblical perspective.

What Happens When the Holy Spirit Comes on People?: The OT Prophets and the Day of Pentecost

Understanding the similarities and differences between Filipino spiritual practitioners and biblical prophets is important to informing any contextualized theology of the Spirit in doctrine for the Philippines. Any number of approaches to understanding the Spirit's work might be undertaken, however, the focus here will be on how the Spirit of God moved upon people and how they reacted. This will enable us to compare what the Bible teaches about this activity of the Holy Spirit and how it might be perceived by ordinary Filipinos. Even here, however, space constraints do not allow an exhaustive treatment of the subject.

The OT Prophets

While the instances of the Spirit of God moving on people in the OT are more sporadic than in the NT, they are instructive here. One similarity between Philippine spiritual practitioners and the OT prophets was the apparent impermanence of the Spirit. The Spirit of the Lord would come upon the OT prophets for a purpose and depart when his work was done.

But some drastic differences contrast with this similarity. First, the prophets never lost consciousness, although there may have been cases (i.e. Saul in I Sam. 10:9-11) where they temporarily lost control of the mental faculties. Also, as Roger Stronstad notes, the activity of the Spirit in the OT was mainly prophetic in nature,[18] whereas demonic spirits possess Filipino spiritual practitioners mainly for healing and divination.

More importantly, there was a substantial difference in the Holy Spirit's purpose through the prophets, as opposed to the spirits' purpose through the spiritists. The activities of the spiritists are always anthropocentric, with the devil's motive being to deceive people. On the other hand, the activities of the biblical prophets were always theocentric—focused on God and his purposes, which are diametrically opposed to that of the spiritists and the demons that possess them.

The Day Of Pentecost

Roger Stronstad draws a direct connection between the activity of the Holy Spirit in the OT and Intertestamental period to Lukan pneumatology:

---

[18]Roger Stronstad, *The Charismatic Theology of St. Luke*, (Peabody, MA: Hendrickson Publishers, 1984), 14.

In general terms, Old Testament and Jewish Hellenistic historiography furnished Luke with the model for writing his two-volume history of the origin and spread of Christianity. Moreover, the Charismatic motifs of the Hebrew and Greek Bibles, such as the transfer, sign, and vocational motifs, influence Luke's theology of the Holy Spirit. In addition to the influence of these Charismatic motifs, the Septuagint furnishes Luke with the terminology to describe the activity of the Holy Spirit in the lives of Jesus and His disciples. Finally, Luke-Acts contrasts with the intertestamental belief in the cessation prophetic inspiration; rather, it reports the restoration of prophetic activity after four centuries of silence.[19]

Here, I will examine Lukan pneumatology in general and the Day of Pentecost in specific. Two respected Pentecostal scholars, Roger Stronstad and Robert Menzies, have done some excellent work in this area. For Stronstad, the Holy Spirit is the Charismatic Spirit that endows believers with gifts, specifically the vocal gifts of prophecy and *glossolalia*, or speaking in tongues, for speaking in God's name and for his glory.[20] Menzies essentially agrees, rooting Lukan pneumatology in Joel's prophecy of a great outpouring of the Spirit in the last days. In doing so he makes a compelling argument that speaking in tongues is the initial, physical evidence of the baptism in the Holy Spirit and should be normative to every believer.[21]

Lukan pneumatology, for Menzies, is also clear in texts such as Luke 11:11-13.[22] I certainly agree with Menzies, but take a slightly different tack when it comes to this particular passage.

---

[19] Stronstad, 31-32.
[20] Stronstad, 24.
[21] Robert Menzies, *Pentecost: This is Our Story*, (Springfield, MO: Gospel Publishing House, 2013), 35.
[22] Menzies, 91-96.

What is critical to note here is the underlying assumption of God's omnipotence and providence. This promise to receive exactly what is requested is good news to people coming out of an animistic background, who fear that if they ask God for the Holy Spirit they may instead become demon possessed.

Most Pentecostals believe that the baptism of the Holy Spirit empowers the believer to be Christ's witness. Menzies presents a compelling argument that this empowerment is a key reason for the explosive growth of the Pentecostal/Charismatic movement around the world, much of which is taking place among people whose worldviews are heavily animistic. In comparing this to the situation in the Philippines, most Filipinos easily understand the connection between spirit possession and spiritual power. What is not always obvious to them, mainly because they seldom question it, is the source of that spiritual power. This is where Pentecostals rightly part company with spiritual practitioners.

Since the Day of Pentecost in Acts 2 provides the most complete story in the NT of the outpouring of the Spirit we will look at it here through the lens of Filipino culture to see parallels and contrasts with the Filipino view of spirit possession. First, the Holy Spirit came upon the believers *en masse*, an experience that was also repeated in Acts 10:44-47 and 19:1-6. I am not arguing that this group experience should be normative, although it is common in Pentecostal circles. By contrast, I simply note that in the animistic practices of which I am aware, only one person at a time becomes possessed.

Second, when the Holy Spirit came on believers they never lost consciousness, whereas animistic practitioners do lose consciousness. While it cannot be said that the believers on the day of Pentecost necessarily understood all that was going on inside of them, they were well aware of their surroundings and knew they were experiencing the arrival of the Holy Spirit as both Joel and Jesus had prophesied (Joel 2:28-32; Acts 1:4-8). They were also well aware of the impact their experience was having on unbelievers outside their door (2:7-14). Furthermore, it is assumed that Luke was writing this somewhere around AD 60-64 and that his information likely came from some of the apostles themselves. Their ability to recall the event in vivid detail thirty years after the fact attests to their clear awareness of what happened that day, although it is possible that Luke may have also had access to those who merely witnessed the disciples speaking in tongues but did not participate. Nevertheless, the clear awareness of Peter immediately after being baptized in the Spirit, as well as the way Luke writes about the Day of Pentecost sharply contrasts with the experience of Filipino spiritual practitioners. All of my interviews in this regard and all the literature I have reviewed are in agreement that the practitioners *always* go into an altered state of consciousness and do not personally recall what happened while they were spirit possessed. Furthermore, there is nothing in the Acts 2 account that suggests any of the disciples lost consciousness.

Third, not only were the believers mentally cognizant of their surroundings, Acts 2:4 suggests that they remained in control of their physical faculties, moving their own mouths in speaking as the Spirit gave the utterance. While one must be careful to press this too far as some believers, myself included, have testified to losing control of their mouths when baptized in the Spirit, this is in contradistinction to the spiritists who always surrender control of their entire bodies to the spirits to perform healing or deliver oracles through them.

Fourth and most important is the issue of speaking in tongues. When doing my doctoral research, I was surprised to discover that nearly twenty-six AG respondents said they understood that the infilling of the Spirit involved speaking in tongues *before* they became Christians. Unfortunately, the research questionnaire was not designed to ask why this was. I have long pondered how this could be and have come up with two possibilities. One, it's possible, maybe even probable that a family member or friend preceded them into the Pentecostal movement, was baptized in the Holy Spirit and testified about their experience to family members and friends. But another possibility cannot be ignored. Filipino spiritual practitioners across the spectrum use mantras known as *orasyons*, drawn from the Spanish word for prayer, in innumerable situations. These may be written or spoken and are also known as "Latin prayers." While I have made no effort to establish their etymology, Melba Maggay, as mentioned earlier, may be correct when she speculates that these unintelligible "prayers" may have come from the time when the Catholic mass was said in Latin.

The function and the use of *orasyons* must be critically assessed here as they function as incantations and are an integral part of numerous animistic rituals. Filipinos believe that if these incantations are said with precise accuracy, the ritual will successfully give the devotee whatever they want or need. The meaning of the actual words is irrelevant because the words themselves are believed to have magical power. If the incantation fails to bring the desired result, it is believed that it was not done correctly.

Setting aside the discussion of *glossolalia* and *xenolalia*, under which these "Latin" prayers might be anthropologically classified, the idea of speaking in an unknown tongue being connected to supernatural power is not difficult for Filipinos to grasp. I must hasten to add, however, that using *orasyons* does normally not require spirit possession and that *orasyons* can be written as well as spoken. The critical difference between the baptism in the Holy Spirit is in the location of the spiritual power and in its purpose or function. For an animist the power is in the words themselves but for the follower of Jesus, the power is in a person, the Holy Spirit. For the animist the incantation itself is an impersonal and amoral spiritual force called magic, but for the believer, the source of power is God himself.

Regarding function, the focus of using incantations is to do the will of the individual, be it good or bad. On the other hand, the purpose of the baptism in the Holy Spirit is to empower believers to do the will of God. One can easily see how Filipinos might be confused on this issue. The need to bring clarity regarding the source and purpose of the baptism in the Holy Spirit is abundantly clear and the implications for discipleship are enormous.

Key Teachings Related to the Baptism in the Holy Spirit

The fulfillment of the Great Commission in Matthew 28:16-20 calls for making disciples. While there are many components involved in do this, most of which are well beyond the confines of this essay, teaching a sound theology in both demonstration and doctrine within the Filipino cultural matrix is vital key to helping people follow Christ.

Power Encounter: Deliverance and the Purpose of Holy Spirit Baptism

One of the research questions focused on the key components that brought people to Christ. Over forty percent of the of the respondents, who were given the opportunity to say yes or no to each category, indicated that they came to Christ because they were delivered from demons.[23] The baptism in the Holy Spirit is essential and desperately needed by people coming from an animistic background. Former animists need power

---

[23] Johnson, 2004, 211.

encounters. The first power encounter they need, however, may be deliverance from evil spirits. The New Testament is replete with examples, both in teaching (i.e. Eph. 1:18-21; Phil. 2:9-11; Col. 1:15-19) and in deed (i.e. Matt. 9:32-33; 17:14-21; Mark 5:1-17; Luke 4:33-37; Acts 5:16; 8:5-8; 16:16-18; 19:11-12) regarding the supremacy of Christ over demonic power and this victory needs to be proclaimed both through study of the Word and through demonstration. People that have been involved in animistic practices, especially if they have experienced actual demon possession, need to be set free. Amulets, talismans and other animistic paraphernalia need to be destroyed by the user (Acts 19:18-19).

But the second encounter, Spirit baptism, is needed to draw experience oriented people into an experience with God which alters their life purpose. This Spirit baptism is a power encounter that enables believers to be witnesses for Christ (Acts 1:8), a reality that Luke consistently demonstrates in the book of Acts (see Acts 2:1-41; 8:14-25; 10:44-48; 19:1-7). My own life was revolutionized by the Spirit's empowering, drawing me out of the evangelical church in which I had been raised and into the Pentecostal movement. I have now served as an Assemblies of God minister for more than thirty years, most of them in evangelistic ministry in the Philippines that, through the grace and power of the Holy Spirit, has resulted in numerous churches being planted.

The Power of the Holy Spirit to Protect Christians from Demons

While former animists need teaching on the power to deliver people from demons and the power and purpose of Spirit baptism, they also need assurance regarding God's protection of Christians against demonic spirits. Questions like "Does God have the power to protect people from demon possession when they are seeking the baptism in the Holy Spirit" are vitally important. Scriptures like Psalms 91:1-4 and Luke 11:9-13 are incredibly good news and help people deal with their fear of the spirit world. Doctrines like the providence of God and the supremacy of Christ over the powers of darkness (i.e. Col. 2:14-15) are critical to bringing people out of the bondage of animism and into God's glorious light. Even teaching on the Trinity can be helpful, an explanation of the fact that the Holy Spirit is on the same level (Hiebert's first tier) as the Father and the Son, far exceeding power level of the spirits.

The Differences Between the Baptism in the Holy Spirit and Demonic Power

Disciples of Christ must be made aware of the critical differences between the baptism in the Holy Spirit and the power used by spiritists for healing and fortunetelling, etc. First, they are different in source. People must be taught about the different sources of supernatural power. Filipinos seldom ask about the spiritists' source of power, but knowing the true power source is critical to understanding the true gospel. The power that possesses the spiritists is from Satan while the power of God is the source of the Holy Spirit baptism.

Second, as mentioned earlier, Spirit baptism and demonic power are diametrically different in purpose. Animists seek spiritual power for anthropocentric reasons such as healing, cursing enemies and especially, through fortunetelling and divination, to control their future. Satan's motives are to draw people away from God through deception. But the purpose of the Holy Spirit is to empower believers to be his witnesses, to walk under the anointing of the Spirit in preaching the gospel, healing the sick, casting out demons, setting the captive free and declaring the arrival of the Kingdom (Matt 10:5, 8; Lk 4:16-18;

Ac 1:8). In short, the Spirit empowers us to see men and women drawn to Jesus Christ, the Author and Finisher of our faith. A study of Spirit baptism and the resulting missionary work through Spirit empowered disciples in the book of Acts may help believers to clearly see the passion of God for the lost and the plan and purpose of God for churches and individuals.

Third, the experience of the baptism of the Holy Spirit and the power of the demonic are different. In Filipino animism, only specialists have access to demonic power for healing, divination, etc. But Joel 2:28-29 is clear that the power of the Holy Spirit is available to *every* believer. Bob Menzies brilliantly connects Joel's motif here to Lukan pneumatology, citing passages such as Acts 2:1-4, 16-18, and 2:38-39, making clear that this outpouring is for every believer in every generation.[24]

Another difference in experience relates to falling down or "falling under the power." For years I wondered why some pastors in the Philippines believe that the evidence of the baptism in the Holy Spirit is being slain in the Spirit. Only recently has it dawned on me that this falling to the floor is what often happens when spiritual practitioners become demon possessed. Apparently these pastors assume that the physical reaction is the same when people become filled with the Holy Spirit. While I have heard accounts of people being slain in Spirit and speaking in tongues at the same time, people need to be taught that being slain in the Spirit is not necessary for and not the same thing as receiving Holy Spirit baptism.

Fourth, another critical difference between Spirit baptism and demonic power is the dynamic of love. Romans 5:5 says, "… God has poured out his love into our hearts by the Holy Spirit, whom he has given us." The Apostle Paul exhorts believers to be encouraged by the comfort of God's love, the fellowship of the

---

[24] Menzies, 77-80.

Spirit and the Lord's tenderness and compassion in order to love one another and be one in spirit and purpose (Phil. 2:1-2). Jesus taught the great commandments–to love God and others (i.e. Lk 10:27 et al).

One day I asked a spiritist if he loved God. He responded by saying that he loved the people in his community that came to him for healing. After affirming his feelings for the people, I restated my question. He had no answer. Indeed. Not only was he missing the love of God, there is also no love between the spiritists and the spirits that empower them. The relationship is purely utilitarian. Once the spirit has completed his work, it leaves the spiritist. The Spirit of God, however, not only pours the love of God in our hearts, he also abides with the believer forever (Jn 14:16). In other words, the Holy Spirit is *sui generis*, wholly other than the demons that possess the spiritists.

The horizontal love relationships with other believers is just as critical, in part because most animists come from group focused cultures. The fellowship of the Spirit, as mentioned above, encourages a loving unity among believers. When they come to Christ, the animists' social group of family and friends may turn against them. Incorporating them into the Body of Christ, where they can be nurtured, cared for and be held accountable, is essential to their walk with God.

The final difference between the baptism in the Holy Spirit and the power encounters animists have with the spirits is the issue of alliance. The allegiance of the spiritist is to his or her possessing spirit. The allegiance of the ordinary people is to the spiritists or spirit that gives them what they want. But the work of the Holy Spirit in general, and the Baptism in the Holy Spirit in particular, points to an allegiance to Jesus Christ whether or not the Lord gives us what we want. This, more than anything else that has been written here, is where Spirit filled believers part company with spiritual practitioners. The Holy Spirit leads the believer into allegiance to Christ and no other. From Genesis to Revelation, the Bible is abundantly clear that our allegiance to Christ must be absolute. God will tolerate no rivals (i.e. Ex. 20:1-6; Isaiah 45:22, et al), although one must not expect new believers to grasp this immediately as this will likely take some time. People from animistic backgrounds must make a clean break from the past at some point, destroying all animistic paraphernalia and trusting Christ to meet their needs. Where possible, biblically based cultural functional alternatives must be sought and implemented, such as an annual church anniversary service, which is dedicated to God, as opposed to town fiestas, which is dedicated to the local patron saint.

Conclusion

The purpose of this paper has been to demonstrate a theology of Holy Spirit baptism in doctrine as it relates the Philippine animistic context. Looking through the portal of Filipino culture, the concept of spiritual power is well known as is the concept of giving utterances while in contact with the spirit realm. The purposes, however, are vastly different and these differences must be clearly understood in light of God's word.

Teaching regarding deliverance, and the differences regarding sources of power, purpose, experience, love dynamics and allegiance are only some of the many issues that must be dealt with in training believers regarding Holy Spirit baptism. The concepts articulated here call for experiencing the power of God in one's life as well as encountering the truth through diligent study of God's word in the company of other believers with the ultimate goal of giving one's allegiance to Christ alone.

PUBLICATIONS BY WONSUK MA

BOOKS:

- Edited (with Robert P. Menzies), *Pentecostalism in Context: Essays in Honor of William W. Menzies* (Sheffield: Sheffield Academic Press, 1997).
- *Until the Spirit Comes: The Spirit of God in the Book of Isaiah*, JSOTS 271 (Sheffield: JSOT Press, 1999).
- Edited (with Julie C. Ma), *Asian Church and God's Mission: Studies Presented in the International Symposium on Asian Mission in Manila, Jan 2002* (Manila: OMF Lit., 2003).
- Edited (with William W. Menzies and Hyeon-sung Bae), *David Yonggi Cho: A Close Look at His Theology and Ministry*, AJPS Series 1 (Baguio, Philippines: APTS Press, 2004).
- Edited (with Robert P. Menzies), *The Spirit and Spirituality: Essays in Honor of Russell P. Spittler* (London: T. & T. Clark, 2004).
- Edited (with Timothy Kiho Park), *Global Mission and Korean Church: Essays in Memory of Jin-guk Ju* [in Korean] (Seoul: Mission Times; Pasadena: Institute for Asian Mission).
- Edited (with Kiho Park) *Calling: Here Am I, Send Me Lord* [in Korea] (Seoul: Qumran, 2010).
- (With Julie C. Ma) *Mission in the Spirit: Towards a Pentecostal-Charismatic Missiology* (Oxford: Regnum 2010).
- Edited (with Brian Woolnough) *Holistic Mission: God's Plan for God's People*, Regnum Edinburgh 2010 Series (Oxford: Regnum Books, 2010).
- Edited (with S. Hun Kim), *Korean Diaspora and Christian Mission* (Oxford: Regnum Books, 2011).
- Edited (with Kenneth Ross), *Mission Spirituality and Authentic Discipleship* (Oxford: Regnum Books, 2013).
- Edited (with Veli-Matti Kärkkäinen and J. Kwabena Asamoa-Gyadu) *Pentecostal Mission and Global Christianity*, Regnum Edinburgh Centenary Series (Oxford: Regnum Books, 2013).
- 'Asian Pentecostalism in Context: a challenging portrait', in Amos Yong and Cecil M. Robeck, Jr (eds.), *Cambridge Companion to Pentecostalism* (Cambridge: Cambridge University Press) (forthcoming).
- 'Life and Power: The Spirit of God in Isaiah', in Trevor J. Burke & Keith Warrington (eds.), *A Biblical Theology of the Spirit* (SPCK) (forthcoming).

DISSERTAION/THESIS:

- "The Spirit of God in the Book of Isaiah and Its Eschatological Significance" (Ph.D. dissertation, Fuller Theological Seminary, 1996; Supervisor: Leslie C. Allen).

JOURNAL ARTICLES:

- "Brief Guidelines to Motivating Cell Leaders," *Horizon: A Communication Paper of the Far East Advanced School of Theology* 1 (March 1985), pp. 3-4.
- "The Spirit of God in Isaiah 1-39," *Asia Journal of Theology* 3 (1989).
- "Missiological Challenges of Pentecostal Theology," *Full Gospel Weekly News*, Nov, 1996 (in Korean).
- "The Spirit of God among the Leaders of Ancient Israel and of Igorot Christians," in *Pentecostalism in Context: Essays in Honor of William W. Menzies* (Sheffield: Sheffield Academic Press, 1997), pp. 291-316.
- "A 'First Waver's Looks at the 'Third Wave': A Pentecostal Reflection on Charles Kraft's Power Encounter Terminology," *Pneuma* 19 (1997), pp. 189-206.
- "The Work of the Holy Spirit in a Social Dimension: A Pentecostal View," in *Sanctification of a Christian in the Work of the Holy Spirit* (in Korean; Seoul: International Theological Institute, 1997).
- "Toward an Asian Pentecostal Theology," *Asian Journal of Pentecostal Studies* 1:1 (1998), pp. 15-41.
- "Tasks and Challenges for Korean Pentecostal Churches in the Twenty-First Century," *Journal of Korean Pentecostal Theology* 1 (1998), pp. 216-264 [in Korean].
- "Biblical Basis for Pentecostal Mission," *Toward the Nations* 1 (May-June), pp. 12-15 (in Korean).
- "A Look at Modern Pneumatology in the Old Testament Perspective," *The Spirit and Church* 1, pp. 25-36 (in Korean).
- "'If It Is a Sign': An Old Testament Reflection on the Initial Evidence Discussion," *Asian Journal of Pentecostal Studies* 2:2 (1999), pp. 163-175.

- "Pentecostal Biblical Studies: Yesterday, Today, and Tomorrow," in *The Globalization of Pentecostalism: A Religion Made to Travel*, eds. Murray W. Dempster, Byron D. Klaus and Douglas Petersen (Oxford: Regnum, 1999), pp. 52-69.
- "Modern Pneumatologies from an Old Testament Perspective," in *Collected Essays of Korean Pentecostal Society*, ed. Yeol-soo Eim (Seoul: Korean Pentecostal Society, 2002).
- "Tasks and Challenges for Korean Pentecostal Churches in the Twenty-First Century," *Australasian Pentecostal Studies* 5-6 (2001): 63-94.
- "Three Types of Ancestor Veneration in Asia: An Anthropological Analysis," *Journal of Asian Mission* 4:2 (2002), pp. 201-215.
- "360 Degree Mission" [in Korean]. *Korean Mission Quarterly* 1:4 (Summer): 10-11.
- (With Julie C. Ma) "'Empowering the Asian Church for God's Mission': An Introductory Reflection," in *Asian Church and God's Mission*, pp. 5-7.
- "Evaluation and Prospects of Pentecostal Spirituality" (in Korean), *Monthly Church Growth Journal*, May 2003 (Seoul, Korea), pp. 43-48.
- "The Effect of Rev. Cho's Sermon Style for Church Growth on the Development of Theology," in *Charis and Charisma: David Yonggi Cho and the Growth of Yoido Full Gospel Church*, edited by Myung Sung-hoon and Hong Young-gi (Oxford: Regnum Books International, 2003), 159-171.
- "Charismatic Leadership and Human Development: A Biblical Rationale for Pentecostal Educational Ministry," in *Reflections on Developing Asian Pentecostal Leaders: Essays in Honor of Harold Kohl*, ed. Kay Fountain (Baguio, Philippines: APTS Press, 2004), pp. 285-303.
- "Toward the Future of David Yonggi Cho's Theological Tradition," in *David Yonggi Cho: A Close Look at His Theology and Ministry*, AJPS Series 1 (Baguio, Philippines: APTS Press, 2004), pp. 255-72.
- "The Empowerment of the Spirit of God in Luke-Acts: An Old Testament Perspective," in *The Spirit and Spirituality: Essays in Honor of Russell P. Spittler* (London: T. & T. Clark, 2004), pp. 28-40.
- "Asian Pentecostalism: A Religion Whose Only Limit Is the Sky," *Journal of Beliefs and Values* 25:2 (Aug 2004), pp. 191-204.
- "A Response to David S. Lim," *Journal of the American Society for Church Growth* 15 (Spring, 2004), pp. 29-33.
- "Full Circle Mission: A Possibility of Pentecostal Missiology," *Asian Journal of Pentecostal Studies* 8:1, pp. 5-27.
- (With Julie C. Ma,) "Jesus Christ in Asia: Our Journey with Him as Pentecostal Believers," *International Review of Mission* 94 (2005), pp. 493-506.
- "Asian (Classical) Pentecostalism: Theology in Context," in *Asian and Pentecostal: The Charismatic Face of Christianity in Asia*, eds. Allan Anderson and Edmond Tang (Oxford: Regnum Books, 2005), pp. 59-91.
- "Doing Theology in the Philippines: A Case of Pentecostal Christianity," *Asian Journal of Pentecostal Studies* 8:2 (2005), pp. 215-233.
- "Asian Pentecostalism" [in Korean, trans. by Dokyun Hah], *Holiness Church and Theology* 13 (Spring, 2005, Seoul Theological University), pp. 195-217.
- "Edinburgh and Seoul: Korean Church in World Mission" [in Korean], *Korean Mission Quarterly* 17 (Fall 2005), pp. 57-64.
- "Missionary Orientation and Theological Schools in the Field: A Philippine Case Study" [in Korean], in *Korean Church and Global Mission: Essays in Memory of Jin-guk Ju*, eds. Wonsuk Ma and Timothy Kiho Park (Seoul: Mission Times; Pasadena: Institute for Asian Mission, 2006), pp. 245-264.
- "Pentecostal Eschatology: What Happened When the Wave Hit the West End of the Ocean," in *The Azusa Street Revival and Its Legacy*, eds. Harold Hunter and Cecil M. Robeck, Jr. (Cleveland, TN: Pathway), pp. 227-242.
- "'When the Poor Are Fired Up': The Role of Pneumatology in Pentecostal-Charismatic Mission," *Transformation* 24:1 (Jan 2007), pp. 28-34.
- "Pentecostal Worship in Asia: Its Theological Implications and Contributions," *Asian Journal of Pentecostal Studies* 10:1 (Jan 2007), pp. 136-52.
- "'In Jesus' Name...': Power Encounter from an Asian Pentecostal Perspective," in Violeta V. Bautista, John F. Baxter, Wonsuk Ma, et al., *Principalities and Powers: Biblical Reflections in the Asian Context* (Manila: OMF Lit., 2007), pp. 21-40.
- "The Spirit of God in Creation: Lessons for Christian Mission," *Transformation* 24:3 & 4 (July & Oct 2007), pp. 222-30.
- "The Southern Church and Global Christianity: An Interview with Wonsuk Ma," *Asian Christian Review* 1:3 (Winter, 2007, Japan), pp. 3-10.
- "The Spirit and Mission: Two Ripples of Pentecostal Mission," *Lausanne World Pulse* (http://www.lausanneworldpulse.com/themedarticles.php/925, April 4, 2008).

Publications by Wonsuk Ma 229

- "The Third Ripple: Deeper And Wider Mission Engagement," *Lausanne World Pulse* (http://www.lausanneworldpulse.com/themedarticles.php/926, April 4, 2008).
- "God's Creation: The Source for Mission in the Spirit," in *Med Kristus til Jordens Ender: Festskrift til Tormod Engelsviken*, eds., Kjell Olav Sannes, Egil Grandhagen, Terje Hegertun, Knud Jorgensen, Kristin Norseth, Rolv Olsen (Tronheim, Norway: Tapir Akademisk Forlag, 2008), pp. 65-76.
- (With Julie Ma) "Spiritualität in der Mission – gelernt vom einheimischen Missionar Tito," in *Mission Erfüllt? Edinburgh 1910 – 100 Jahre Weltmission: Jahrbuch Mission 2009* (Hambrug: Missionshilfe Verlag, 2009), pp. 136-42.
- "Discerning What God Is Doing among His People Today," in Huibert van Beek, ed., *Revisioning Christian Unity: The Global Christian Forum* (Oxford: Regnum, 2009), pp. 80-92.
- "A Missionary Call? Not Exactly . . . ," in Kiho Park and Wonsuk Ma (eds.), *Calling: Here Am I, Send Me Lord* [in Korea] (Seoul: Qumran, 2010), pp. 226-241.
- (With Cathy Ross, Thomas Harvey and Naomi Rose) "Theme Nine: Mission Spirituality and Authentic Discipleship," in Daryl Balia and Kirsteen Kim (eds.), *Edinburgh 2010: Witnessing to Christ Today* (Oxford: Regnum Books, 2010), pp. 222-244.
- "Pentecostal Theological Education in Asia," in Dietrich Werner, David Esterline, Namsoon Kang, Joshva Raja (eds.), *Handbook of Theological Education in Global Christianity: Theological Perspectives, Regional Surveys, Ecumenical Trends* (Oxford: Regnum Books, 2010), pp. 729-735.
- (With S. Hun Kim) "Introduction", in S. Hun Kim and Wonsuk Ma (eds.), *Korean Diaspora and Christian Mission* (Oxford: Regnum Books, 2010), pp. 1-7.
- "A Millennial Shift of Global Christianity and Mission: An Initial Reflection", in S. Hun Kim and Wonsuk Ma (eds.), *Korean Diaspora and Christian Mission* (Oxford: Regnum Books, 2010), pp. 11-23.
- (With S. Hun Kim) "Postscript", in S. Hun Kim and Wonsuk Ma (eds.), *Korean Diaspora and Christian Mission* (Oxford: Regnum Books, 2010), pp. 283-88.
- "David Yonggi Cho's Theology of Blessing: Basis, Legitimacy and Limitations," *Evangelical Review of Theology* 35:2 (April 2011), pp. 140-159.
- (With Cathy Ross) "Theme 9: Mission Spirituality and Authentic Discipleship", in *Edinburgh 2010: Mission Today and Tomorrow*, Regnum Edinburgh 2010 Series, eds. Kirsteen Kim and Andrew Anderson (Oxford: Regnum Books, 2011), pp. 183-89.
- "The presence of evil and human response in the Old Testament," in William K. Kay and Robin Parry, eds., *Exorcism and Deliverance: Multi-Disciplinary Studies* (Milton Keynes: Paternoster, 2011), pp. 27-44.
- 'Grace Korean Church, California: Mission form Margins', *International Bulletin of Missionary Research* 36:2 (April, 2012): 65–71.
- 'The Theological Motivations for Pentecostal Mission', in Emma Wild-Wood and Peniel Rajkumar (eds.), *Foundations for Mission*, Regnum Edinburgh Centenary Series 13 (Oxford: Regnum Books, 2012), 220-35.
- (With Julie C Ma) 'The Making of Korean Pentecostal Missionaries: Our Personal Journey', in Arto Hämäläinen and Grant McCung (eds.), *Together in One Mission: Pentecostal Cooperation in World Evangelization* (Cleveland, TN: Pathway, 2012), 159-176.
- (With Kenneth R. Ross) 'Introduction: The Spiritual Dimension of Mission', in Wonsuk Ma and Kenneth R. Ross (eds), *Mission Spirituality and Authentic Discipleship* (Oxford: Regnum Books, 2013), 1-9.
- (With Kenneth R. Ross) 'Conclusion: Spirituality as the Beating Heart of Mission', in Wonsuk Ma and Kenneth R. Ross (eds), *Mission Spirituality and Authentic Discipleship* (Oxford: Regnum Books, 2013), 225-33.
- 'Blessing in Pentecostal Theology and Mission', in W Ma, V-M Kärkkäinen and J. K.Asamoa-Gyadu (eds.), *Pentecostal Mission and Global Christianity* (Oxford: Regnum Books, 2013), n.p.
- (With Veli-Matti Kärkkäinen and J. Kwabena Asamoa-Gyadu) 'Introduction: Pentecostalism and World Mission', in *Pentecostal Mission and Global Christianity* (Oxford: Regnum Books, 2013), n.p.
- (With Veli-Matti Kärkkäinen and J. Kwabena Asamoa-Gyadu) 'Conclusion', in *Pentecostal Mission and Global Christianity* (Oxford: Regnum Books, 2013), n.p.
- 'Life, Justice and Peace in the Spirit: A Korean Pentecostal Reflection', *Ecumenical Review* 65:2 (July 2013), 225-57.
- 'A Theological Journey of an Institution through the Eye of an Alumnus-Staff: A Case of Asia Pacific Theological Seminary', *Asian Journal of Pentecostal Studies* (2013). (forthcoming).

DICTIONARY AND ENCYCLOPEDIA ENTRIES:

- "Philippines," *New International Dictionary of Pentecostal and Charismatic Movements*, Stanley M. Burgess, et al, eds. (Grand Rapids: Zondervan), pp. 201-207.

- "Villanueva, Eddie C. (1946-)," *New International Dictionary of Pentecostal and Charismatic Movements*, Stanley M. Burgess, et al, eds. (Grand Rapids: Zondervan), p. 1177
- "Philippines For Jesus Movement (PJM)," *New International Dictionary of Pentecostal and Charismatic Movements*, Stanley M. Burgess, et al, eds. (Grand Rapids: Zondervan), p. 988
- "Asia, East," and "Korea," *Encyclopedia of Pentecostal and Charismatic Christianity: A Religion and Society Encyclopedia*, ed. Stanley M. Burgess (New York & London: Routledge, 2006), pp. 46-49.
- "Korea," *Encyclopedia of Pentecostal and Charismatic Christianity: A Religion and Society Encyclopedia*, ed. Stanley M. Burgess (New York & London: Routledge, 2006), pp. 276-281.
- "Korean Christian Spirituality," in Glen G. Scorgie (ed.), *Dictionary of Christian Spirituality* (Grand Rapids: Zondervan, 2011), 564-65.

REVIEWS:

- Book Review of *Divine Threads within a Human Tapestry: Memoirs of Phil Parshall* in *Journal of Asian Mission* 3:2 (2001): 285-288.
- Review of Barry L. Ross, *Our Incomparable God: A Commentary on Isaiah 40-55* (Pune, India: Fountain Press, 2003) in *Journal of Asian Evangelical Theology* (2004), pp. xx-xx.
- Review of Scott W. Sunquist, ed. (with David Wu Chu Sing and John Chew Hiang Chea, as associate editors), *A Dictionary of Asian Christianity* (Grand Rapids: Eerdmans, 2001) in *Journal of Asian Mission* 6:2 (2004), pp. 272-75.
- Review of Gina Maria Tagasa, direct. *Sa Kandungan ng Langit* [Heaven's Cradle]. Manila: White Windows Production, 2003 in *Journal of Asian Mission* 6:1 (2004), pp. 109-111.
- Review of David Aikman, *Jesus in Beijing: How Christianity Is Transforming China and Changing the Global Balance of Power* (Washington, DC: Regnery Publishing, 2003) in *Asian Journal of Pentecostal Studies* 8:1 (2005), pp. 185-88.
- Review of Gary Hal Graff, *Can a Christian Have an Unclean Spirit?* (El Cajon, CA: Christian Service Network, 1999) in *Pneuma Foundation* (http://www.pneumafoundation.org/article.jsp?article=/article_0051.xml, 2006)
- Review of *Global Pentecostalism: The New Face of Christian Social Engagement* by Donald Miller and Tetsunao Yamamori (Berkeley, CA: University of California Press, 2007) in *Transformation* 25:4 (2008), pp. 274-76.
- Review of James Robinson, *Word and Spirit in Ezekiel*, Library of Hebrew Bible/Old Testament Studies 447 (New York & London: T & T Clark, 2006) in *Journal of Biblical and Pneumatological Research* 2 (2010), pp. 128-37.

PUBLICATIONS BY JULIE MA

BOOKS:

- *When the Spirit Meets the Spirits: Pentecostal Mission to an Animistic Tribe of the Northern Philippines* (Frankfurt: Peter Lang, 2000).
- Edited (with Wonsuk Ma), *Asian Church and God's Mission: Studies Presented at the International Symposium on Asian Mission, Manila, January 2002* (Manila: OMF Literature, 2003).
- *Mission Possible: Biblical Strategies in Reaching the Lost* (Oxford: Regnum Books, 2005).
- (With Wonsuk Ma), *Mission in the Spirit: Towards a Pentecostal/Charismatic Missiology* (Oxford: Regnum Books, 2010).

JOURNAL ARTICLES:

- "Growing Churches in Manila: An Analysis," *Asian Journal of Theology* (Jan 1996).
- "A Pentecostal Woman Missionary in a Tribal Setting: A Case Study," a paper presented at World Council of Churches Consultation with Pentecostals, Nov, 1997, Bossey, Switzerland, and published in *Cyberjournal for Pentecostal-Charismatic Research* 3 (1998) [http://www.pctii.org].
- "Santuala: A Case of Pentecostal Syncretism in the Northern Philippines," a paper read at the Theological Symposium for Asian Pentecostal Leaders, the 18th Pentecostal World Conference, Seoul, Korea on Sept 21, 1998. Also to be published in *Asian Journal of Pentecostal Studies* 2:2 (1999).
- "Light: Missiological Implication" published in *Journal of Asian Mission* 1:2 (September 1999).
- "Korean Pentecostal Spirituality: A Case Study of Jashil Choi," *Asian Journal of Pentecostal Studies* 5:2 (2002), pp. 235-254. Also published in *The Spirit and Spirituality: Essays in Honor of Russell P. Spittler* (London: T. & T. Clark, 2004), pp. 245-260.
- (With Wonsuk Ma,) "Jesus Christ in Asia: Our Journey with Him as Pentecostal Believers" (Plenary address in Asian Consultation of Global Christian Forum, Hong Kong, April-May, 2004), subsequently published in *International Review of Mission* 94 (Oct 2005), pp. 493-506.
- "Asian Religious Worldviews and Their Missiological Implications" published in *Journal of Asian Mission* 7:1 (2005).
- "Pentecostalism and Asian Mission" (paper presented in Annual meeting of Missiology in Chicago, May 2006), subsequently published in *Missiology in International Review*, Vol. XXXV:1 (Jan. 2007), pp. 23-37.
- "Growth of Christianity in Asia and Its Impact on Mission," *Encounter Mission Ezine*.
- "Korean Mission in Global Leadership," *Korean Mission Quarterly*, 6:4 (Sept. 2007), pp. 55-62.
- "North-East Asia," in *Christianity Worldwide: A.D. 1800 Onwards* (1989) (London: SPCK, forthcoming).
- "Eschatology and Mission: Living the 'Last Days' Today," *Transformation: An International Journal of Holistic Mission Studies* 26:1-4 (June. 2009), pp. 186-198.
- "A Critical Appraisal of Korean Mission Movements: Challenges for Western Mission," *Encounter Mission Ezine.* 2009.
- "Pentecostal Education" (the paper placed in the Edinburgh 2010 website).
- "Challenges, Contributions and Commitment of Pentecostals in Missionary Work Among Other Faith," *International Journal of Pentecostal Missiology* (forthcoming).
- "Significant Role of Asia Pacific Theological Seminary and Missionary Training Institute for Equipping Asian Church for Mission," *Asian Journal of Pentecostal Studies* (forthcoming).
- The Role of Christian Women in the Global South *Transformation Journal* (forthcoming).

CONTRIBUTIONS TO COLLECTED WORKS:

- "A Comparison of Two Worldviews: Kankana-ey and Pentecostal," in *Pentecostalism in Context: Essays in Honor of William W. Menzies*, eds. Wonsuk Ma and Robert P. Menzies (Sheffield: Sheffield Academic Press, 1997).
- "Pentecostal Challenge in East and Southeast Asia," in *Pentecostalism in Globalization*, eds. Marry Dempster and Byron Klaus (Oxford: Regnum Books, 1999).
- "'A Close Encounter with the Transcendental': Proclamation and Manifestation in Pentecostal Worship in Asian Context," in *Asian Church and God's Mission: Studies Presented at the International Symposium on Asian Mission, Manila, January 2002* (Manila: OMF Literature, 2003), pp. 127-145.
- (With Wonsuk Ma) "'Empowering the Asian Church for God's Mission': An Introductory Reflection," in *Asian Church and God's Mission: Studies Presented at the International Symposium on Asian Mission, Manila, January 2002* (Manila: OMF Literature, 2003), pp. 5-7.

- "Church Planting: Pentecostal Strategy for Mission," in Reflections on Developing Asian Pentecostal Leaders: Essays in Honor of Harold Kohl, ed. Kay Fountain (Baguio, Philippines: APTS Press, 2004), pp. 323-55.
- "Asian Women in Ministry," in *Asian and Pentecostal: The Charismatic Face of Christianity in Asia*, eds. Allan Anderson and Edmond Tang (Oxford: Regnum Books, 2005).
- "Fundamental Mission Issues of the Korean Church and Implications to Global Mission Leadership" [in Korean], in *Korean Church and Global Mission: Essays in Memory of Jin-guk Ju*, eds. Wonsuk Ma and Timothy Kiho Park (Seoul: Mission Times; Pasadena: Institute for Asian Mission, 2006), pp. 107-121.
- (With Wonsuk Ma) "Die Dynamik in der heutigen Missionsbewegung," in *Mission Erfullt?* (Hamburg: Missionshilfe Verlag, 2009), pp. 128-142.
- "Changing Image: Women in Asian Pentecostalism," in *Women in Pentecostal-Charismatic Leadership*, eds. by Estrelda Alexander and Amos Yong (Eugene, OR: Pickwick pub., 2009), pp. 203-214.
- (With Allan Anderson) "Pentecostalism," in *Atlas of Global Christianity*, eds, by T. M. Johnson & K. Ross (Edinburgh: University of Edinburgh Press, 2010), pp. 100-103.
- "A Critical Appraisal of Korean Missionary Work," in *Korean Diaspora and Christian Mission* eds. S. Hun Kim and Wonsuk Ma (Oxford: Regnum, 2011), pp. 131-145.
- "Challenges, *Contributions* and Commitment of Pentecostals in Missionary Work Among Other Faiths," in *Witnessing to Christ in a Pluralistic Age: Christian Mission among Other Faiths* eds. by Lalsangkima Pachuau and Knud Jorgensen (Oxford: Regnum Books, 2011), pp. 79-89.
- "Challenges, Contributions and Commitment of Pentecostals in Missionary Work Among Other Faiths," in *Mission Erfullt?: Edinburgh 1910-100 Jahre Weltmission* eds. by Verena Gruter (Hamburg: Missionshilfe Verlag, 2011), pp.136-142.
- (With Wonsuk Ma) "The Making of Korean Pentecostal Missionaries: Our Personal Journey", in Arto Hämäläinen and Grant McCung (eds.), *Together in One Mission: Pentecostal Cooperation in World Evangelization* (Cleveland, TN: Pathway, 2012), pp. 159-176.
- Pentecostal Evangelism, Church Planting, and Church growth in *Pentecostal Mission* (Oxford: Regnum Book, forthcoming).
- "A Critical Appraisal of Korean Missionary Work" in Understanding Asian Mission Movements eds. KangSan Tan, Jonathan Ingleby and Simon Cozens (UK: Wide Margin, 2011), pp. 77-102.

DICTIONARY AND ENCYCLOPEDIA ENTRIES:

- "Animism and Pentecostalism, A Case Study," in *The New International Dictionary of Pentecostal and Charismatic Movements*, eds. Stanley M. Burgess and Eduard M. van der Maas, revised and expanded edition (Grand Rapids: Zondervan, 2002), pp. 315-318.
- "Animism and Pentecostalism," *Encyclopedia of Pentecostal and Charismatic Christianity: A Religion & Society Encyclopedia*, ed. Stanley M. Burgess (New York: Routledge, 2006), pp. 26-27.

Profiles of Contributors

Allan Heaton Anderson is Professor of Mission and Pentecostal Studies at the University of Birmingham, where he has been since 1995. He is from Southern Africa and author of many books and articles on global Pentecostalism, including Spreading Fires (SCM & Orbis, 2007), To the Ends of the Earth (Oxford, 2013), and An Introduction to Pentecostalism (Cambridge, 2014).

J. Kwabena Asamoah-Gyadu is Baeta-Grau Professor of Contemporary African Christianity and Pentecostal/Charismatic Theology at the Trinity Theological Seminary in Legon, Accra, Ghana where he is Director of Graduate Studies. Prof. Kwabena Asamoah-Gyadu is also a member of the Board of Trustees of the Oxford Center for Mission Studies, UK.

John Carter serves as a non-resident faculty member of APTS and in 2006 was named President Emeritus. In 2012, he was elected Chairman of the APTS Board. He is also Chairman of the Board of the World Alliance for Pentecostal Theological Education (WAPTE), which is affiliated with the Pentecostal World Fellowship. He has published numerous articles in the field of education and spoken at national and international conferences of educators in the U.S., Europe and Asia. His teaching interests involve the application of psychological principles to the design and implementations of learning systems of various kinds, and the development of ministry leaders. He teaches Leadership, College Teaching, Educational Psychology and Curriculum Development.

Teresa Chai (PhD, Fuller Seminary) is a faculty member at Asia Pacific Theological Seminary filling the John Bueno Chair of Intercultural Studies for June 2013 – March 2015, Global Mission Center Director, Administrative Committee member and Book Review Editor for APTS journal AJPS. She was the President of Alpha Omega International College, Malaysia and had served in this Bible College for over ten years from April 2003 – December 2013. For eight years, she served in Bangladesh with the United Bible Societies and a Danish mission. Teresa Chai is an ordained minister with the Assemblies of God Malaysia. She teaches in Bible schools and seminaries in China, India, Malaysia, Romania, Samoa, Singapore and Thailand. Her most recent publications are a chapter entitled *Pentecostal Theological Education and Ministerial Formation*, Chapter 19, in Regnum Edinburgh centenary series, Mission Spirituality and Authentic Discipleship, Volume 14, 2013 and a book review in *Pneuma*, a journal.

R. G. dela Cruz was a resident faculty member of Asia Pacific Theological Seminary, Baguio, Philippines for many years. He was also a postgraduate tutor in the Department of Theology and Religion at the University of Birmingham, UK. He is currently an adjunct professor in the Church Ministries Department at Valley Forge Christian College, Phoenixville, PA.

Rose Engcoy served as Faculty/Dean of Women (1981-1982), and as Registrar (1982-1990) at Immanuel Bible College. Before that, she was an Instructor in Chemistry at the University of the Philippines, (1975-1977, 1980-1981). Her ministerial experience includes being a church worker in Iloilo Bethel Temple (1974-77, 1980-81) and a pastor's wife at New Creation Koinonia (1986-2000). Since 1998, she was the Assistant Director and latterly Coordinator of the Asia Pacific Research Center at APTS. She does oral history research on the beginnings of Pentecostal groups especially in the Philippines. Currently, she is the Registrar of ICI Global University, Philippines.

Harold D. Hunter (PhD, Fuller Theological Seminary) is currently Director of the IPHC Archives & Research Center. Denominational executive positions, seminary teaching, and ecumenical dialogues have taken him to at least 70 countries. Hunter actively engages the World Council of Churches, Eastern Orthodox Churches, and the National Council of Churches USA (NCCUSA) Faith and Order Commission.

Dave Johnson has been an ordained Minister of Assemblies of God USA since 1986. He was appointed Missionary with Assemblies of God World Missions (USA) in 1994 and has full professional proficiency in Tagalog, the national language of the Philippines. His publications include *Theology in Context: A Case Study in the Philippines* (Baguio City, Philippines: APTS PRESS, 2013); being the Managing Editor, *Full Life Study Bible: Cebuano Language Edition*: Springfield., MO, USA: Life Publishers, 2012; *Led By the Spirit: The History of the American Assemblies of God Missionaries in the Philippines*. Manila: ICI Ministries, 2009; Managing Editor *Ang Ganap na Buhay Biblia (Full Life Study Bible). Tagalog Edition*. Springfield, MO, USA: LIFE Publishers, 2004; *An Analysis of the Worldwide and Religious Beliefs of the Waray People of the Philippines and the Factors Leading to the Growth of the Assemblies of God in the Regions With Implications for the Development of a Contextual Theology For the Waray*. D-Miss dissertation in Asia Graduate School of Theology, 2004; and *A Study of the Animistic*

Practices of the Waray People of the Leyte-Samar Region of the Philippines. Master's Thesis, Asia Pacific Theological Seminary, 2000.

Veli-Matti Kärkkäinen (Dr.Theol.Habil., University of Helsinki) is Professor of Systematic Theology at Fuller Theological Seminary, Pasadena, CA and Docent of Ecumenics at the University of Helsinki. A native of Finland, he has also lived and taught theology in Thailand. He has participated widely in the ecumenical, theological, and interreligious work of the World Council of Churches, Faith and Order, and several international bi-lateral dialogues. He travels widely to give lectures and participate in consultations and seminars.

Kirsteen Kim PhD is Professor of Theology and World Christianity at Leeds Trinity University, UK. She is a graduate of Fuller Theological Seminary and received her PhD from the University of Birmingham, UK in 2002. She was Research Coordinator for the Edinburgh 2010 project and served as vice-moderator of the Commission for World Mission and Evangelism of the World Council of Churches (2007-2013). Kim is the editor of *Mission Studies*, journal of the International Association for Mission Studies, and among other publications, she is the author of two books on the Holy Spirit: *The Holy Spirit in the World* (Orbis 2007) and *Joining in with the Spirit* (SCM 2012) and co-author of *Christianity as a World Religion* (Continuum 2008) and *A History of Korean Christianity* (2014).

Robert Menzies completed his Ph.D. studies (New Testament) at the University of Aberdeen, Scotland under the supervision of I. Howard Marshall in 1989. He has authored a number of books on the work of the Holy Spirit, including *Spirit and Power: Foundations of Pentecostal Experience* (Zondervan, 2000), which he co-authored with his father, and *Pentecost: This Story is Our Story* (GPH, 2013). Dr. Menzies is an adjunct professor at Asia Pacific Theological Seminary in the Philippines. He has taught at Bible schools and seminaries in the Philippines, Australia, Fiji, Indonesia, Malaysia, Japan, Russia, Holland, Korea, and the United States. Dr. Menzies' writings on the work of the Holy Spirit in the New Testament have served as a catalyst for fresh thinking in this area. For the past 20 years Dr. Menzies, along with his wife, has lived and served in China. The Menzies have two daughters who grew up in China and now live in the U.S. with their husbands. Dr. Menzies is currently the Director of Synergy, an organization that seeks to enable rural village people in Southwest China to live productive and fruitful lives.

Ekaputra Tupamahu is currently a Ph.D. student in New Testament and Early Christianity at Vanderbilt University, Nashville, TN. He went to Asia Pacific Theological Seminary and finished both M.A. and M.Div. degrees in 2005. He then taught at Satyabhakti Advanced School of Theology in Malang, Indonesia, for three years before moving to California to pursue further education at Claremont School of Theology in 2009. While studying at Claremont, he served as a pastor of an Indonesian congregation in California from 2010 to 2012.

Amos Yong is Professor of Theology and Mission and director of the Center for Missiological Research at Fuller Theological Seminary in Pasadena, California (effective 1 July 2014). His graduate education includes degrees in theology, history, and religious studies from Western Evangelical Seminary (now George Fox Seminary), Portland State University, Portland, Oregon, and Boston University, Boston, Massachusetts. He also obtained an undergraduate degree from Bethany University of the Assemblies of God. He has authored or edited over thirty volumes. He and his wife, Alma, have three children – Aizaiah (married to Neddy), on the pastoral team at New Life Church (Renton Washington) and in a masters in theology program at Northwest University (Kirkland, Washington); Alyssa, a graduate of Vanguard University (Costa Mesa, California); and Annalisa, a student at Point Loma University (San Diego, California). Amos and Alma reside in Pasadena, California.

www.ingramcontent.com/pod-product-compliance
Lightning Source LLC
Chambersburg PA
CBHW051636230426
43669CB00013B/2327